# Negotiation

# Negotiation
## Strategies for Mutual Gain

The Basic Seminar of the
Program on Negotiation
at Harvard Law School

## Lavinia Hall editor

**SAGE Publications**
*International Educational and Professional Publisher*
Newbury Park   London   New Delhi

*For information address*:

 SAGE Publications, Inc.
2455 Teller Road
Newbury Park, California 91320

SAGE Publications Ltd.
6 Bonhill Street
London EC2A 4PU
United Kingdom

SAGE Publications India Pvt. Ltd.
M-32 Market
Greater Kailash I
New Delhi 110 048 India

Printed in the United States of America

**Library of Congress Cataloging-in-Publication Data**

Main entry under title:

Negotiation: strategies for mutual gain: the basic seminar of the
  Harvard Program on Negotiation / [edited by] Lavinia Hall.
    p.   cm.
  Includes bibliographical references and index.
  ISBN 0-8039-4849-2 (hard).—ISBN 0-8039-4850-6 (pbk.)
  1. Negotiation.  2. Conflict management.  3. Interpersonal
conflict.  4. Harvard Law School.  Program on Negotiation.
I. Hall, Lavinia.
BF637.N4N44  1993                                        93-30441
302.3—dc20


93  94  95  96  10  9  8  7  6  5  4  3  2

Sage Production Editor:  Astrid Virding

# Contents

Introduction     vii

**I. Frameworks for Effective Negotiation**     **1**

1.  Negotiation Power: Ingredients in an
    Ability to Influence the Other Side
    *Roger Fisher, William Ury,* and *Bruce Patton*     3

2.  The Neutral Analyst: Helping Parties
    to Reach Better Solutions
    *Howard Raiffa*     14

3.  Facilitated Collaborative Problem Solving
    and Process Management
    *David Straus*     28

**II. Applying Mutual Gains to Organizations**  41

4. The Courthouse and Alternative Dispute Resolution
   *Frank E. A. Sander*  43

5. Resolving Public Disputes
   *Lawrence Susskind*  61

6. Why the Labor Management Scene Is Contentious
   *Robert B. McKersie*  77

7. Searching for Mutual Gains in Labor Relations
   *Charles C. Heckscher*  86

8. Options and Choice for Conflict Resolution
   in the Workplace
   *Mary P. Rowe*  105

**III. Perspectives on Individual Negotiators**  121

9. Conflict From a Psychological Perspective
   *Jeffrey Z. Rubin*  123

10. Her Place at the Table: Gender and Negotiation
    *Deborah M. Kolb*  138

11. Style and Effectiveness in Negotiation
    *Gerald R. Williams*  151

**IV. Appendices**

I. Sample Curriculum on Negotiation
   and Dispute Resolution  177

II. Case Clearinghouse Materials  185

Bibliography  186

Index  199

About the Authors  206

# Introduction

*The work of righteousness shall be peace and the effect of righteousness, quietness, and assurance forever.*

Isaiah 32:17

*We have thought of peace as passive and war as the active way of living. The opposite is true. War is not the most strenuous life. It is a kind of rest cure compared to the task of reconciling our differences. From war to peace is . . . from the futile to the effective, from the strategic to the active, from the destructive to the creative way of life. . . . The world will be regenerated by the people who rise above these passive ways and heroically seek, by whatever hardship, by whatever toil, the methods by which people can agree.*

Mary Parker Follett

▶ This book is for people in all fields who need to deal with conflict and resolve issues on a continual basis. Conflicts, improperly managed, within or between organizations or between individuals, are frustrating and waste valuable resources of time, energy, and finances. The Harvard Program on Negotiation is dedicated to improving the processes of reaching agreements. It assumes that conflicts, managed well, can provide the impetus for growth, constructive change, and mutual benefit. Ideas for settling disputes, improving communication, and changing the nature of certain debates are covered in this book.

*Negotiation: Strategies for Mutual Gain* is about breaking the paradigm of winning and losing and transforming negotiation into a search for improved solutions to problems. While many successful businessmen, judges, lawyers, therapists, and other people act on this instinctively, the common wisdom still holds that nice guys finish last and that asking for more than you want or need ensures that you will get your minimum.

An assumption of the Harvard Program on Negotiation is that there is nothing so practical as good theory, and nothing more stimulating to good theory than engaging in practice. While fully developed academic theories are as yet few in this relatively new area of study, the invention of new techniques and their creative application to everyday situations and negotiations is quite productive, as I think this volume attests.

This is a collection of key ideas and process strategies about negotiating and resolving disputes more effectively. All of the authors have been lecturers in the seminar of the Program of Negotiation at Harvard Law School. Each of their lectures is organized around a key idea in their work and expands on their particular approach to dispute resolution and problem solving. In some cases the lectures have simply been edited; in others, it was necessary to construct a separate chapter because of the format of the original lecture. In the case of Roger Fisher's presentation, we decided that the chapter on power from his 1991 edition of *Getting to Yes,* co-authored with Bill Ury and Bruce Patton, was the best version.

The book itself is an outgrowth of a popular semester-length seminar that is given each year at Radcliffe by the Harvard Program on Negotiation. It is open to graduate students and professionals. I designed it and was its main instructor during its initial 3 years. The idea for the seminar as the core of the program was the brainchild of Lawrence Susskind, then executive director of the Program on Negotiation, who obtained initial funding from the

Hewlett and Exxon foundations to help spread the word about the academic work and fieldwork being done in negotiation. He asked me to create a seminar that would be a window on the field of negotiation and dispute resolution ideas developed by faculty and affiliated practitioners. I remain grateful for the chance it provided to work with enthusiastic theorists, practitioners, and students of negotiation and dispute resolution.

Designing and teaching the seminar provided fertile ground for honing my own mediation skills, because the faculty often saw different issues as most worthy of being emphasized and presented a wide range of exciting ideas, case studies, and simulations. To some degree, the pedagogy of the course follows literary critic Kenneth Burke's idea of developing "perspectives by incongruity." Rather than reconciling the contradictions and gaps in the lecturers' approaches vis-à-vis each other, the students and I needed to spend substantial time debating and integrating the ideas presented into their own frameworks of negotiation and dispute resolution practice. It allowed, indeed required, them to synthesize things for themselves in order to develop their own work. Pedagogically speaking, we were learning to learn.

*Negotiation* (much as the structure of the course does) attempts to present a set of ideas, organized around frameworks for improving negotiation; the challenges to applying these ideas in organizational settings; and some analyses of individual behavior in negotiation. It is hoped that the format offers readers the chance to pick and choose among its ideas for integration into their own practice at work, at home and in a variety of negotiations where its ideas prove useful.

In *Negotiation,* the most compelling and unifying theme is the critical importance of good process. Virtually all of the authors, from Roger Fisher in his analysis of the elements of negotiation power, to Gerry Williams's description of lawyers' negotiating, emphasize the need for negotiators to develop awareness and constructive processes. All of the authors are positive in outlook and firmly believe that reframing how we negotiate and problem solve is highly possible; they are also realistic and demonstrate how hard it is at times to change ingrained habits. These brief, bird's-eye looks at some of the most interesting ideas in negotiation and dispute resolution work today should hearten us all about the possibilities of improving outcomes by improving the processes we use to reach them.

For those interested, the full curriculum and pedagogical design of the course itself is presented in Appendix I. It was first given in the fall of 1985 and has been given annually since then. Approximately half of the participants are graduate students and the balance are professionals (lawyers, psychotherapists, planners, managers) seeking ways to incorporate negotiation and dispute resolution techniques and practice into their work. The approach is intentionally cross-disciplinary; the premise is that negotiation is not a field in itself but rather a set of process and analytic skills that can be applied to good effect in courts, diplomacy, city planning, and inside corporations and government agencies.

I would like to thank all the contributors for their time and work in helping the Program on Negotiation and the National Institute for Dispute Resolution, which will share all proceeds from this book. Thanks also to all those lecturers who have participated over the six years of the program. The National Institute for Dispute Resolution provided funding for the book's production, and I must thank Michael Lewis and Madeleine Crohn also for their support and patience when it took longer than anticipated. Esther Siskind helped in the early stages of copy editing, and Maria Hortaridis and Meemee Swofford were an enormous help in final typing and production.

Chris Christensen of Harvard Business School taught a seminar about teaching that helped me think about how to present these ideas. Finally, I am grateful to past and present students of the seminar who continue to demonstrate what learning to learn by unfreezing old habits and integrating these techniques into practice really means.

All proceeds from this book will be divided between the Program on Negotiation at Harvard Law School and the National Institute for Dispute Resolution to further their work.

Lavinia Hall
Lincoln, MA

# PART I

# Frameworks for Effective Negotiation

## Introduction

▶ In Part I, the three chapters outline some key aspects of the techniques for which their authors are best known. The authors are united in the primary importance that they attribute to process. Process, here, is used to distinguish the *way* negotiations are conducted from their substance. Fisher, Ury, and Patton, in their chapter on negotiating power, outline the elements of principled negotiation as the source of real power. Their concept of a BATNA (walk-away alternative) is used by other authors in the book and is a universally useful calculation to make in preparing for any negotiation. The principles that they set forth serve as a checklist for the negotiator to take into negotiations.

Raiffa's approach is highly analytic; it offers a number of creative options for generating potential zones of agreement and criteria for deciding how to divide up those areas. His neutral advice offers ways to avoid inefficiency and waste in negotiations. Raiffa's examples,

1

drawn from his experience as a neutral adviser, show that good negotiation theory translates directly into practice.

Straus's chapter on collaborative problem solving stresses the value of inclusivity in its concern with representative voice, and in its admonition to "go slow to go fast"; in other words, to spend time initially to develop a process for addressing the problems that need to be resolved, rather than jumping to solutions too early. Using a facilitator to manage the process, particularly when there are many participants and many interests at stake, can be the first step toward success.

All of the authors offer coherent techniques and incisive ideas for readers to integrate into their own negotiation frameworks. Being aware that these elements of process design have a major effect on the substance of the outcome, and not merely the tone of the negotiations, can be a revelation for many new students of negotiation, and even for experienced negotiators. All negotiators, I believe, can find techniques to incorporate into their own negotiating frameworks from among ideas presented in this first part.

# 1

# Negotiation Power: Ingredients in an Ability to Influence the Other Side

ROGER FISHER

WILLIAM URY

BRUCE PATTON

▶ How you negotiate (and how you prepare to negotiate) can make an enormous difference, whatever the relative strengths of each party.

## Some Things You Can't Get

Of course, no matter how skilled you are, there are limits to what you can get through negotiation. The best negotiator in the world will not be able to buy the White House. You should not expect

EDITOR'S NOTE: This chapter is a portion of the new material included in the second edition of *Getting to Yes* (Fisher, Ury, & Patton, 1991). Copyright © 1981, 1991 by Roger Fisher and William Ury. Reprinted by permission of Houghton Mifflin Co. All rights reserved. It is one of 10 "answers to questions people ask." The second edition of *Getting to Yes* is recommended both to those who do not know the first edition and to those who do.

success in negotiation unless you are able to make the other side an offer they find more attractive than their BATNA—their Best Alternative To a Negotiated Agreement. If that seems impossible, then negotiation doesn't make sense. Concentrate instead on improving your BATNA and perhaps changing theirs.

## How You Negotiate Makes a Big Difference

In a situation where there *is* a chance for agreement, the way you negotiate can make the difference between coming to terms and not, or between an outcome that you find favorable and one that is merely acceptable. How you negotiate may determine whether the pie is expanded or merely divided, and whether you have a good relationship with the other side or a strained one. When the other side seems to hold all the cards, how you negotiate is absolutely critical. Suppose, for example, that you are negotiating for an exception to a rule or a job offer. Realistically, you may have little recourse if the other side denies your request and little to offer if they grant it. In this situation, your negotiation skill is everything. However small the opportunity for success, the way in which you negotiate will determine whether you are able to take advantage of it.

## "Resources" Are Not the Same as "Negotiation Power"

Negotiation power is the ability to persuade someone to do something. The United States is rich and has lots of nuclear bombs, but neither has been of much help in deterring terrorist actions or freeing hostages when they have been held in places like Beirut. Whether your resources give you negotiating power will depend on the context—on who you are trying to persuade and what you want them to do.

## Don't Ask "Who's More Powerful?"

Trying to estimate whether you or your counterparts are more "powerful" is risky. If you conclude that you are more powerful, you may relax and not prepare as well as you should. On the other hand, if you conclude that you are weaker than the other side, there is a risk that you will be discouraged and again not devote sufficient attention to how you might persuade the other side. Whatever you conclude will not help you figure out how best to proceed.

In fact, a great deal can be done to enhance your negotiation power even when the resource balance is one-sided. Of course there will be negotiations where, at least in the short term, the best cards are held by the other side. But in this increasingly interdependent world, there are almost always resources and potential allies that a skilled and persistent negotiator can exploit, at least to move the fulcrum, if not ultimately to tip the balance of power the other way. You won't find out what's possible unless you try.

Sometimes people seem to prefer feeling powerless and believing that there is nothing they can do to affect a situation. That belief helps them avoid feeling responsible or guilty about inaction. It also avoids the costs of trying to change the situation—making an effort and risking failure, which might cause the person embarrassment. But while this feeling is understandable, it does not affect the reality of what the person might accomplish by effective negotiation. It is a self-defeating and self-fulfilling attitude.

The best rule of thumb is to be optimistic—to let your reach exceed your grasp. Without wasting a lot of resources on hopeless causes, recognize that many things are worth trying for even if you may not succeed. The more you try for, the more you are likely to get. Studies of negotiation consistently show a strong correlation between aspiration and result. Within reason, it pays to think positively.

## There Are Many Sources of Negotiation Power

How do you enhance your negotiating power? This **whole book** is an attempt to answer that question. Negotiation power has many sources. One is having a good BATNA. Provided they believe you, it is persuasive to tell the other side that you have a better alternative. But each of the four elements of the method **outlined in Part II of this book**—people, interests, options, and objective criteria—is also a source of negotiation power. If the other side is strong in one area, you can try to develop strength in another. To these five we would now add a sixth, the power of commitment.

*There Is Power in Developing a Good Working Relationship Between the People Negotiating.* If you understand the other side and they understand you; if emotions are acknowledged and people are treated with respect even when they disagree; if there is clear, two-way communication with good listening; and if people problems are dealt with directly, not by demanding or offering concessions on substance, negotiations are likely to be smoother and more successful for both parties. In this sense, negotiation power is not a zero-sum phenomenon. More negotiation power for the other side does not necessarily mean less for you. The better your working relationship, the better able each of you is to influence the other.

Contrary to some conventional wisdom, you will often benefit from the other side's increasing their ability to influence you. Two people with well-deserved reputations for being trustworthy are each better able to influence the other than are two people with reputations for dishonesty. That you can trust the other side increases their ability to influence you. But you also benefit. You can safely enter into agreements that will benefit both sides.

Good communication is an especially significant source of negotiating power. Crafting your message with punch, listening to the other side, and showing that you have heard can all increase your persuasiveness. John F. Kennedy was justly famous for his skill at the first of these, crafting a forceful message: "Let us never negotiate out of fear. But let us never fear to negotiate."[1]

A message does not have to be unequivocal to be clear and effective. In many cases, helping the other side understand your thinking—even when you are of two minds about something—can reduce their fears, clear up misperceptions, and promote joint problem solving. Consider the supplier who makes what she thinks is a competitive bid for a business supply contract. The purchaser likes the bid and the bidder, but is worried that the bidder's firm, which is new to the market, may not be able to manage the volume needed to meet his peak requirements. If the purchaser says simply, "No, thank you," and then pays more to hire another firm, the bidder may assume that the purchaser disliked her bid. And the bidder would have no opportunity to persuade the purchaser that she could handle the needed volume. It would be better for both if, instead, the purchaser shared both his interest in the bid and his concerns.

Good listening can increase your negotiation power by increasing the information you have about the other side's interests or about possible options. Once you understand the other sides' feelings and concerns, you can begin to address them, to explore areas of agreement and disagreement, and to develop useful ways to proceed in the future. Consider, for example, the elderly man whose doctors wanted to move him from his current hospital to one with specialized facilities. The doctors repeatedly explained how the specialized hospital would be better for him, but the man refused to budge. Knowing that the man was acting against his own best interests, the doctors dismissed his reasoning as irrational. One intern, however, took the man seriously and listened carefully to why he did not want to move. The patient told of how he had suffered repeated abandonments in his life and his fears that moving might result in another. The intern set about addressing this concern directly, and the man happily agreed to be moved.

Showing that you have heard the other side also increases your ability to persuade them. When the other side feels heard **by** you, they are more apt to listen to you. It is comparatively easy to listen when the other side is saying something that you agree with. It is harder to listen to things with which you disagree, but that is the very time it is most effective. Listen before you launch into a rebuttal. Make sure you understand their view; and make sure that they know you understand. Once the other side knows that you understand what they have said, they cannot dismiss your disagreement as simple lack of understanding.

*There Is Power in Understanding Interests.* The more clearly you understand the other side's concerns, the better able you will be to satisfy them at minimum cost to yourself. Look for intangible or hidden interests that may be important. With concrete interests like money, ask what lies behind them. ("For what will the money be used?") Sometimes even the most firmly stated and unacceptable position reflects an underlying interest that is compatible with your own.

Consider the businessman who was trying to buy a radio station. The majority owner was willing to sell his two-thirds of the station for a reasonable figure, but the one-third owner (and current manager of the station) was demanding what seemed an exorbitant price for her third. The businessman had raised his offer several times to no avail, and he was beginning to consider abandoning the deal. Finally, the businessman inquired more deeply into the second owner's interests. He learned that the second owner had less interest in money than she did in continuing to manage a radio station of which she was a part owner. The businessman offered to buy only that portion of the owner's share he needed for tax reasons and to keep her on as manager. The second owner accepted this offer at a price that saved the businessman almost a million dollars. Understanding the seller's underlying interests had greatly enhanced the buyer's negotiating power.

*There Is Power in Inventing an Elegant Option.* Successful brainstorming increases your ability to influence others. Once you understand the interests of each side, it is often possible—as in the radio station example above—to invent a clever way of having those interests dovetail. Sometimes this can be done by devising an ingenious process option.

Consider the sealed-bid stamp auction. The auctioneer would like bidders to offer the most they might conceivably be willing to pay for the stamps in question. Each potential buyer, however, does not want to pay more than necessary. In a regular sealed-bid auction each bidder tries to offer slightly more than their best guess of what others will bid, which is often less than the bidder would be willing to pay. But in a stamp auction the rules are that the highest bidder gets the stamps at the price of *the second highest bid*. Buyers can safely bid *exactly* as much as they would be willing to pay to get the stamps, because the auctioneer guarantees that *they will have to pay it*! No bidder is left wishing that he or she had bid more, and the high bidder is happy to pay less than was offered. The auctioneer is happy knowing that the difference between the highest and second highest bids is usually smaller than the overall increase in the level of bids under this system versus a regular sealed-bid auction.[2]

*There Is Power in Using External Standards of Legitimacy.* You can use standards of legitimacy both as a sword to persuade others, and as a shield to help you resist pressure to give in arbitrarily. ("I would like to give you a discount, but this price is firm. It is what General Motors paid for the same item last week; here is the bill of sale.") Just as, by finding relevant precedent and principles a lawyer enhances his or her ability to persuade a judge, so a negotiator can enhance his or her negotiation power by finding precedents, principles, and other external criteria of fairness and by thinking of ways to present them forcefully and tellingly: "I am asking for no more and no less than you are paying others for comparable work." "We will pay what the house is worth if we can afford it. We are offering what the similar house nearby sold for last month. Unless you can give us a good reason why your house is worth more, our offer remains firm and unchanged." Convincing the other side that you are asking for no more than is fair is one of the most powerful arguments you can make.

*There Is Power in Developing a Good BATNA.* As we argue in Chapter 6, a fundamental way to increase your negotiation power is by improving your walk-away alternative. An attractive BATNA is a strong argument with which to persuade the other side of the need to offer more. ("The firm across the street has offered me 20 percent above what I am now earning. I would rather stay here. But with the cost of living, unless I can get a good raise soon, I will have to consider moving on. What do you think might be possible?")

In addition to improving your overall BATNA (what you will do if the negotiations fail to produce an agreement), you should also prepare your "micro-BATNA"—if no agreement is reached *at this meeting*, what is the best outcome? It helps to draft in advance a good exit line to use if a meeting is inconclusive. ("Thank you for sharing your views and for listening to mine. If I decide to go forward, I will get back to you, perhaps with a fresh proposal.")

Sometimes it is possible, quite legitimately, to worsen the other side's BATNA. For example, a father we know was trying to get his young son to mow the lawn. He offered a significant amount of money, but to no avail. Finally, the son inadvertently revealed his BATNA: "But Dad, I don't need to mow the lawn to get money. You, uh, leave your wallet on the dresser every weekend. . . . " The father quickly changed his son's BATNA by not leaving his wallet out and making clear that he disapproved of taking money without asking; the son started mowing the lawn. The tactic of worsening the other side's BATNA can be used to coerce or exploit, but it can also help insure a fair outcome. Efforts to improve one's own alternatives and to lower the other side's estimate of theirs are critical ways to enhance our negotiating power.

*There Is Power in Making a Carefully Crafted Commitment.* One additional source of persuasive power deserves attention: the power of making commitments. You can use a commitment to enhance your negotiating power in three ways: You can commit to what you will do, for example, by making a firm offer. You can, with care, make a negative commitment as to what you will not do. And you can clarify precisely what commitments you would like the other side to make.

*Clarify What You Will Do.* One way to enhance your negotiating power is to make a firm, well-timed offer. When you make a firm offer, you provide one option that you *will* accept, making it clear at the same time that you are not foreclosing discussion of other options. If you want to persuade someone to accept a job, don't just talk about it; make an offer. By making an offer you give up your chance to haggle for better terms. But you gain by simplifying the other side's choice and making it easier for them to commit. To reach agreement, all they have to say is "yes."

Making an offer of what you will do if they agree to the terms you are proposing is one way to overcome any fear the other side may have of starting down a slippery slope. Without a clear offer, even a painful situation may seem preferable to accepting "a pig in a poke," especially if the other side fears that a favorable indication will encourage you to ask for more. In 1990, the U.N. Security Council sought to influence Iraq to withdraw from Kuwait by imposing sanctions. The Council's resolutions clearly stated that Iraq must withdraw but did not state that upon withdrawal sanctions would end. If Saddam Hussein believed that sanctions would continue after Iraq withdrew, then those sanctions, though unpleasant, provided no incentive for Iraq to leave.

The more concrete the offer, the more persuasive. Thus a written offer may be more credible than an oral one. (A real-estate agent we know likes to have a client make an offer by stacking bundles of hundred-dollar bills on the table.) You may also want to make your offer a "fading opportunity" by indicating when and how it will expire. For example, President Reagan's inauguration in 1981 created a fading opportunity in the negotiations for the release of the American diplomatic hostages held in Iran. The Iranians did not want to have to start negotiating all over again with a new U.S. administration.

In some cases, you may also want to clarify what you will do if the other side does not accept your proposal. They may not realize the consequences of your BATNA for them. ("If we can't get heat in our apartment by this evening, I will have to call the health department's emergency line. Are you aware that they charge landlords a $250 fine when they respond and find violation of the statute?")

*Consider Committing to What You Will Not Do.* Sometimes you can persuade the other side to accept an offer better than their BATNA by convincing them that you cannot or will not offer more ("Take it or leave it"). You not only make an offer; you tie your hands against changing it. . . . Locking into a position has significant costs; locking in early limits communication and runs the risk of damaging the relationship by making the other side feel ignored or coerced. There is less risk in locking in after you have come to understand the other side's interests and have explored options for joint gains, and it will do less damage to your relationship with the other side if there are credible reasons independent of your will to explain and justify your rigidity.

At some point, it may be best to put a final offer on the table and mean it. Doing so tends to influence the other side by worsening their micro-BATNA. At this point if they say "no," they no longer have open the possibility of reaching a better agreement with you.

*Clarify What You Want Them to Do.* It pays to think through the precise terms of the commitment you want the other side to make. This insures that your demand makes sense. "Susan, promise *never* to interrupt me again when I am on the telephone" could easily be disastrous if Susan took her promise literally in an emergency. You want to avoid a sloppy commitment that is overboard, fails to bind the other side, leaves out crucial information, or is not operational.

Especially when you want the other side to do something, it makes sense to tell them exactly what it is you want them to do. Otherwise they may do nothing, not wanting to do more than they have to. In the fall of 1990, for example, the ability of the United States to influence Saddam Hussein was undercut by ambiguity about what would satisfy the United States. At different times, the withdrawal of Iraqi troops from Kuwait, the destruction of Iraqi nuclear facilities, the dismantling of Iraq's military capability, and the overthrow of Saddam Hussein all seemed to be possible U.S. goals.

## Make the Most of Your Potential Power

To make the most of your negotiating power, you should use each source of power in harmony with other sources. Negotiators sometimes look for their strongest source of power and try to use it alone. For example, if a negotiator has a strong BATNA, he or she may confront the other side with it, threatening to walk away unless the last offer is accepted. This is likely to detract from the persuasive power of the negotiator's arguments about why the offer is fair. If you are going to communicate your BATNA, it would be better to do so in ways that respect the relationship, leave open the possibility of two-way communication, underscore the legitimacy of your last offer, suggest how that offer meets the other side's interests, and so forth. The total impact of such negotiation power as you have will be greater if each element is used in ways that reinforce the others.

You will also be more effective as a negotiator if you believe in what you are saying and doing. Whatever use you are able to make of the ideas in this book, don't wear them as though you were wearing someone else's clothes. Cut and fit what we say until you find an approach that both makes sense and is comfortable for you. This may require experimentation and a period of adjustment that is not so comfortable, but in the end, you are likely to maximize your negotiation power if you believe what you say and say what you believe.

# Notes

1. Inaugural Address, January 20, 1961.

2. A process similar to this can be used in all kinds of allocation decisions, even when the issue is as volatile as where to site a hazardous waste facility. See Howard Raiffa, *A Hypothetical Speech to a Hypothetical Audience About a Very Real Problem* (1985), Program on Negotiation Working Paper No. 85-8, available from the Program on Negotiation at Harvard Law School, Pound Hall 513, Harvard Law School.

# 2

# The Neutral Analyst: Helping Parties to Reach Better Solutions

## HOWARD RAIFFA

▶ In this chapter, I want to consider how an outside, third-party intervener can use analysis to help parties resolve a conflict in a better fashion. I come to this problem with the bias or observation that a lot of discord is settled in inefficient ways. I contend that very often people come to much less than optimal outcomes and joint gains are left on the table that could have been exploited.

There are several types of third-party interventions that can help parties to reach agreements and more efficient agreements. A *facilitator* helps with the logistics in the proceedings of meetings. A *mediator* guides or helps people come to a voluntary agreement. An *arbitrator* tries to understand the issues on all sides and then imposes an agreement, as a judge.

When I describe what I do as a neutral analyst most people do not know if I am a mediator or an arbitrator. To me, there are no hard-and-fast rules for everything that each does, and I am not going to dwell on the distinctions between mediation, arbitration, and other forms of third-party intervention. Rather, I want to

describe some methods that an intervener might use based somewhat on some of my experiences as an intervener in real conflicts,
on laboratory experiments, and on my reflections of what could
have been done in many real-world settings.

## Third-Party Methods

The first category of intervention activities is those ordinarily
undertaken by a facilitator: convening meetings, leading discussions, preparing neutral minutes, and attesting to the good faith of
the bargaining procedure. The biggest contribution of third parties
in an intervention may be getting the parties together, taking
minutes, and telling people what they have agreed to unwittingly.

The second category is those activities that set the ambience:
maintaining the rules of civilized debate, diffusing personality
conflicts, and helping reticent speakers. At the heart of many
disputes are personality problems. If I were to train mediators to
mediate in small claims court and labor disputes, I would emphasize the importance of dealing with personality problems.

The third category is the third party's role in the exchange of
information. In distributive bargaining you divide up a fixed-size
pie. In integrative bargaining, you can make that pie grow through
the exchange of information. The third party is most important in
integrative bargaining problems. Some feel that all problems are
integrative, but I believe that there are some problems that are not.
There are situations in which there is a seller and a buyer, each is
only concerned about price, and neither will budge.

## Distributive Bargaining Problems

An example of a distributive bargaining problem is a situation in
which there is a buyer and a seller, each has a reservation price in
mind, but each is willing to bargain. The seller quotes a high price
and the buyer says, "Nonsense, I'm only willing to offer you this."
The seller and the buyer talk about the good and bad aspects of the
item and they each make new offers. This keeps on going until they
eventually get stuck. The seller says that he or she will not go below

a certain price and the buyer says that he or she will not go over a certain price. It may be that there is no zone of agreement. However, it may be that there is a zone of agreement but the buyer and the seller are not willing to divulge their rock-bottom prices because they fear that they will be taken advantage of if they do.

Now let us bring in a third party. Confidential information could be disclosed to the third party. If the third party can get the parties to disclose confidentially their bottom line or reservation prices, the third party can determine whether there really is a possibility for agreement. If there is, the third party can encourage the parties to keep at it. If there is not, he or she can tell the parties to give up because there is no hope.

## Integrative Bargaining Problems

A typical situation involves two parties, unimaginatively labeled A and B, who must agree on the resolution of several issues, only one of which might involve money or prices. A and B typically will differ on the importance of the issues; they might differ on their perceptions of the future and how it will affect any agreement they might arrive at, they might have different trade-offs for money up front versus money in the future, they might have strong differences in their attitudes toward risk, they might have different quasi-legal constraints on what they could do, they might attach different values to certain symbolic acts, they might be used to different processes for negotiating, or they might have different ethical or word standards about what is fair or legitimate or appropriate.

In such integrative negotiating problems the parties often do not reach an agreement when agreements are possible or they might reach an agreement that is jointly inferior. Essentially they do not know how to exploit their differences effectively and end up by splitting a small pie rather than constructively creating and sharing a much larger pie.

Many disputants refuse to go to a third party because they fear that their power might not be recognized by the third party and that they will lose control over the proceedings. Instead, they engage in adversarial, strident bargaining which features and emphasizes win-lose, rather than win-win, elements. They exaggerate and misrepresent their sides, come to agreements, and sign contracts that are not Pareto efficient; in other words, they will leave joint gains on the table that could have been divided.

## Postsettlements, Rules Manipulation, and Neutral Analysis

There are several intervention mechanisms that an intervener can use to improve these agreements. The first is what I call *postsettlement-settlement.* Some parties may be willing, if they already have the security of a contract, to try to improve on what they have agreed through a second round of negotiation. In this postsettlement-settlement phase they will try to squeeze out more joint gains. This intervention is not widely used. I have used it in a limited number of real-life situations and have often used it very effectively in the laboratory.

In another type of intervention, which I call *rules manipulation,* the intervener, rather than play the role of a typical mediator or arbitrator, sets up a dynamic mechanism such as a bidding procedure to resolve a conflict that would ordinarily be resolved in a different fashion. For example, commercial disputes that are settled in this country by competitive bidding, auctions, or market mechanisms, are settled in other countries through negotiation. We have competitive bidding for off-shore oil tracts; in the UK this is negotiated. Different cultures use different mechanisms to resolve disputes and such alternatives could be exploited by the intervener.

Today, in economic theory, there is a burst of activity among mathematical economists and games theorists who are looking at rules manipulation. They are studying the way people behave and misrepresent information in negotiations to determine whether rules can be changed and procedures constructed so that the negotiation process will foster honesty and less strategic posturing. Through the use of truth-generating mechanisms, rational people acting in their own interest will divulge the truth.

The following example will illustrate a situation in which rules manipulation can be used:

> There is a sealed bid auction on a contraption that is very useful. The highest bidder will win the machine. There are only three or four people that are interested. How do they figure out what their bids should be?

One woman feels that the machine is worth $150, and this is what she would bid in an open auction. Should she bid $150 on the sealed bid auction, as well? She will do some thinking about the psychologies of the other people and some strategic analysis to figure out what her bid will be. "How many other people are interested in this machine? I think that the other are not going to pay more than $75, why should I bid $150?"

She finally decides, "I'm going to take a gamble and bid $105." It turns out that the highest bid is $110, and she loses.

Notice the nature of the woman's decision making. She had to figure out what the machine is worth to her and what it is worth to the other bidders and then make a decision. She bid an amount that was less than the machine was worth to her, which resulted in her losing the machine.

Let us now contrast this auction with a different kind of auction that is sometimes called the *philatelist auction*. It is used to auction off rare stamps. In this type of auction, everybody puts in a sealed bid. The highest bidder wins the machine but pays the auctioneer, not the highest bid price, but the second-highest bid price. This new and not very common procedure is currently the darling of the economics community. Let us see why.

Suppose the machine is worth $150 to you. In the first type of auction, you also worry about what it is worth to the other bidders. In the second-highest-bid-price auction, if it is worth $150 to you, you bid $150! You bid *exactly* what you believe it is worth, and you do not do any strategic thinking about the other bidders. There is no advantage in bidding $130 if you believe it is worth $150. If everybody bids below $130, you are just as well off bidding $150, because you pay the second-highest bid. But if you bid $130 and someone bids $140, you would have been better off if you bid $150. This procedure allows you to be honest about what an item is worth. It generates truth and that's why it is exciting.

A third type of intervention that I am interested in is *neutral analysis*. Let us take the example of acid rain in Europe. The countries in Western Europe are disturbed about acid rain and the generation of sulfur dioxide in power plants. Each country has its own particular interest in the problem. There are many scientific uncertainties involved. They would each like to commission their own studies, but most of them do not have the resources to do so.

Neutral analysis could be used in this situation. All the protagonists would work together to build a model showing how sulfur dioxide is created and transported and its effect on lakes, streams, forests, and soil. They would need to decide on an appropriate party to do the neutral modeling, what should and should not be in the model and what flexibilities should be incorporated in the model to suit each party's particular and possibly confidential needs.

## Case Examples

The following is an example of a case in which I was involved. Two brothers were negotiating the price of some shares. One brother, John, was trying to buy out the other brother, Fred.

John said he was willing to buy Fred's shares for $120 per share. Fred demanded $250 per share. In a pas de deux they danced around, and John moved to $160 and Fred moved down to $240 and they got stuck. The focal point in this dispute was the midpoint $200 a share.

John offered to split the difference. Fred responded, "What?! You were willing to go up to $200 and you stuck to $160? Obviously, $160 was an extreme offer. I will treat $200 as your offer, and now we can begin to bargain." What they ended up with was $220. The person who suggests splitting the difference in this adversarial win-lose negotiation is at a disadvantage.

Now let us bring in a third party. The third party comes in when the parties are stuck at $160 and $240 a share. The third party says to each party privately that the focal point is $200 a share and asks whether they would accept $200 if the other side were to agree to it. Each party agrees to the price that the third party suggested (that neither was willing to suggest on his own), on the condition that the third party does not let his brother know that he agreed to it. Another method would be for the mediator to announce to both brothers, "I think that $200 is a fair price. If you both privately tell me it is acceptable it will be a deal."

Another case that I worked on also involved two brothers, Lawrence and Paul, who received a bequest of an art collection from their recently deceased mother. Her will stated that the brothers should equally share the art collection that she diligently collected over a lifetime. The art collection had sentimental value to both brothers.

After reading my book, the two of them approached me to help them resolve their dilemma, because they realized that they could not possibly divide this art collection on their own. They wanted to ensure a balanced outcome, balanced audits, and truth telling, yet they could not negotiate. Each of them had a personal motivation, yet each wanted to be fair. There were sparks between them. The two brothers liked each other and saw each other socially, but there was tremendous sibling rivalry whenever it came to anything that involved business or a trade of anything that had any value. One brother recalled that the other always got the best toy; the other brother confided to me that their mother gave the other a better wedding gift.

I told them that I would try to generate an efficient contract that would exploit all the information I received. I decided that in these negotiations I would represent their mother. I told them that I would keep on reminding them about what their mother would have wanted. They were very close to being enemies, and she certainly would not have wanted that. (There is a difference of opinion among mediators on using this mechanism, but it is often used in certain mediation situations. Divorce mediators often represent the children. Mediators of environmental disputes often represent a party that is not adequately represented at the negotiations.)

We began by agreeing on a set of rules that would be used to negotiate the items. I asked them to specify what kind of balances they wanted to strive for. We talked about what could be done with the paintings. They could jointly donate them to museums or they could individually donate them after they received property rights. They felt that there were just a few items that they would jointly donate and they wanted to allocate property rights for the rest. They agreed that if one of them had property rights to a painting and wanted to sell it, the other person would have the right of first refusal at a 10% discount. In dividing the paintings, they did not feel that a more complicated process such as the fair division Steinhaus procedure[1] would work for them because they were not willing to put dollar values on anything.

There was much anticipated postdecisional regret. For example, they would be very upset if one person got all 20 Macavoy paintings, and Macavoys one day became more valuable, to the benefit of one brother and the distress of the other. In addition, we discussed the possibility that their preference for the paintings might change in the future. This was particularly true because they were in such an emotional state. Someone may really want a particular painting but might lose interest in it 3 months after it was hanging on their wall and feel that they made a mistake. To allay their concerns over postdecisional regrets, they agreed to renegotiate at periodic stages in the future.

It was unclear whether certain pieces should be considered art, jewelry, or furniture; there were stipulations in the will regarding jewelry and furniture. We decided not to resolve all these issues in the beginning but, rather, to begin by dividing the expensive Macavoy paintings because they wanted to determine their equity as soon as possible. We would then move on to the Lundquist and the Gallo paintings, handling one artist at a time.

Up to this point, we never discussed preference for particular items. When we finally came to the point of dividing up the paintings, I communicated with each of them confidentially in order to get lots of information. I asked each of them to do whatever they found natural; to write long letters telling me how they felt about the pieces and the rationale behind these feelings. I asked that they use any system they wanted to measure the strength of their preferences, including rankings or numbers.

I collected this information to determine whether compatible deals could be arranged that would balance the need for equity across artists and equity in fair market values. Occasionally, I had to get more information from them. I put all this information into a spreadsheet on a computer. After analyzing all the information they had given me, I made suggestions to them. This is the role of an analytic intervener. I would show them two allocations and ask them which one they preferred and why. I then used this information to come up with a third allocation to which they both agreed on. After it was all over, they invited me to dinner to show me that they were still brothers. They also agreed that in a couple of years they would go through another round of trading. They also awarded me a bonus because their relationship did not deteriorate during the process.

In my book, *The Art and Science of Negotiation,* I discuss a negotiation that took place between the United States and Panama over the Panama Canal. Ambassador Bunker was given the assignment of representing the United States in the negotiations with Panama. In order to determine what the U.S. position should be, Ambassador Bunker interviewed the principal U.S. parties involved in the conflict: the Commerce Department, the Defense Department, the Army, the Navy, the Air Force, and others. There was a vast difference of opinion. These differences had to somehow be resolved through internal negotiations so that Ambassador Bunker would know how he should negotiate across the table with Panama.

At first glance, President Carter could be thought of as the arbitrator in this internal conflict because he had the power to decide the U.S. position. But if you examine the situation more closely, President Carter could not really impose a decision on the military because they could resign and go political. Therefore, in actuality, President Carter's role was that of a mediator rather than an arbitrator in this internal conflict. But he was a *mediator with clout* and, therefore, had more power.

President Carter and Ambassador Bunker, after weighing the positions of all the parties involved, believed that they had somehow to convince the military to compromise on their position in order to get an agreement. They could have appealed to them on the grounds that it was in the public's best interest, but the military clearly believed it was guarding the public's best interest and that America's position would be weakened if they compromised their position. One way to appeal to the military in this case would be to link this problem to another problem. The president could give the military a slightly bigger budget to buy an extra aircraft carrier to be placed in the southern Pacific Ocean for added protection. This could allay security concerns regarding the Panama Canal issue.

Similarly, in hierarchical organizations the role of the manager is often that of a mediator with clout. The manager can dictate to his or her subordinates, but this does not work in our society because people can quit or they can sabotage procedures. When there are big disputes within a firm, you want to get people to sit down together and do joint problem solving. The manager is often a built-in mediator because of the structure of the firm.

A manager may also be in a situation in which several people are giving him or her contradictory information. The manager can use his or her own analytic staff or hire a consulting firm to serve as neutral analytic intervener to help resolve the issue. This is done all the time in management. Most people do not think of it as mediation, but I do.

Many years ago, I gave lectures to advanced management people at Harvard Business School; these are middle-aged people who are vice presidents and executives of large corporations. When I talked to them about negotiation and I mentioned the terms *mediation* and *arbitration,* they thought immediately of labor mediation or arbitration. They said, "We don't do mediation or arbitration. We're in the marketing group." After much resistance, they agreed to discuss the subject. When we went through a list of what mediators do, they realized that it is *exactly* what they do all the time as managers. They were practicing mediation, and doing it very well, but did not realize that they were doing it. Mothers and fathers also practice mediation with their children all the time but they do not think of it that way.

The next example is a merger case that I do in my course on negotiation at Harvard Business School. It illustrates the need for exchange of information, joint problem solving, and neutral analysis in negotiating settlements. I give the following background information to my students: Magnus is a large electronics firm that is terrific at production, marketing, and distribution but does not have a flair for research. They try to get good researchers to work for them, but good researchers do not want to work for a large manufacturing firm. Magnus decides to try to acquire AIL, a small research firm, and they enter negotiations.

The students divide into two groups, Magnus and AIL. Confidential instructions are given to each side and they are told to negotiate. The Magnus group is told that their bottom-line offer, or reservation price, is $6.5 million. The AIL group is told that their reservation price, the lowest offer that they would accept from Magnus, is $7.2 million. There is no zone of agreement. A lot of figures went into establishing these reservation prices. Each group is given a technical report prepared by their company's research staff, which details how their bottom line, or reservation price, was arrived at.

When given this problem, most students find that they cannot agree. Because there is no zone of agreement, the students just go back and forth on price.

The students rarely look at the calculations that went into the establishment of the reservation prices. The prices are based on each company's perception of what would happen in the future. It turns out that Magnus and AIL arrived at different estimates of the value of AIL because they used different discount rates. While one used a high discount rate, the other used a low one. Differences in the companies' estimates were also due to uncertainty over the future value of the firm.

In this problem, when each side made separate calculations, there was no zone of agreement. Differences in risk perception and the time value of money must be resolved in order to determine whether there is a zone of agreement and an efficient contract can be reached. What is needed is joint problem solving and for each side to divulge information. Once there is agreement on both sides over the figures, the search for an acceptable compromise becomes an analytical problem that could be handed over to an operations analyst.

A mechanism that is often useful in negotiations for which there is uncertainty over the future value of a firm is a *contingent contract.* In a contingent contract, each party agrees to pay a certain sum, with the stipulation that depending on what happens in the future more or less money will be paid. The contract price is reevaluated each year. Although this problem requires financial analysis and most mediators are not trained to do this, a mediator must learn to ask the following questions: What figures and calculations went into these prices? and How can these differences be resolved so that an agreement can be reached? A zone of agreement does not always exist in contract negotiations. A mediator must, therefore, be prepared to use analysis to determine how figures were calculated.

In the second part of the exercise, after most of the students fail to reach a settlement, I change the numbers so that there is a small zone of agreement. In an ideal situation, there would be a zone of agreement—the reservation prices would overlap. If there is a zone of agreement, the two sides, through negotiation, potentially can get a surplus; they can do better than their reservation prices. This is known as beating your best alternative to a negotiated agreement (BANTA), or your walk-away alternative. Given a zone of agreement, most of the students end up settling near their BATNA. Once they get their BATNA, they are satisfied and quit. They are not adventurous about considering alternatives such as the possibilities of risk-sharing plans or contingent contracts.

## Scorable Games

Another case that I use as an exercise in my classes is the Associated Metropolitan Police Organization's (AMPO) labor contract negotiations. AMPO wants to negotiate 10 items including starting salary, vacation pay, and the status of the police review board. The students are paired off: One student represents AMPO, the other represents the city.

In this game, a scoring system is used. Each item to be negotiated has a certain value that allows students to determine how much of one item they would be willing to give up to receive another. Scoring imposes an artificiality that distorts the problem in some dimensions but brings out other factors. There are usually great debates among the students about the values of the trade-offs. However, it is not the player's role (in this simulation exercise!) to question the trade-offs; they are given.

Each side is given confidential instructions and each side is given a different scoring system. The students representing the city are told that they must get a score of 300 (their BATNA) or more. The students representing AMPO are given a different scoring system and are told that they must get a score of 25 or more. They hold negotiations in pairs.

Each pair ends up with different scores and has used different procedures to arrive at their outcomes. The two students in a pair cannot be compared. This is not a zero-sum game; one does not win or lose.

However, all the students representing one side can be compared with each other to a certain extent. If Arnold, who represented the city, received a higher score than all the other students representing the city, you might be tempted to say that he is a better negotiator than the others. However, it may be that Arnold's partner was an easy customer. It may not have been the acumen of Arnold but the weakness of his partner that allowed him to receive such a high score.

In scorable games, when pairs come back with such a range of different outcomes, you can clearly see that there are often joint gains that are not exploited. If pair 1 gets a score of 310, 30 and pair 2 gets a score of 365, 50, one can see that pair 1 could have done better. They could have baked a bigger pie. Most of the time when people negotiate, they are satisfied if they do better than their reservation price (or BATNA). They are not aware that there were joint gains left on the table. Both sides can improve their scores without hurting the other side.

I sometimes vary the dynamics in this game by including a mediator. Then there are three people involved, one representing AMPO, one representing the city, and one mediating. The mediator does not have any of the information or scores that the two sides are given. The parties have the option of deciding whether or not they want to use the mediator. Most students find that they do not know what to do with a mediator. The mediator is not highly trained, and they tend not to use him or her. Those who do use the mediator claim that he or she is not very helpful. However, the students who do use the mediator are surprised to find that on average they do a little better. *Why* do they do better? A mediator is able to generate more truth telling and convey more confidential information than the parties themselves. The mediator who gets to know joint scores can suggest creative alternatives.

I then ask the pairs that did not use a mediator whether they would be willing to go into a second postsettlement-settlement round of negotiations with a mediator to determine whether they could improve their outcomes. They would have to agree to tell the mediator something about their scores, even if they distorted the information, so that the mediator could do some mathematical analysis with a computer program. They would have the option of keeping their original scores if they did not like the outcome they got using a mediator.

Almost all think that they do not have anything to lose by using the mediator to try to embellish this contract in a second postsettlement-settlement phase. However, most people said they would not divulge their true scores because they would want to try to figure out how to do better. In the end, most people end up telling the truth because they do not know in this case how to lie or exaggerate. It is safer to tell the truth. Only through joint problem solving and divulging the truth can you move ahead.

In the laboratory, time and time again, people refuse to use arbitrators and mediators because they think that somebody will gain an advantage. They negotiate, come to a conclusion, and leave. They never think about whether there were joint gains left on the table. The issue of exploiting joint gains is tremendously complicated. Let us look at the AMPO versus city negotiations, a complex integrative negotiation involving several issues to be resolved. There are several possible ways the city and AMPO could go about formulating a contract. Each side could come to the negotiation table with a proposed contract it drew up on its own. Each side would spend a lot of time trying to convince the other side that its contract is better. They may eventually end up revising their contracts and come to a final contract.

Or they can negotiate by building a contract from the bottom up. This is an example of joint problem solving. They would examine one issue at a time and try to compromise. Eventually they would start to trade off among issues. One side would give up something on one issue if the other side gave up something on another issue. What usually happens is that each side pretends that it is giving up a lot and, therefore, expects a lot. It exaggerates what it is giving up and minimizes what it is getting. This distorts the problem. The claiming aspect of the negotiation gets in the way of the creating aspect. Instead of building up the pie, they hide information from each other. In both these scenarios, the final contract most likely will not be efficient and the outcome may be in the Pareto crummy area. With the security of a contract, they might be willing to move on to a second stage of postsettlement-settlement negotiations using a third party with the likely outcome of improved results.

Many of the techniques a third party can do, the parties can do for themselves without the use of an intervener. But it is often the case that the intervener is more knowledgeable about constructive processes of negotiations. Good training for an intervener is good training for the negotiator and vice versa.

These are just some of the techniques that third-party interveners can use to help parties resolve conflicts with better results for all. As I noted earlier, my own interest in assisting people is to avoid inefficient, wasteful extremes and to use all the joint gains.

## Note

1. See Raiffa (1982, pp. 290-291) for a fuller discussion of this and other procedures.

# 3

# Facilitated Collaborative Problem Solving and Process Management

DAVID STRAUS

▶ I am an architect by training. Part of what got me into the field of collaborative problem solving was frustration with education at design school where the creative process was not talked about. Creativity was viewed as something you either had or did not have. However, there were waves of design methodologies sweeping the drafting room that were never discussed. In desperation, I started taking courses in cognitive psychology and began to realize that there were discrete cognitive structures involved in productive thinking. I went to Berkeley to work on a National Institute of Mental Health grant in the area of design methodology; it turned into a study of problem solving.

What is it that is useful to know about how the mind works? What I discovered was that all of problem solving can be viewed as involving a limited set of heuristic strategies: basic concepts of transformation. For example, two of these elemental heuristics are the concepts of *working forward* and *working backward*. Both can be very useful whether you are trying to write a book, solve a math problem, or design a collaborative planning process. These strategies are involved in all problem solving but are rarely taught.

What is needed is for students to be given a set of problem-solving tools at the earliest levels of education. This would require a massive retooling of the teachers and educators in our society. The pressure to introduce these tools into the education process is going to start coming from businesses that are finding that the work force simply is not prepared. Businesses are moving toward collaborative consensus-based problem solving, and the students that are coming out of the education system have no experience in this area.

Conflict can occur at any level of society. There are interpersonal, community, group, organizational, and international level conflicts. Eighty percent of my firm's work is in the private sector, inside large companies that are experiencing all the traditional problems of working with large numbers of stakeholders. We also work with large public-private partnerships.

There is a difference between *negotiation* and *mediation* (the predominant focus of the Harvard Program on Negotiation), and collaborative problem solving and facilitation. The first approach sees conflict as fundamentally a negotiation, sometimes requiring third-party mediation. The second approach views conflict as a problem involving many stakeholders, often requiring third-party facilitation. Mediation relies heavily on caucusing with separate parties. Facilitation operates with all the stakeholders meeting face to face in a collaborative setting. Small group conflicts can often be resolved through meeting facilitation. Complex, multiparty conflicts require the design of large-scale collaborative problem solving processes.

*What are the different ways our society makes decisions?* Our society is based on win-lose decision making. Democracy is based on majority rule where 51% can determine an outcome. In executive and judicial decision making, decisions are deferred to higher authorities, and in these decision-making processes, there is a winner and a loser.

Our experience has been that there is a growing interest in finding alternatives to the win-lose decision-making approach. Negotiation, mediation, facilitation, and collaborative problem solving are all examples of consensus-based win-win approaches.

*Consensus* means that everybody in the group is able fundamentally to live with and support actively the decision. Everyone must feel that the decision is a win for him or her as well as for everyone else in the group. The proliferating number of different courses offered in some aspect of nonadversarial dispute resolution are evidence of this new consensus building trend. What forces are causing this change to take place?

## Forces for Collaboration

One of the major forces for the growing interest in win-win approaches is the lateralization of power. Many of us have a fantasy that when we finally get to head an organization, we will have much power and will be able to make many decisions. However, this is not so. Let us look at the situation of a school superintendent. What groups have the power to block the superintendents, making life very difficult? To name a few: the school board, voters, parents, teachers, the city council, the bus drivers, and the courts.

Similarly, in the private sector, most CEOs do not feel very powerful. The warfare between divisions in large corporations is as bad as it is in communities. In many companies there are multiple divisions with different responsibilities, each trying to protect itself. Each has the power to make things very difficult for the other.

The lateralization of power is a relatively new phenomenon. About 20 years ago, if you were at the top of an organization or government agency, there were relatively few people below you who had the power to block your decisions. Now many more groups have this power. One reason this has occurred is that the complexity and interrelatedness of issues has increased. Second, there is also a growing dissatisfaction and distrust with leadership in the post-Nixon, post-Watergate era from people who are no longer willing to say, "The guys upstairs must know what they're doing." The concept of a leader or manager with complete authority has really changed tremendously. A final factor is the growing number of organized advocacy groups. In a city like San Francisco, on any issue there are at least 20 groups that will surface claiming they represent the interests of the community. This advocacy has gone to such an extreme that we are at a standstill on many issues.

Another force moving us in the direction of consensus based win-win decision making is that experience has shown us that win-lose approaches such as taking disputes to courts, strikes, protests, and riots really produce lose-lose results.

If I have no power and you have all the power, the only thing I can do is to drag you down to a lose-lose situation. I may pay for it by being fired, but at least I pull you down and stop the assembly line. We have gotten very good at figuring out how to stop each other in a variety of ways. Once we recognize that we are only pulling each other down, there will be an interest in moving to a more collaborative win-win approach.

Another force is a dissatisfaction with adversarial processes. People are not very happy after an adversarial divorce or an adversarial dispute among partners in a corporation.

And finally there is a growing body of evidence that there are alternatives and that problems and disputes can be handled differently. Much of our challenge in communities and organizations is simply to show that there is an alternative. Consensus-based win-win decisions are possible most of the time. We have developed a mentality that they are not possible and that conflict is a zero-sum game. This attitude is self-fulfilling.

## Resistances to Collaboration

I have discussed some of the forces that are driving our society toward consensus based decision making. Now let us look at some of the resistances.

One resistance is the phenomenon of leadership. We know much more about how to design and manage collaborative win-win planning processes than we know about the kind of leadership that is needed to support them. The model of leadership that exists to this day is that leaders should have all the right answers even though they themselves know that they do not. Who could get elected by saying, "I don't know all the right answers?"

On the one hand, we are interested in building collaborative processes and, on the other, we are still expecting leaders to come charging in on white horses with the right decisions. Many people who are in leadership roles have been rewarded for being bright, quick, and good problem solvers. Often when these people find themselves as heads of organizations, families, or churches, they try to solve all the problems and make all the decisions themselves and discover that this approach does not work. It is very hard to accept the need to be more collaborative and involve more people in decision making.

If your boss is a Theory X type, who believes in autocratic decision making, it will be hard to convince him or her to involve the rest of the staff in decision making. However, there is a growing body of leaders in both the public and private sectors who are looking for alternative ways of operating more facilitatively, but who simply do not have the tools. They have not received them in business school, engineering school, or elsewhere.

A second reason for resistance to consensus building is the fear of loss of power by those in leadership positions.

A third reason, related to the fear of loss of power, is a reluctance by those in power to legitimize the existence of all parties. If I invite you to the table or to the planning room, I am legitimizing your existence. If I invite the PLO to talk about what should be done in the Middle East, I am acknowledging that they exist. I have tried to put together collaborative processes, particularly at the municipal level, whereby the management will acknowledge only one of several groups that represent a particular stakeholder group. I remember one situation in which a city manager did not want to recognize the black police association and felt that by including the association in the negotiations, it would only legitimize their role.

A fourth reason for resistance is that the knowledge of how to design and manage these processes is not very well known. The thought of involving large numbers of people in figuring out a transportation plan for a city is overwhelming to most people who do not have the tools. They would like to do it but feel that it would be impossible; it would take too much time and be too inefficient. A collaborative process does require more time and money initially, but in the long run, it will save time and money.

Others resist because they have had a bad experience with collaborative approaches. They tried it, it did not work, and they are turned off and cynical. People have to understand that this is a learning process. If you fall down the first time, you do not quit trying to walk.

## Collaborative Problem Solving:
## Tools and Principles

What tools are needed for successful collaborative problem solving? What strategies are useful in specific situations?

Let us begin by looking at the planning process. The American approach to planning has been typically a linear one—for example, to hire some consultants and to come up with a plan. At this point a number of different parties surface and say, "Why weren't we involved?" "Why didn't you notify us?" "You left out such and such." It then takes a tremendous amount of time to try to sell the solution. In fact, this is the most time-consuming part of the process.

An example is the Yerba Buena Convention Center in San Francisco that was proposed back in the 1950s and finally broke ground in the early 1980s. It took 30 years to get it going. A process that takes this long is expensive in terms of lost jobs, lost convention business, and escalating construction costs. In determining the costs and benefits of a planning process, one not only must look at the length of the planning phase (when the plan is devised) but also must consider how long it will take to sell the plan and move to implementation.

There is an alternative to the linear planning process I have described. It is what I call an *accordion* approach. It involves identifying all the key stakeholders and including them in the planning process from the beginning. The key stakeholders themselves determine whether there is a problem and whether they want to work collaboratively to solve it. If so, they work together, step by step, through the planning phase, continually checking back with their constituencies. The participants first work for agreement on the definition of the issues and then go on to solutions. It is important that this accordion collaborative process continues through the implementation phase.

Faced with the possibility of participating in a consensus-based process, many mayors or managers might say, "It sounds fine, but how do I go about operating in this kind of situation without losing my power and responsibility?" They fear that if they enter into a collaborative process, they will somehow get outvoted and will have to abdicate their power or responsibility. The key to dealing with this fear lies in a better understanding of consensus-based decision making.

For example, let us say I have been asked to come up with a decision about which insurance policy to recommend. I have a number of different options for making this decision. I could make a decision and announce it to my staff. Or, I could call my staff in individually and ask each what he or she thought. In this case, I would have a more informed decision. Or I could say, "There are some strong feelings on this issue so let us try to get a consensus." I could ask someone to facilitate the discussion or try to play this role as well. I would set certain ground rules; I would clarify my constraints and the options with which I could not live. Various techniques could be used to work through the phases of collaborative problem solving. One of two things could happen by the end of the meeting. Either we reach consensus (meaning that all of us, including me, can live with and actively support the decision) or we do not reach consensus, in which case the decision falls back to me.

The key to acceptance of collaborative problem solving by leaders is to think about the process as a movement back and forth between formal and informal structures of decision making. It does not replace the formal mechanisms in a city or an organization. The decisions made by a collaborative group usually must be approved by a vote of a formal decision-making authority (i.e., city council or the board of directors). People need to be reminded that their solutions will not be effective unless they can gain the approval of the ultimate decision-making authority.

Establishing such a collaborative process within an organization or city often involves the creation of a parallel structure and neutral territory to surface systemwide issues. This unbound structure does not replace but, rather, supports the formal structure. Because a multistakeholder collaborative process is time consuming, it should only be applied to strategic issues. For important policy issues, it provides a very different kind of format where the city council, the mayor's staff, business organizations and community groups can come together in an environment that is not perceived as being manipulative.

It is essential that the key decision makers agree to participate in a collaborative process and that they see it as an integral part of their decision making. There are distinctions between some citizen-involvement processes and effective collaborative problem-solving processes. When the mayor and his or her key staff people show up, or the CEO shows up, participants begin to feel that this process is being taken seriously and that there is a real possibility for their ideas to be implemented.

# Designing a Consensus-Based Planning Process

The following principles are useful to consider in every consensus-based process. They are very simple and yet often difficult to implement. But if you do not attend to these principles and try to cut corners, they will come back to haunt you.

### Representation

The first principle is that if you really are serious about developing consensus, you have to include from the beginning all the stakeholders who have the power to make decisions, are responsible for implementing them, are affected by them, and have the power to block them. You have to do what is called a *stakeholder analysis.* The tendency is to want to exclude certain groups because they will cause trouble. The truth is that if groups are cut out of the process, they may do more harm than if they are included. In most cases, the person who everybody thought would be the alligator turns out to be the pussycat, if he or she is really brought into the process. Often, identified alligators are just frustrated. Once they see that there is a constructive way to work through an issue, they can become strong supporters of the process.

If you are making decisions by consensus, it does not make any difference how many people represent a particular point of view as long as all the other key points of view are also represented. It is much easier to keep the process open and permeable rather than to argue ahead of time about exactly how many from each organization should be involved.

Grouping people according to interests does not allow for new coalitions to form or for stereotypes to be broken down. We are working on a master plan for downtown Denver. One of the issues being negotiated is historic preservation. We cannot assume that all developers are on one side, all historic preservationists are on another, and all community people are on a third. The lines that form do not fall by sector but, rather, by all sorts of blends that change according to the issues.

## Agreeing on the Problem

A second fundamental principle for designing a consensus building planning process is that if you do not agree on the problem, you will never agree on the solution. We all tend to jump to solutions and positions before we discuss the issues and our basic interests. The success of a collaborative planning process depends on clarifying and legitimizing interests and reaching consensus on the definition and root causes of a problem before moving on to solutions.

## Owning and Designing the Process

A third principle is that the participants have to own the process from the very beginning. The third party cannot come in and say, "This is what we are going to do." As a third-party consultant, you must assist the participants to design the process themselves.

A typical collaborative planning process might proceed through the following phases: Process design, task force startup and education, problem definition and analysis, alternative solutions, evaluation, decision making, and implementation. How these phases are orchestrated is part of the skill and technology of what we call *process management.*

## Concentric Rings of Involvement

Another basic principle is called *concentric rings of involvement.* Large scale collaborative processes can become overly structured and bureaucratic quite easily. A steering committee can begin to think of itself as *the* community and close its doors to all newcomers. It is important to find ways to involve people who want to join after the process has begun. There are a variety of mechanisms that can be used to keep boundaries permeable. Additional parties can be included in task forces. Participants burn out and drop out, particularly if the process continues for a number of years. Others can be brought in to replace those that no longer want to participate.

### Committing Time, Energy, and Resources

It takes time, energy, and money to make collaborative processes work. People will believe that you are serious when resources are committed. A large-scale collaborative planning process can easily cost $200,000 a year and require the commitment of a full-time process manager or executive director.

### An Open and Visible Process

The process must be open and visible. You cannot build broad-based consensus that no one knows about. It is also important to look for some short-term successes along the way.

### Teaching New Behavior

And finally, the quality of what happens and the way people behave in the face-to-face sessions really makes a difference. If the meetings are seen as manipulative, the process will fall apart. Many parties may at first find it difficult to drop their old ways of operating. Managers must be coached on how to participate effectively and taught a new set of leadership tools.

Advocates must also be taught how to participate effectively in a collaborative process. It does not work to come crashing into the middle of a meeting shouting your demands. You will only meet resistance. There is a saying: "Check your guns at the door, but don't throw them away." An advocacy group can always fall back to its guns of protest or lawsuit. It is just the threat of fallback that keeps participants engaged in trying to seek consensus. However, in this process there is a different set of ground rules governing effective participation. You do not have to scream louder than everyone else to be heard.

The exciting thing about collaborative processes is that they are educational and they empower people. People can take the skills back to their own organizations. When these skills are disseminated throughout a community, the community is able to handle conflicts in more constructive ways.

# Cases Studies

### Case 1: Newark, New Jersey

Newark, New Jersey, is an example of East Coast urban decay. Vacant lots are scattered between houses–the city looks like a guy with his teeth knocked out. Some major industries do exist, one being Prudential Insurance Company. A senior executive from the Pru said, "We can't tolerate this continued deterioration. We won't be able to attract employees to this city anymore." He got all the key actors–the mayor, the city council, the heads of most of the major organizations and community leaders–to agree to come to a meeting to explore options for working together to change the situation. He did not know how to go about managing the process and who should run this first meeting. He knew that there was a desire to work together, and at the same time, he knew that there were many complex issues involved. At this point, he turned to my firm for facilitation and process design assistance.

We helped the group design an agenda and facilitated their first 2-hour meeting. The agenda included listing some of the major issues facing the city and beginning to develop a vision of the future. It was important to realize that they were not going to solve all the problems in a 2-hour meeting. The big decision that the group had to make during the meeting was whether they were willing to consider investing the time and resources to work together and operate collaboratively. They decided to do so and self-selected a group of people, a process design committee, to recommend how to proceed. Because the level of trust was so low, 25 of 60 people, including the mayor, volunteered for the process design committee.

We served as third-party facilitators and consultants to this committee. We gave them tools to help them assess an alternative planning process. The group, however, wanted some immediate successes to test the effectiveness of this kind of collaborative process. The committee tried to come up with specific options that would bring quick results, including cleaning up one of the corridors coming into the city, creating a job generation program, and dealing with some specific housing issues.

The process design committee members went back to the large group, which had by this time grown from 60 to 100 people. The committee offered the above options. (At this early point in the process there is always a test as to whether consensus can be reached.) The group of 100 was able to reach consensus on these three short-term task forces despite strong challenges between the neighborhood and the business communities. The fact that the whole group could resolve their differences gave it confidence that consensus was possible. The process design committee was encouraged to design the rest of the strategic planning process.

The citizens of Newark created a nonprofit organization called the Newark Collaboration Process. After much negotiation, an executive committee was formed to manage the effort. This committee does not make unilateral content decisions but is responsible for the administration and management of the overall process. Money for a staff was raised and Hewlett-Packard donated computer resources.

What has happened in Newark is very exciting. There is a very different kind of feeling in the city now. Substantial investments have been made and economic development has occurred in Newark. Recent articles in *The New York Times* and elsewhere describe a "renaissance" occurring in Newark and attribute this change to the fact that this community is demonstrating that it can work together.

### Case 2: The Federal Bureau of Land Management

Some organizations test collaborative processes internally before testing them with external stakeholders. The U.S. Bureau of Land Management (BLM) recognized the need to develop collaborative processes to deal with large environmental disputes. The BLM was involved in designing one of the largest land use plans ever attempted in the United States, encompassing the whole California desert. More than 150 stakeholder groups had been identified. Meanwhile, BLM had created a 200-person staff organization to do the actual drafting of the plan. These 200 people were sequestered in a building in Southern California and divided up into groups, according to expertise and subject area (i.e., wildlife, recreation, etc.). These groups were at war with one another. All were suboptimizing, coming up with proposals according to their particular interests and values.

The BLM had no idea how to reconcile these internal conflicts. Our job as facilitators was to get the various divisions to talk with one another and develop a clear process to enable them to come up with a common plan. After these internal interest groups demonstrated some success applying collaborative processes among themselves, the BLM began to use these processes to collaborate with many of the external stakeholder groups. In the end, the BLM created a truly collaborative and successful process for resolving most of the issues in the California Desert Plan, one that reconciled the internal agency's experts and that acknowledged and dealt with the special interests of various stakeholders.

I do not know anyone who claims that all issues can be resolved through collaborative problem solving and negotiation. These processes are not panaceas. However, I also believe that they should be considered before turning to more adversarial processes. In the cases that I have cited, facilitation and consensus-building process allowed solutions to be developed and implemented cooperatively by formerly adversarial parties. Turning conflicts into constructive opportunities for positive results is what this work is all about.

# PART II

# Applying Mutual Gains to Organizations

## Introduction

▶ Creating awareness of how different players perceive the real problem and helping to change locked-in, unproductive habits are the themes in this part about applying these problem-solving frameworks to organizations. The authors speak from their experiences in different settings and analyze the obstacles to applying their process frameworks in specific contexts.

Sander's chapter on the range of dispute resolution techniques being used by the legal profession and courts is heartening. Saving time, energy, and money of the court system and individuals are goals, but they must not outweigh the overriding concern for fairness and the constitutional guarantees of due process.

Susskind applies his ideas to building consensus around how-to issues in public debate and demonstrates some successes that have been achieved using process skills. He views the processes as supplemental aids to existing public systems but to the extent that regulatory negotiation and other processes transform the way that public debate takes place, the change may be transformative rather than merely supplemental.

McKersie and Heckscher show how difficult unfreezing old habits can be, even in a climate in which those habits are self-defeating. They offer a number of suggestions and hopes for employment relations in the long run, while recognizing that many unionized organizations will need to make some painful adjustments if cooperative, mutual gains decision making is ever to become the predominant mode of collective bargaining. Although there are success stories, they are not the rule; their chapters point out why that is so and how some of the ideas and techniques presented here can help to change the existing paradigm.

Rowe offers many interesting insights around the issue of choice in organizational settings. Rather than arguing for one way of doing things, she urges that employers set up systems in which their employees help to create and select the option of their choice. Perhaps more than any other chapter, this one emphasizes that there is no one right way to resolve anything and that an individual's freedom to create his or her own dispute resolution process is a prerequisite for a successful system within an organization.

# 4

# The Courthouse and Alternative Dispute Resolution

FRANK E. A. SANDER

## Introduction

▶ This chapter introduces alternative dispute resolution (ADR) mechanisms and the ways in which they can be further integrated into the court system. I will start with an overview of dispute resolution and then focus on some specific processes within the court system. I use three concepts to examine disputes and their resolution: *the dispute pyramid, the process spectrum,* and *inside-the-court and outside-the-court mechanisms.*

## The Dispute Pyramid

The dispute pyramid (Figure 4.1) is an inverted pyramid. At the top of the pyramid is what Bill Felstiner, Richard Abel, and Austin Sarat (1980-1981) call *perceived injurious experiences* (PIES); a person feels hurt about something. The next level of the pyramid

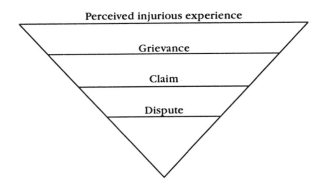

**Figure 4.1.** The Dispute Pyramid

is the identification of a culprit, the person who is responsible for the injury. There is now a grievance against someone. As you move down the inverted pyramid, the injured party would make a claim against the culprit. However, not all people make claims. For example, you might want to take some sort of action against your employer if she or he transfers you to a job that you do not like. But you realize that it would be difficult to get another job and that you need to get along with your employer, so you do not make a claim. It all depends, in dispute resolution jargon, on what alternatives you have available to you, what your best alternative to a negotiated agreement (BATNA) is. Not everybody who has voiced a grievance will make a claim. If a claim is made, it will likely become a dispute. But not all claims become disputes because some culprits believe that the injured party is correct and agree to compensate them.

One of my students who works at the Harvard Mediation Small Claims Program told me of a case she was attempting to mediate. After identifying herself as a mediator and explaining what a mediator does, the defendant responded, "The plaintiff is absolutely right, I owe him that money." My student was very upset because she did not have a chance to mediate the case, which shows you that we are not always trying to settle disputes, but sometimes trying to learn how to mediate. Clearly this is a claim that did not become a dispute, because the respondent accepted the claim.

**Figure 4.2.** The Process Spectrum

Once we have a genuine dispute, there are many alternatives available to resolve them. Some disputes go to court, where a variety of mechanisms are used. Others go to an assortment of noncourt complaint mechanisms such as labor arbitration, ombudsmen, and consumer complaint mechanisms such as the Better Business Bureau. Some of these cases eventually wind up in court, but most of them do not.

What can be learned from the dispute pyramid is that the courts are used to resolve only a tiny proportion of people's perceived injurious experiences. Law schools should not be spending all their time on such a small part of the dispute resolution universe. We are, therefore, trying to convince law schools to spend more time focusing on alternative methods of dispute resolution. We are making gradual progress; increasingly, some of these concepts are being introduced. Courses are being offered in negotiation, mediation, and other forms of alternative dispute resolution.

## The Process Spectrum

Another useful tool for examining dispute resolution processes is the process spectrum (Figure 4.2). As one moves along the spectrum from right to left, third-party involvement increases. At the extreme right end there is *avoidance* which is comparable with the level of the dispute pyramid at which a person decides not to voice a claim. Once a claim becomes a dispute, there are several processes that can be used to resolve it. The most common form of dispute resolution is bargaining or negotiation, a field that has grown considerably over the past 15 or 20 years. There is increased third-party involvement in the resolution as you move along the spectrum from negotiation to mediation and finally to adjudication. There are essentially three types of adjudication: adjudication in courts, arbitration, and that in administrative agencies.

A dividing line exists between negotiation and mediation. To one side of the line people handle disputes on their own, either by not voicing a claim or by negotiating. The processes to the left of the line—mediation and adjudication—involve third parties. However, the really important dividing line exists between mediation and adjudication because mediation, although a third-party process, is really more akin to negotiation than to adjudication. I think the key to understanding dispute resolution is understanding the significance of the dividing line between mediation and adjudication.

In teaching mediation, I ask people to take a relatively simple problem such as an uncomplicated divorce or a simple dispute between two neighbors; I then ask them first to resolve the dispute by adjudication and then by mediation. Think about what happens.

When people play the roles of the disputants as well as the third party, they feel entirely different in the two processes. In mediation, the disputants feel much more in control of the process. They come up with and, therefore, own the result; the mediator does not tell them what the answer is. The mediator is simply a catalyst. In adjudication, the disputants have to be very careful not to alienate the adjudicator, because she or he can impose a solution on them. Their whole argumentation is entirely different. They play up to the adjudicator, which is what happens in most courts between the lawyers and the judge.

The third party also feels different in these two processes. In mediation, the third party typically feels less responsibility for the substance of the agreements, although this depends on the type of dispute. This raises the issue of the ethical responsibility of the mediator. Many argue that the primary criterion for judging a mediation is whether the parties are satisfied with the outcome, not whether the results are fair and well-reasoned and serve as a precedent for the future, criteria that would apply in judging a court decision. Susskind has argued that, at least in the public sector, mediation outcomes should be judged by whether they are fair, efficient, wise, and stable.[1]

In the mediation chapter of the book *Dispute Resolution* (Goldberg, Sander, & Rogers, 1992) there is a hypothetical Socratic dialogue that addresses this issue. Does the mediator have the same kind of social responsibility as the adjudicator in producing an ethical decision? Should the mediator withdraw if she or he strongly disagrees with and does not wish to bless an arguably unfair decision with which both parties are satisfied? The conclusion is that the ethical responsibility of a mediator depends on the nature of the relationship between the parties and the kind of dispute that is involved.

In the environmental area, and perhaps also in the family area, there is generally a public interest in the outcome of the dispute, and the parties themselves are often not sophisticated; often too, there are bargaining imbalances between the parties. In these cases, the mediator may have an ethical and social responsibility to ensure a fair decision, similar to, if not the same as, a judge. By contrast, in the labor sphere, where you have sophisticated people who regularly deal with each other, most mediators feel that the goal does not extend much beyond producing a result with which both parties are satisfied.

Before I leave the world of mediation, it is worth noting that there are two distinct forms of mediation. In one, which may be termed *rights based,* the mediator looks to the rights that the disputants would have in court, and with that guideline as a benchmark, tries to help the disputants resolve the dispute within those parameters. For example, in a personal injury case, such a rights-based mediator might seek to predict the likely result in court if the case went to trial and then use that information to help the parties reach an acceptable settlement.

A different approach is one that focuses on the *interests,* or needs, of the parties. Take, for example, a dispute between two partners of a small manufacturing business, one of which has contributed the capital and the other an invention. Assume that the inventor partner has come forth with a product that was initially rejected by the capital partner, but that the latter now wants to appropriate this product for the partnership. The rights-based approach would look to the outcome if this case were to go to court and seeks to use that *shadow* to facilitate a settlement. An interest-based approach would look to the needs of the parties (such as the inventor's need to exercise his creative powers while the supplier of capital wants to make sure that the inventor does not use the business to feather his own nest).

Inherent in this approach is the desirability of fashioning a new relationship between the two disputants that will address the general question of the inventor's relation to the company with respect to future inventions and that may incidentally yield an acceptable solution to the present dispute. For example, regardless of what a court might decide in this situation, the disputants after canvassing various options might decide that a fair solution in such cases would be for the inventor to get 25% of the royalties off the top and then to contribute the remainder to the partnership. Or they may decide to formulate a much more complex arrangement. But the key point is that mediation will attempt to explore the interests of each disputant and then come up with some accommodative resolution.

## Hybrid Dispute Resolution Mechanisms

Let us return now to the process spectrum. Galanter (1984) at the Wisconsin Law School coined the term *litigotiation*. He says that most cases are really disposed of through litigotiation, a combination of litigation and negotiation. There are many hybrid processes that combine some aspects of the primary processes discussed above, including fact finder, neutral expert, minitrial, summary jury trial, mediation-arbitration, and final offer arbitration. All are described in this chapter.

*Fact Finder.* A fact finder combines some aspects of mediation and arbitration. A fact finder is similar to a mediator in that she or he is a disinterested third party who determines the facts but has no authority to impose a decision on the parties. However, a fact finder, based on his or her conclusions from the case, can weigh in on the side of one of the disputants. For example, a fact finder in a labor dispute can find that the union is correct in saying that a fair wage to pay for a particular job is $7 rather than $5 an hour. The effect of such a finding is, therefore, similar to quasi-adjudication.

*Final Offer Arbitration.* Final offer arbitration is a hybrid of negotiation and adjudication used in baseball player salary disputes and in public sector bargaining, particularly for the police and fire departments. Each side comes up with its best offer. The third party must pick one of the offers but cannot select a compromise between the two. In form, the process is similar to adjudication or arbitration in that the third party chooses and imposes the outcome. But, in effect, it is similar to negotiation in that it presses the disputants to compromise and make more reasonable demands because they know that the third party will pick the most reasonable offer. It encourages the disputants to come up with their own result, but if they are unable to, it offers a third-party decision as a failsafe.

*Mediation-Arbitration.* Mediation-arbitration is known in the field as med-arb and is a mechanism commonly used in labor disputes. The process begins with mediation. If the parties cannot settle, the mediator takes off the mediation hat, puts on the arbitration hat, and imposes a solution. Some academics in the dispute resolution field are very troubled by this method, because they think that it commingles two very different processes in a nonconstructive manner. The parties in a mediation often give the mediator information in confidence. If the mediator suddenly becomes a judge, she or he can impose a decision based on confidential information received from one of the parties during the mediation. However, people in the labor field advocate this method and use it all the time. I am reminded of the Maine farmer who, when asked whether he believes in infant baptism, said, "Believe in it? Hell, I've seen it done." Of course, this issue of role confusion can be avoided if the arbitrator is a different person than the mediator, but then there is also a concomitant loss in efficiency.

Another variant, used in South Africa, is call *arb-med.* There, the neutral, after hearing the case, writes a decision that is then placed

in a sealed envelope and put aside. Only if the subsequent mediation fails to produce an agreement is the envelope opened.

## Inside-the-Court and Outside-the-Court Mechanisms

I will now focus on a third way of looking at dispute resolution
by considering inside-the-court and outside-the-court mechanisms.
There are many outside-the-court dispute resolution mechanisms
that are used regularly: labor arbitration, commercial arbitration,
consumer protection mechanisms such as the Better Business Bureau, internal grievance mechanisms in prisons and hospitals,
neighborhood justice centers, media complaint mechanisms such
as *action lines,* private divorce mediation, and environmental mediation. Some of the disputes that are initially brought to these mechanisms may ultimately go to court but in most cases that does not
happen.

Edwards (1986) and others in the legal field are concerned that
"ADR may be dangerous to your health." They are worried that
alternative dispute resolution (ADR) may usurp the important role
of the courts in vindicating public rights concerning such issues
as employment discrimination, desegregation, fair housing, social
security, and other public rights issues. He does not want to see
alternative mechanisms used to bargain away these rights. Edwards's
message is that ADR is a useful approach for cases that are not in
the courts and that do not address public rights and values.

This is a legitimate concern except that there really is no clean
separation between inside- and outside-the-court processes and
between public and private uses. In fact, one of the big challenges
in this field is to develop a dynamic interplay between court and
noncourt processes (i.e., between mediation and adjudication) to
achieve more desirable solutions. For example, if you have an
environmental case in which the polluters will not sit down with
the pollutees, the victims, you may need the court or a statutory
requirement such as an environmental impact statement to force
the polluters to deal with the pollutees. But the courts are not a
good place to resolve complex environmental disputes. What is
needed is some creative interplay between the court, which can
use its power to get people to the bargaining table, and negotiation

or mediation, with its many advantages such as greater flexibility, ownership of the outcome, diversity of solutions, and maximizing joint gains.

## Overcoming Obstacles to Settlement

Why do people bring cases to court and why do cases not settle once they are filed in court? The transaction costs, including lawyers' fees and waiting time, are so high in court cases that there is a strong incentive to settle without court intervention. Despite these incentives, there are at least five major reasons why cases do not settle out of court. It is important to examine these reasons and the ways in which ADR mechanisms can be used to overcome these obstacles to settlement. (These ADR mechanisms will be discussed at greater length later on.)

1. *The parties have different information and facts.* Mechanisms that could be used to resolve this impediment to settlement are facilitation and other third-party processes (such as mediation) as well as a structured information exchange such as a minitrial.

2. *The parties may have different assessments of the same information.* They may agree on what the facts are, but each party believes that if the case is brought to court, it has a good chance of winning. One outside-the-court mechanism that can be used to resolve these differences is an experienced lawyer or retired judge who can give the parties an educated appraisal of the likely court outcome. This is commonly called *case evaluation,* or *early neutral evaluation.* As will be apparent below, the minitrial or summary jury trial can also serve this purpose.

3. *There are constituency problems between the lawyer and client.* In some cases the lawyers feel that the case could be settled right away, but their clients do not understand the issue and will not agree to settle. In other cases, the clients think that the case could be settled right away, but their lawyers have let the case take on a life of its own, beyond the simple business problem that it originally was. Therefore, most ADR settlement mechanisms require the presence of the clients and the lawyers at all critical times in the settlement process.

*4. There is a different willingness to settle.* Typically, the plaintiff is very eager to try to settle the case but the defendant is not, because the status quo favors the defendant. Therefore, the defendant drags his or her feet, slowing down the process. Under these circumstances, some kind of sanctions may be needed for unreasonable refusal by the defendant to participate in the settlement process.

*5. Finally, there are emotional considerations.* Defendants and plaintiffs often refuse to settle out of court as a matter of principle. A plaintiff will often say, "I don't care whether I get a cent, but I want that bastard to pay." And the defendant may say, "I'm willing to pay any amount of money, but not to that S.O.B. who's suing me in this outrageous action." A federal judge in Boston worked out a solution to a case like this whereby the defendant paid the money to the judge's favorite charity and everybody was happy. The plaintiff got his wish that the defendant pay. The defendant got his wish that the plaintiff not collect any money. This was a very innovative solution to a not uncommon problem.

Let us look in detail at some of the mechanisms that can be used by the overburdened court system to resolve these issues and reduce the number of cases being brought before it. These mechanisms break down into two categories: *categorical referral* and *individual referral.*

## Categorical Referral

Categorical referral is a mechanism by which the legislature takes certain categories of cases out of the courts and requires that an attempt be made to resolve them through other mechanisms. For example, in California, contested child custody cases must first go to mediation before they can go to court. In Massachusetts, all medical malpractice claims have to be brought before a three-person tribunal—consisting of a doctor, a lawyer, and a judge—to determine whether there is probable cause that the doctor was negligent. If the panel finds probable cause, the case goes to court. If the panel finds no probable cause, the plaintiff has to put up a bond for the defendant's costs before the case can go to court.

One of the most familiar kinds of categorical referral is *court-annexed arbitration*. In about 18 states and some dozen federal district courts, cases involving personal injury, malpractice, consumer, and other money claim cases below a certain dollar amount are required first to go to arbitration. Exceptions are typically made for cases that involve civil rights and public values. The arbitration takes place outside the court, but we call it court annexed to distinguish it from voluntary arbitration, such as that used in labor cases in which the union and the company agree, in their collective bargaining agreement, to submit every dispute under the agreement to final and binding arbitration. The union and the company thus voluntarily waive their right to go to court.

Categorical referral and court-annexed arbitration are most often mandated by statute but at times by court rule. These mechanisms are only conditional diversions from the court; there are always provisions that the cases can ultimately go to court because constitutional provisions usually require access to the courts.

Categorical referral and court-annexed arbitration raise several issues and concerns. Is it fair to the plaintiffs that there be a mandated extra step that they must go through? How effective have they been in reducing the number of cases that have to go to court? Are they keeping the right cases out of court?

Let us look at the Massachusetts medical malpractice tribunal. It was instituted in the mid-1970s when there was growing concern about the increasing number of malpractice suits and doctors could not get insurance. This process has been challenged in court in regard to the legality (even though ultimately there is access to the court) of requiring plaintiffs in a medical malpractice case to go to the tribunal and then to court, whereas plaintiffs in a legal malpractice case would not have to do this. The courts have given varying answers to this question but have generally upheld its legality, particularly when there is a compelling reason for the diversion such as a malpractice crisis and court congestion.

Early data showed that approximately half the cases get screened out of the courts through the tribunal. In 40% of the cases, it is determined that there is probable cause. In the other 60%, it is determined that there is no probable cause but about 25% of these (15% of all the cases) ultimately go to court because the plaintiff decides to put up a bond.

Many cases are thus being kept out the courts, which makes the doctors happy. But the key question is: Are the right ones being kept out? Studies must be done to compare the cases that were found not meritorious, but were brought to the court anyway (the 15% mentioned above) with those that were found meritorious, to determine whether the juries reached different conclusions. If not, then the screening process is not adequately doing its job.

As regards court-annexed arbitration, the existing studies suggest that if the programs are set up carefully the mechanisms work quite well. Ideally, what is needed is an experiment in which cases are randomly assigned to the court and to arbitration. The two methods can then be compared to determine the differences between them. Such a study was recently done in North Carolina, and it showed that arbitration disposed of cases faster and resulted in greater disputant satisfaction with the outcome and procedure.[2]

An example of a creative interplay between court mechanisms and noncourt mechanisms is the following. In California, there were 137 claims in a land fraud case. Once the court set the general principles for the case, the rest of the claims were referred to arbitration.[3] Using this simpler and more informal procedure avoided recourse to the federal court for a series of routine fact determinations. The potential is there for many such collaborations and innovations.

## Individual Referral

Individual referral, whereby each case is looked at and referred to a particular mechanism, is used by the court in a number of states. Individual referral mechanisms include mediation (sometimes through a special master), neutral experts, and minitrials and summary jury trials.

*Special Master.* In recent years, courts have appointed special masters to do three things:

1. To do fact-finding in a complicated case.
2. To supervise the implementation of a decree. The special master would help implement the decision in a large-scale institutional litigation case such as a constitutional challenge to prison conditions.

3. To resolve a complex multiparty dispute and to be responsible for making recommendations to the judge.

This can raise similar questions to those raised by the med-arb mechanism discussed earlier. Suppose the mediator has talked with the parties confidentially, as mediators often do, and following the parties' failure to agree, recommends a possible solution to the court. Is that proper? The parties may object that they have not been heard in a formal process. Many of these questions have yet to be fully worked out.

*Neutral Expert.* A neutral expert is used when there is a technical question that is preventing the resolution of a case. Courts have power, under Federal Rule of Evidence 408, to bring in a neutral expert—even against the desires of the parties—to give evidence on the critical issue in the case.

*Minitrial and Summary Jury Trial.* Perhaps the most interesting devices are the minitrial and the summary jury trial. Both of these were invented in the 1970s.

The minitrial was invented in 1976 by some lawyers who had a major case that had been going on for about 3 or 4 years and had run up over a $1 million in attorneys' fees. In an effort to resolve the case they developed a structured information exchange, which some newspaper subsequently dubbed minitrial. I think the term *information exchange* is more descriptive.

Here is how it works. Each party presents the essence of its case in any manner that it chooses, for example, through documents, lawyer talk, or even a key witness. The whole process is very informal. The length of the proceeding and the types of evidence allowed are determined by the parties at the outset. The key requirement is that top decision makers of both sides, such as the presidents of the companies in a corporate dispute, as well as their lawyers, must be present at the proceeding. There is usually also a presider, who might be a retired judge, a lawyer or other neutral party. After the plaintiff's presentation—which may last a half day or so—the defendant gets to ask questions and vice versa. But the neutral presider does not play the role of a judge; he or she rather acts as a kind of master of ceremonies.

When each side thus fully understands the strength and weakness of each other's case, the two settlement officials sit down together to try to resolve the issue, usually from a business, rather than a legal, approach. In the first minitrial, involving a case that had been in litigation for 3 to 4 years, the dispute was resolved by the two businessmen in 37 minutes. It then took the lawyers 3 months to draw up the necessary papers.

If the parties cannot come to an agreement, the minitrial presider will give an opinion concerning the likely court outcome based on his or her experience. The presider may say exactly what he or she thinks would happen in court, or may say, "I think that there is a 66% chance that the plaintiff will win and the likely damages will be between $2 and $3 million." The parties then sit down with this additional information and try again to settle the case.

A minitrial is not suitable for every case, particularly those with high emotional stakes and those that involve a legal issue for which the parties want an interpretation of a statute or a binding precedent. These cases may best be resolved in court.

A summary jury trial is similar to a minitrial except that there is a mock six-person jury. The parties present their summary case as in the minitrial and the jury makes a judgment. The lawyers then have the opportunity to converse with the jury to learn how they assessed the case, which can be very helpful to them in working out a settlement. Judge Enslen of the U.S. district court in Michigan used summary jury trials in two interesting cases. One was a complex waste dumping case with 93 claims. The plaintiff and the defendant each picked their best case and the judge picked one case in between. The three cases went to three different summary juries. Once these three *boundary* cases were settled, the outcomes and information were used to settle all the other 90 cases.

Another interesting summary jury case involved a baby who was severely burned by very hot water. The plaintiff sued the manufacturer of the heater, claiming that the temperature valve was defective. The case was sent to a summary jury trial and the jury found for the defendant. When the parties spoke with the jury afterward, the jury told them that although the baby was terribly injured they did not think that the defendant was responsible. The jury, however, made it clear that if they had found liability, they would have awarded huge damages. The defendant's lawyer then told his client that although this jury did not find him liable one could not predict what another jury might do if the case were to be taken to court. He advised his client that it was his moral responsibility to give some money to the plaintiff; some would call this public relations. The defendant paid several hundred thousand dollars, and the case was settled and did not go to court. This is another example of an imaginative resolution where both the defendant and the plaintiff were able to get most of what they wanted.

All these mechanisms involve taking different ingredients and putting them together in some imaginative way to produce a process. The beauty is that they can be adapted to particular cases; the parties, with the judge, can design their own process to best meet their situation. It is like going into a candy store, choosing a little of this and a little of that and coming up with a Halloween mixture suited to your taste.

## Sanctions and Incentives

Court cases fall into two categories: those in which the defendant and the plaintiff are looking for better ways to resolve the dispute and those in which, as I mentioned earlier, one party is dragging his or her feet and does not want to settle or wants to delay settlement of the case. These parties may use outside-the-court mechanisms to further delay the settlement of the case, in that these mechanisms can potentially add one more layer to the process if the case eventually ends up in court. There are compulsory mechanisms and sanctions that can be used to prevent this from occurring.

In many court-annexed arbitration programs, such as the so-called Michigan mediation program, the party that appeals an arbitration decision to court, must improve his or her result by a certain factor (10% in Michigan), or she or he will be responsible for either the cost of the arbitration or, at times, the cost of the court proceeding. In some systems the costs are automatic and mandatory. For example, if the plaintiff got a judgment for $50,000 in arbitration and then takes the case to court to try to get a larger settlement, the final judgment would have to be at least $55,000 in the court, or the judge could impose costs on the plaintiff for taking the case to court. If the defendant were appealing the $50,000, the final judgment would have to be less than $45,000.

There is going to be a lot of litigation over these sanctions, particularly if they are high, because there will be people who will feel that they are an unconstitutional impairment of their access to court. But unless you have sanctions, outside-the-court mechanisms may simply add another layer to the process. The sanctions will have to be fine-tuned so that they will not interfere with constitutional rights, yet be severe enough to act as a deterrent against duplicative appeals.

If you were a court reformer trying to bring more ADR mechanisms into the courts, how would you fit this smorgasbord of mechanisms and processes together into a coherent court system? What should be the relationship between the court and these various mechanisms? What are the implications of combining the processes? Should categorical methods or individual methods be used?

## The Multidoor Courthouse

The multidoor courthouse is a new concept that is being experimented with in Washington, D.C., and Houston, Texas, under an American Bar Association (ABA) project with which I am involved, as well as in some other places. The basic idea is that each case that comes to court will be analyzed by an intake person and referred to the mechanism or sequence of mechanisms that is most responsive and effective for that particular kind of case. There needs to be a sophisticated screening of cases to determine which mechanism best suits a case. The criteria would include such factors as the relationship of the parties and the nature of the dispute.

There is a strong belief that mediation is one of the most effective mechanisms for resolving disputes involving parties who have a long-term, interdependent relationship that will continue in the future, because mediation can help to strengthen that relationship. If the parties had a one-time encounter and they are trying to determine who was at fault in some particular event, adjudication may be most effective. If the parties are aiming for the creation of a precedent, adjudication is necessary. Mediation does not usually create a precedent, which in most situations would be considered an advantage but in some, a disadvantage (particularly where a general policy needs to be formulated for the future). One advantage of the multidoor courthouse is that we will learn a lot more about what kinds of mechanisms work for particular kinds of cases.

Every person should have access to a variety of dispute resolution mechanisms to resolve their cases. These mechanisms must be available through the courts because, as Willie Sutton said when asked why he robbed banks, "That's where the money is." The courts are where the cases are and the money is. If there are cases that are more effectively dealt with by mediation or another form of ADR, these mechanisms must be made publicly available. Currently, if the parties to a dispute want to have their case mediated, they may have to pay a private dispute resolution provider to have their dispute resolved. But if they go down to the courthouse, they can get an adjudication free of charge, clearly an economic disincentive to the use of mediation.

The multidoor notion can have many applications. For example, an organization can set up a system whereby its disputes would be handled by the particular mechanisms most suited for their resolution. Or the courts can set up a multidoor courthouse by subject type. A court may decide that this process is suitable for family disputes but too complex for other disputes. Or lawyers can use this approach when they are canvassing possible dispute resolution options with clients.

The more I work in this area, the more I think that public education is a key issue. We need a "Perry Mediator" show on television to make people aware of the fact that there are other ways to resolve disputes. There are some exciting programs going on in high schools and grammar schools that educate children in conflict resolution. They wear T-shirts that say "I'm a Conflict Manager." Clients are increasingly putting pressure on lawyers to use these methods. So are judges.

I see the day, whether it is in the year 2000 or later, when the whole range of dispute resolution mechanisms discussed in this chapter will no longer be seen as arcane alternatives to litigation but, rather, as the central means of resolving disputes.

# Notes

1. Susskind and Cruikshank (1987).
2. Clarke, Donnelly, and Grove (1987).
3. See, for example, *Kamm v. California City Development Co.*, 509 F.2d 205 (9th Cir.), 1975: Trial court in land-fraud class action was justified in dismissing class action on basis of agreement that defendant would use arbitration to process potential multiple claims against it.

# 5

# Resolving Public Disputes

LAWRENCE SUSSKIND

▶ This chapter is about dispute resolution from my perspective as a researcher and as a mediator of conflicts in the public sector. I describe a couple of specific cases to give some life to my prescriptions. More detail is contained in *Breaking the Impasse.*[1]

## Public Policy Disputes in Perspective

There are several categories of public disputes. The first is one in which two parties fight over a single item. This includes the classic distributive bargaining situation: Whatever Party A gets, Party B loses.

A second category is one in which two parties contend over many issues. In this instance, there are opportunities for integrative or *mutual gains* bargaining, because trades can be made across issues.

Many parties battling over one issue characterizes a third category of disputes. The Law of the Sea negotiations, for example, were multilateral negotiations focused on the allocation of mineral resources in the sea bed.

The most difficult is the fourth class of disputes: many parties contesting many issues. These are the disputes that I tend to get involved in as a mediator. In public disputes, there are almost always many parties and many issues. The disputes are further complicated by the fact that we often do not know who represents some of the stake-holding interests. Sometimes people who think that they are parties are not accepted by the others; and people who say that they represent parties do not. The issues change rapidly and the parties think about them in very different ways.

Let us consider public disputes at all three levels of government: federal, state, and local.

In this country, we often take public policy disputes to the legislative arena for resolution. We dump them into the legislative hopper and wait for resolution. If we do not like the resolution that emerges, we put the unacceptable outcome into the judicial hopper. If we still do not like the results, we send it back to the legislative arena. Sometimes a dispute begins in the executive branch, after a law has been passed. An example is the Clean Air Act. Congress said, "There shall be clean air!" and left the Environmental Protection Agency (EPA) with the task of figuring out how best to achieve this goal. Then ensued the traditional administrative process of setting standards. When people did not like the standards EPA came up with, they challenged EPA in court. When they were dissatisfied with the court's response, they lobbied Congress to rewrite the Clean Air Act.

Not only do disputes move from one branch of government to another but they also move from one level to another. If you do not like a local law, you can go to the state legislature to try to have it preempted or changed. If you cannot get what you want there, maybe Congress will do something for you.

We use this rather unstable system in the United States to settle three kinds of disputes: disputes over policy priorities, disputes over the allocation of resources (not only financial, but fixed resources such as land, air, and water), and disputes over standards describing acceptable levels of risk.

Decisions are made in the legislative arena by voting, usually preceded by lobbying and logrolling (trading favors). In the judicial arena, decisions are made, presumably, with reference to the rule of law. In the executive or administrative arena, decisions are made by relying on technical expertise.

The conventional system of public dispute resolution does not produce results that are good enough for us to be satisfied. Indeed the results are often perceived as unfair by many of the parties with a stake in a dispute. Furthermore, the results are often not as efficient as we would like them to be in terms of minimizing costs. In addition, good solutions are often disregarded because the system of dispute resolution is awkward and cannot find them. Many outcomes are not stable. Often the stakeholders are not committed to them and key parties have not really accepted them. Finally, the results of many dispute resolution efforts are not really as wise as hindsight allows us to believe they should have been.

Because conventional public dispute resolution procedures do not produce results that are sufficiently fair, efficient, stable, or wise, I think that we should search for better ways of handling these kinds of conflicts. I am interested in ways of *supplementing* the conventional system for resolving public disputes in the hope that we can produce results that are perceived as fairer by those affected; demonstrably more efficient—produced in less time with less expense; more stable; and in retrospect, wiser. When I say that I am interested in supplementing the current system, I do not mean that we need alternatives to it or that we need to replace it. I cringe when people talk about alternative disputes resolution (ADR) as a "new" system. I do not believe we should eliminate representative democracy in the United States.

## Consensus Is the Goal

I think that the key to producing better outcomes is to seek consensus. In order for a result to be perceived as fairer than what the conventional system produces, all the people affected by it must feel that it is better than what the conventional system would have produced. The only way to reduce the costs and time associated with making and implementing decisions is to ensure that people who need to live under them do not try to undermine them. If you have consensus, there is a chance that decisions will remain stable. The implementation, not just the invention, of the solutions will be more efficient. People will say, "I can live with that solution. I'll behave and I'll comply because I believe that it is a fair, appropriate solution."

I expect some skepticism in regard to my notion that consensus is at the heart of doing better. Some people say, "If everyone agrees, the solution must be wrong." They believe that if a settlement satisfies everybody, it must be mediocre—a compromise decision. If people are happy with it, it is probably not the smartest solution because the smartest solution is not likely to be popular. I do not believe that any of these claims is correct.

Consensus is achieved when a neutral party can turn to all the participants and ask, "Can everybody live with this agreement?" and they respond "yes." If everybody concludes that they cannot think of a solution that is better for them while still satisfying the concerns of others, and they do not think that additional time and energy will produce a better result, then they will say yes. If someone says (in good faith), "No, I can't live with it," then the parties must keep working. A better outcome guarantees that all stakeholders feel that their interests have been better served.

As a practicing neutral, what I have tried to do over the last 15 years is to experiment with consensus building at all three levels of government. My goal has been to demonstrate, on a pilot basis, that better results can be achieved by supplementing the conventional system with consensus building. Several examples are presented in my book *Breaking the Impasse*. I have worked with federal and state courts to implement supplementary consensus-building activities in an effort to produce better outcomes. My colleagues and I have also been working to convince administrative agencies at the federal, state, and local levels to experiment with consensus-building supplements to conventional administrative processes.

Our consensus-building efforts have succeeded at the state and local levels and we are on the verge of doing something akin to the bipartisan Social Security negotiations at the congressional level. You will remember that during the Social Security debate, the normal procedure of battling along party lines, between committees, and between the executive and the legislative branches was suspended. Congress said, "This is a real emergency! Let's get our act together, form a bipartisan committee and get a resolution." Although noteworthy, this process did not have all the attributes of a full-fledged consensus-building supplement; rather, it was a desperate attempt to strike a compromise.

What, then, are the key attributes of a consensus-building supplement to the conventional system?

First, the real stakeholders—the people who have a stake in the policy, standard, or resource allocation choose representatives who reflect their interests. They do not use general-purpose elected officials; they select representatives specifically for the occasion to participate in face-to-face problem-solving sessions.

Second, the stakeholders agree that consensus is their goal. They do not just sit down to talk a while, and then vote in a majority-rule fashion. Their goal is to keep working until everyone's interests are satisfied or they all agree that this is impossible.

Third, the process is assisted by a neutral party acceptable to all the representatives who helps to manage the face-to-face dialogue. This person must not have a stake in the outcome. I distinguish between unassisted party-to-party negotiation and assisted negotiation. In my view, multi-issue disputes are too complicated to resolve without neutral assistance.

The Social Security bipartisan effort did not meet all of these criteria. Although it was consensus seeking and it was face to face, it was negotiated by elected legislative leaders and it was not assisted by a neutral.

I have conducted a series of demonstrations using consensus building in each of the contexts mentioned above and I want to report that we do get better results. We have conducted some demonstrations dozens of times and we keep getting better results. These results are:

- *Fairer* in the eyes of the people participating.
- More *efficient;* efficiency means less time, cost, and waste.
- More *stable;* the parties are still living by the agreements and are still committed to them, they want to make them work.
- *Wiser;* it is harder to prove that the agreements are wiser.

I am prepared to be told that anything experimental can work a few times, or that because I was part of evaluating it, people do not trust my findings. I am also prepared to be told that it will be hard to institutionalize these concepts. Thus my job for the next 10 years, as I see it, is to make sure that we do change normal practice.

I make a distinction between disputes about rights (whether or not something ought to be done) and disputes about how to do something, given that there is agreement that it ought to be done. Consensus building processes can be used to help with the second type of dispute but not the first. Consensus building is ineffective in constitutional battles such as whether we should have prayer in the schools. These are the kinds of issues that the courts must decide. Consensus building will not work for issues such as whether we should have nuclear power. The Clamshell Alliance and the Public Service Company of New Hampshire will not come together in a consensus-building process to decide whether the Seabrook Power Plant should be built. Rather, consensus building can help decide questions such as: Given that you are going to build a nuclear power plant, where should it be located? How big should it be? What impacts should be allowed? How should it be monitored? To which standards should it be held? The question in places like Seabrook, New Hampshire, is still "Should we have nuclear power?"

In the negotiation literature, some analysts talk about reservation price (the minimum a seller can settle for and the maximum a buyer will pay), bottom line, or walk-away positions: What it is that you have to have before you will say okay. What they fail to address is the gap between reservation price and aspirations (what buyer and seller would like to get, ideally). Fisher and Ury (1981) say that you should walk into a negotiation knowing your best alternative to a negotiated agreement (BATNA). However, you do not want to settle for an outcome that is just a little bit better than your BATNA. You have higher aspirations and would like to get much more.[2]

Suppose a situation in which a group has been working for a year, and everyone in the group is satisfied except for one person who keeps saying, "Well, you have met my fundamental interest, but I really would like more." The rest of the group may say, "We are stopping. Can you live with it or not?" At that point the person might say, "No, I can't live with it. I really want much more. I want more because that person over there got much more than his minimum, so now I demand much more than the minimum I told you I had to have in the beginning." If the group decides to stop at this point, it is still very likely, judging from experience, that the informally negotiated consensus-based decision will in fact be adopted by the conventional system because it is so close to being perfect.

# Case Studies From Practice

Let me give some examples from practice. The first case falls into the federal administrative category. It involves negotiated rule making (sometimes referred to in Washington, D.C., by the horrendous nickname *regneg,* for regulatory negotiation). The EPA is one of several federal agencies experimenting with negotiated rule making.

## EPA

How do we usually draft regulations in the United States? Congress sets a goal. Sometimes it is very specific (i.e., "There shall be clean air by 1991.") Readers who are not familiar with federal administrative procedures may be surprised to learn that statutes, no matter how many pages they contain, are not enough. The law does not say who should do what tomorrow and the next day, and the next day to achieve the objectives of the legislation. Regulations are necessary to implement statutes.

An agency, in this case the EPA, drafts regulations. In preparing a draft, sometimes the agency seeks outside advice and other times it does not. Sometimes it says, "We know how to do this. We have a bunch of technical people in our agency who can figure this out." Other times, it appoints a scientific advisory committee.

An agency announces that it will be drafting regulations by publishing a notice of proposed rule making in *The Federal Register.* The next thing that the public sees is the draft regulations promulgated in *The Federal Register.* Then a period known as *review and comment* begins. During that time, the agency has to subject itself to the outrage of all those who do not like the draft. People comment in writing (under the *ex parte* rule of the Administrative Procedures Act direct conversation is not allowed between the agency and the people who are upset). Public hearings or meetings are also held so that people can testify as to why they think the regulations are wrong and should be changed.

After everybody gets a chance to voice his or her concerns about the draft regulations, the agency must decide whether to admit it made a mistake. That is, it is supposed to respond to all comments, revise the draft, and publish the final rule. This long, complicated process can take years, and there is more: People not satisfied with the final rule can challenge it in court. Four out of five rules promulgated by the EPA in 1985 went to court. A rule can be challenged on several grounds. The rule's or the legislation's constitutionality can be challenged. Claims can be made that the regulation does not meet the intent of the legislature or that the agency has been *arbitrary and capricious* in reviewing the scientific evidence.

Courts rarely settle substantive disagreements about standards. How could the court know whether a standard should be set at six or nine parts per billion? Cross-examination of witnesses or a jury is not going to get us any closer to what the standard ought to be. In fact, most of the time, the court says, "It's really not up to us. Do it again," and the whole process starts over. If it decides that the standard is okay, then the group that is aggrieved will go to Congress to seek a change in the law.

Negotiated rule making offers an alternative to this process. In half a dozen negotiated rule makings at the EPA we brought together everybody who would be likely to complain during the review and comment period and everybody who would be likely to challenge a rule in court. The parties included the agency and representatives of all stakeholders. We said to them, "Let's all sit down and draft the regulation together. Let's develop and review the data together, and let's assess the alternatives together." We were adding a step to the conventional rule-making process. After the draft rule is published, there would still be an opportunity for review and comment. No one's right to litigate is precluded. If they fail to reach consensus, they go back to where they were and continue along the conventional route.

A neutral convener begins by contacting a list of people who have objected to, or commented on, similar regulations as well as others who have an interest in the issue. Coming up with such a list is not difficult. The convener describes his or her role and the steps in the process and asks each party if they would like to participate. The convener makes clear that he or she has no stake in the outcome.

Interested parties have several incentives to participate in such a process: (1) they know that if they do not, the agency will have no choice but to continue down the conventional road and eventually create a regulation; (2) there are substantial costs associated with lobbying Congress and the EPA as well as with litigation: They have the option of either continuing to pay those costs or trying this new process for a few months; and (3) they always retain the power to veto any decision.

After contacting all interested parties, the convener creates a long list of potential stakeholder representatives. The convener must be sensitive to the clustering of interests. He or she asks all the parties if they feel that their interests would be adequately represented if only some of the potential participants were at the negotiating table. If the parties are not satisfied with the list, more representatives can be added or individuals can attend the first meeting and can be added to the list if they feel that their interests are not adequately represented.

Because the parties know how much hard work is coming, a relatively small number of serious participants are prepared to participate. Groups designating a person to represent them want to send somebody that knows something about the issue, even if they have to hire someone special to represent their concerns.

Through this process, the convener is trying to pare down the number of people needed at the table. My colleagues and I have debated the desired number of representatives; some prefer 15 while I think that this number is too small and tend to prefer 30 or 40.

The first rule for which we tried the negotiated rule-making procedure concerned the economic penalties that would be imposed on manufacturers of air-polluting truck engines. Eight years after the passage of the Clean Air Act, there were no economic penalties in place on manufacturers of engines that did not meet the industry leader standard. Without penalties, there would be no incentive to invest in making cleaner engines. Interested parties included truck-engine manufacturers, air environmental groups, state air-pollution control agencies and manufacturers of parts that are sold to truck-engine manufacturers.

There are often imbalances in representation. General Motors, Ford, Toyota, and all the truck-engine manufacturers are competitors so each of them was determined to sit at the table. Environmental groups, on the other hand, have a lot of things that they are working on and a small number of staff to represent them. They agreed that the Natural Resources Defense Council (NRDC) would represent them in the negotiation. Based on the political clout and the numerical representation of the parties, seven trucking manufacturers and one environmental representative, you might assume that this would be a recipe for an utterly imbalanced outcome.

As it turned out, though, it was more difficult for the seven parties than it is for the one, because the seven parties had to do all kinds of extra work to deal with their internal conflicts. In this particular negotiation, everybody agreed that the NRDC had the most influence. The NRDC representative knew more about the scientific and technical aspects of the issue than most of the other representatives and he was able to use that knowledge in ways that counteracted the political clout of the other participants. Political clout does not help a party come up with a creative response to a conflict. Because there was no voting, what really counted was each party's ability to understand the interests of the other side, what they really cared about, and then to be creative in inventing some resolution that responded to their interests and, at the same time, gave the others what they needed. The more you know about the substance of an issue, the easier it is to be creative.

Early attempts to set up negotiated rule making met with several obstacles. The Office of Management and Budget (OMB), the Federal Advisory Committee Act, and many legal problems stood in the way. The first problem involved covering the costs imposed on the participants. Low-income advocacy groups or environmental groups that have one office in the middle of the country need some financial support to enable them to come to Washington, D.C., once a month. Funding was supposed to come from the agency and be turned over to a neutral party to manage. However, the federal government has a prohibition against compensating *interveners* in administrative processes. The argument we made was that in this early stage, the parties are not actually interveners because the rule had not yet been promulgated. In addition, although interveners cannot be compensated, members of advisory committees can be. So, for OMB's purposes, we called the group an advisory committee and solved this problem.

The funds in the resource pool were used not only to pay expenses, but also to hire technical consultants. When there is unequal technical ability among the parties there is a problem. The resource pool was used to provide technical assistance for the group as a whole, not just for one party. This created an opportunity for joint fact-finding and lessened the gap in technical expertise.

Moreover, matching funds from a private foundation were provided in case there was any kind of expense that federal auditors said could not be funded with public money. You might ask, "How are you ever going to institutionalize the system if it depends on private foundation grants?" Congress recently passed negotiated rule-making legislation that called for $1 million to be placed in a kitty under the control of the Administrative Conference of the United States, obviating the need to get each agency to agree to create a pool for each rule.

Another problem related to the *ex parte* rule is: "How could the EPA sit at the table and discuss a rule with all these people?" We overcame this problem by arguing that no rule had been promulgated; the group was just talking about writing a rule.

Many of these initial problems were caused by overzealous lawyers working in the general counsel's office at the EPA and the Justice Department. We solved every problem they raised. We now have a standard procedure: A convener is hired, interested parties are contacted, others add themselves, and the group is formally appointed as an advisory committee so that resources can be provided. At the first meeting, there was a day-long training session built around a simulation; a hypothetical, mock negotiated rule-making involving a new chemical called *Dirty Stuff*. All the parties were given roles that are not similar to their normal roles (i.e., industrialists play the role of environmentalists). The parties have to draft a rule. By simulating what is going to happen, people learn about how they can negotiate in ways that will be advantageous to all sides.

Once the group has been convened, it drafts protocols or guidelines. It identifies the responsibilities of the neutral, it discusses its agenda and work plan and it sets timetables. The agency explains what will occur if an agreement is not reached. Everybody understands their BATNA, their alternative to an agreement. At this point, the group moves into a joint fact-finding phase with adequate financial resources. The whole process I have described up to this point is called *prenegotiation* and it is the most difficult part. If you can get through this stage, the rest of the negotiation will usually be easy by comparison.

The parties then sit down at the table with an agenda, a timetable, funds for fact-finding and other kinds of technical analyses. They begin with the first issue on the agenda. A technical subcommittee may be formed to work on this issue. The whole group explores the options suggested by the subcommittee. For up to several days they lock themselves in a room and work together. Sometimes they all sit around a table and sometimes they caucus; sometimes committees present proposals that have been prepared before the full meeting. When they have gotten as far as they can on an issue, the convener writes a report summarizing what the group has covered and on what they have agreed. (This document provides a record that should satisfy federal record-keeping requirements.)

When there are many issues on the agenda, the parties invent options for the first agenda item and then they move on, item by item. They do not come to closure on any item. After inventing options for each issue, they try to come up with a single text that covers all the issues. This is accomplished by trading and packaging: "If you give me something on issue one, I will give you something on issue three, because issue one is most important to me and issue three is most important to you." When the package has been created, the parties are asked whether they want to make further changes or whether they can live with it as it is. They continue making changes until all parties feel that they can live with the result.

This process may take several months and a lot of hard work. At this point, they may think that they are done, but they are not. Each representative must now take the agreement back to the group he or she represents. Then they must come back together. Often they must say, "I'm very sorry. I never imagined that my people would be as concerned as they were about this issue." What is different this time, though—if everything has worked well—is that the parties have a working relationship that allows them to proceed more speedily through any final changes that are required to meet the interests of all sides.

The next stage is to link informally negotiated agreements to formal government decision making. The proposed regulations are promulgated and hearings are held. If nobody opposes them, the negotiation was a success. The agreement and the process will be perceived as better than the status quo, especially if the costly delays associated with litigation have been avoided.

If someone in the EPA looks at the final draft created by the parties and says, "I know that I didn't want to be involved, but I don't like the draft and section three ought to be changed," there is a big problem. If the draft is promulgated with agency-imposed changes the negotiating parties will back out. On the other hand, the agency has the right to change the draft. If it does so, though, in a way that violates the negotiated agreement, it will pay a price. Everybody is going to be very angry, not only about the substantive changes but about all that time spent and not getting what they thought had been agreed. What we suggest is, if the agency has to change something after the review and comment period is completed, it should send the proposed changes to everyone in the group before releasing anything officially. There have been many negotiated rule makings at the EPA; almost all have been successful.

A facilitator should always mail copies of negotiation proceedings to anyone who is interested. Also, all the meetings must be announced and open to the public and the press.

The negotiated rule making process does not work for every type of rule. One rule that the EPA considered negotiating was the *de minimus* rule for low-level radioactive waste. The question was What amount of low-level radioactive waste would qualify producers as small-quantity generators thereby subjecting them to less stringent procedures for disposing of waste? The answer from the environmental community was very simple: zero. Industry said, "There has to be some reasonable number." This issue was not amenable to negotiated rule making because the parties were not able to agree on whether an action should be taken. This process is good for deciding how rather than whether to take action.


## Camden, New Jersey

Another case I mediated involved the funding and building of a regional sewerage district in Camden, New Jersey. It was on the state rather than federal level, and it involved the judicial rather than the executive branch. As background, 14 years ago, the state of New Jersey passed a law making a number of towns in Camden County part of a regional sewerage district. The creation of the district was necessary in order to qualify for federal EPA grants for building sewer systems. Because new growth was going to occur and old septic systems were breaking down, New Jersey believed that forming regional districts to build new sewage treatment plants was a good idea.

Immediately, the small towns in the proposed region opposed the idea. "Why should we be part of an expensive regional system? Our existing sewerage systems work fine. We will allow you to put a pipe through our town. If we want to hook up in the future, we will pay at that time."

The city of Camden said, "We can't afford to pay for a new sewerage system. We're going bankrupt. We intend to sue so that we don't have to be part of the system." Camden was one of the poorest cities on the East Coast. The notion that they would have to assess each household to cover the expense of a new system meant that as much as 50% of the land in the city might be taken by tax title.

The nearby suburban communities like Cherry Hill said, "If the little towns aren't going to pay, and the big city isn't going to pay, we are not going to be part of the district either. We don't want to end up paying all the costs."

Everybody sued. The case wound its way through court. Meanwhile, the sewage district that was created by law to implement the sewer system had no money coming in because no one would join. So it borrowed money to start work. It built a building so that it had a place for its new staff. It could not apply for federal grants to cover the cost of engineering studies because the communities would not agree to become part of the regional district.

As time went on, the suit got bumped up and down the system. Ten years after the controversy started, the EPA ended federal subsidies for sewer grants. By that time, the agency was $70 million in debt. The EPA and the state environmental protection agency attempted to shut down all inadequate treatment plants that were polluting the area.

A few years later, another judge got to hear the case. This judge thought that the situation was ridiculous and should have been settled long ago. He declared a moratorium on all sewer hookups in the county. This got everybody's attention, especially the Homebuilders Association. The central city was in a renaissance and the small towns were experiencing rapid growth. Suddenly, the judge told them that all development would stop until they settled the suit. The judge decided to appoint a person, a special master, to work with the towns to get a consensus on the design of the new sewer system and the allocation of the costs of construction and operation.

I was appointed special master. It was my job to build a consensus; a colleague in New Jersey was my comediator. The judge told us not to work on the issue of whether or not the towns should be included in a regional district because that was a constitutional question that would have to be decided separately. He suggested that we work on the assumption that all the communities would be part of the system and would be required to pay a fair share of the costs of construction and operation. As special master, we had no power to recommend or impose a solution. The judge told the parties that they could choose not to participate, and that they still had the right to raise constitutional questions as to whether they could be forced to join the regional agency. He gave us 6 weeks. The moratorium created enormous pressure to resolve the conflict. If they could not agree, the case would have to go through further litigation.

We began by meeting privately with all the parties to have them tell us, confidentially, what their concerns and interests were, what they thought ought to happen, what they thought the others could live with and what they could accept. We met with them all as well as with representatives from the state and federal governments, congressional representatives, and the attorneys. Representation was not a problem in this case because we knew who all the parties to the suit were. We insisted that all the lawyers come with their clients, and made it clear that we would be talking directly to the litigants.

After getting the group together, the first thing we did was to get the group to agree on which technical consultants would evaluate the proposed engineering plans that the agency had drawn up. We also needed to assess the financing plan that the agency proposed and make a model to forecast, under various sets of assumptions, the long-term costs. All the parties were presuming incredibly high costs. The city of Camden said that they were going to go bankrupt because the agency had designed a "gold-plated system." They thought that they would have to pay at least a $1,000 a year per household.

How did they arrive at that number? They made it up–they looked at the numbers and said $1,000. To get the parties to agree on a set of more realistic numbers, we had to develop a joint fact-finding process that allowed them to pool information and build a new model to forecast costs under various design and financial assumptions.

We drafted procedural protocols, agreed to an agenda of issues and a timetable, and then proceeded with joint fact-finding. After the fact-finding, we began the process of inventing options. We did this by holding confidential meetings with each party in which they told us the issues most important to them and the ones on which they would compromise. We then convened the full group of 150 participants and proposed a series of system design options. Should we have two separate treatment systems, or would it be more cost-effective to have one system? What was assumed about how old systems would be maintained and hooked up to the new system? We discussed the options, received comments, and tried to reach as much closure as we could. We went through all the issues on the agenda in this way. Then the mediation staff drafted a composite proposal based on our confidential conversations and group meetings with the parties. We created a total package and sent it to the representatives for discussion with the communities that would be affected by the decision. We brought everybody back together and asked whether they could live with the packaged agreement. When they said no, we went another round. We made changes until we had an agreement.

We returned to the judge and said, "Judge, you won't believe it, but we have an agreement." The judge called a formal hearing, invited all the parties and their lawyers, held up the agreement, and said, as I cringed, "Is everybody completely happy with this?" They responded no! The judge turned to us and said, "I thought you said there was an agreement." We told him that there was, but that he had asked the wrong question! He should have said, "Can everybody live with the agreement?" We asked him for a few more weeks to try to put an agreement back together. He agreed, with a stern reminder about all the pressures on him because of the development moratorium.

We went through another full cycle and the most amazing thing happened. A totally new option emerged: We created a completely different formula for allocating costs among the communities. Working with the same parties and the same data, we came to a completely different agreement. The agreement was drafted, all the parties checked back with their constituents, and we gave it to the judge.

The judge held another meeting and looked over at us and winked. After 14 years, there was agreement. "Can everybody live with this agreement?" Everybody said "yes." The conventional process was an incredibly expensive and inefficient way to resolve an allocation dispute. The process should have been a consensual one from the beginning. Nobody had ever brought the parties together, nobody had ever asked them to imagine what they could live with. The regional authority had never tried to work with its member communities to gather data jointly or generate options. In fact, the agency bitterly fought the consensus-building process every step of the way. They claimed, "It is our responsibility. We've done a plan. We've spent the money. We know the answers."

After the agreement was reached, the parties dropped their law suits. The judge issued an order requiring the agency to draft a service agreement that embodied all the principles of the consensual agreement. At that point, the case entered the postnegotiation phase in which the informal agreement was transformed into binding commitments. The agreement was complicated. It included mechanisms proscribing procedures for review, monitoring, renegotiation, and the mediation of subsequent disputes between the communities and the agency. Note that this dispute resolution process did not replace the court system, rather it supplemented it. Dispute resolution, mediation, and consensual decision making were grafted onto the judicial process.

## Institutionalizing New Forms of Public Dispute Resolution

These cases illustrate the relevance of the steps in the consensus-building process and show that, in fact, consensual approaches can work in the political world of public disputes at the federal, state and local levels. My view is that by *supplementing* the conventional system we can resolve disputes and reach results that the parties and analysts can say are fairer, more efficient, more stable, and wiser. I do not think that we should eliminate representative democracy.

A current challenge is to create state offices of mediation, entities within each state that will broker the use of consensual processes for resolving public disputes. These small offices may or may not deliver mediation services themselves. Their primary purpose is to encourage people in agencies to use consensus building when an agency is involved in a dispute.

State mediation offices generally put up some money to pay a neutral person to conduct preliminary conflict assessments. If the parties decide to keep working, the disputants may have to come up with a way of paying for the services of the neutral. State mediation offices can supply the parties with a list of neutrals from which to choose.

Quite a few states have experimented with this concept, including Florida, Hawaii, Massachusetts, Minnesota, Ohio, and Oregon. Maine, New Hampshire, Texas, and several other states are also contemplating creating state offices of mediation. The goal is to move from a few experiments to institutions that support this mode of resolving all major public disputes.

## Notes

1. Susskind and Cruikshank (1987).

2. Raiffa (1982) deals with the gap between BATNA and aspirations somewhat more than Fisher and Ury (1981), particularly in his analysis of optimal versus inefficient agreements.

# 6

# Why the Labor Management Scene Is Contentious

ROBERT B. McKERSIE

▶ In this chapter I apply what I know from the world of industrial relations to the general arena of negotiation. This is a challenge for those of us who work in industrial relations, because we tend to get caught up in the institutional arrangements, history, and parties rather than focusing on central negotiation issues. What I see as important, with respect to labor negotiations, is not so much the bargaining process, but rather the context, the backdrop around which any particular negotiation has to be understood. I explore some of the issues with which labor negotiators are wrestling today, the context in which they are working, the strategies that employers are pursuing, and finally, how these problems are being solved through cooperation.

## The Context

In the first chapter of the book *The Transformation of American Industrial Relations* (Kochan, Katz, & McKersie, 1986), my co-authors and I discuss three levels of labor management relations: the collective bargaining level, the corporate strategy level, and the workplace level. Usually negotiations are thought to be played out on the collective bargaining level, but one cannot understand what is really going on in industrial relations unless one looks at the other two levels as well.

One can think of three prototypical labor management systems within which these three levels interact. First, under the traditional system, the assumption at the strategic level is that management manages and unions, at least in the United States, do not get very involved in corporate decisions. The purpose of unions in the traditional system is to take wages out of competition so that firms do not compete against one another to get lower wage rates, and unions have been quite successful in most industries in establishing a standard rate.

On the workplace level, the dominant theme has been job control with grievance systems culminating in arbitration. As a result, unions have become heavily involved in administering complicated agreements. This system was in place for 30 or 40 years and, indeed, succeeded as long as industries continued to grow.

The second system, the nonunion system has always been with us in this country, but has grown rapidly, particularly since the 1970s beginning with such key companies as IBM and Hewlett Packard. One can no longer talk about negotiating in a traditional system without reference to the fact that "in the next pasture," there may be a nonunion operation, which most likely is more productive and less costly.[1] This economic reality places a lot of pressure on the traditional system.

In a nonunion system there often are grievance procedures and good fringe benefits. At the workplace level, many nonunion companies have developed high commitment systems, using the concepts of human resources and human relations to design a whole array of ideas to get workers identified within the enterprise via work groups and increased participation. Again, these ideas have placed pressure on the traditional union system, which historically was in the lead regarding innovations in fringe benefits and wage patterns. Now, with the nonunion system experimenting with participation at the shop floor level, the traditional system finds itself playing catch-up.

Is there a third system emerging, specifically, a transformation of the traditional union system? I think the answer is yes; there are new forms of governance. We see for the first time, for example, corporations in which union representatives are on the board of directors. There is much more participation by unions in major business decisions; for example, union members are learning about new technology and can react to decisions about where plants will be sited. On the collective bargaining level, there is much more emphasis on employment security and on gain sharing. On the workplace level there is an effort, on the part of the unionized sector, to realize some of the same flexibility that many of the leading nonunionized sectors have achieved.

Often, when people read our book *The Transformation of Industrial Relations*[2] they think that we are saying that a new, transformed system clearly has emerged. But if you read us closely, we are not going that far out on the limb. Our general point is that although some relationships have changed, many parts of the system remain entrenched in traditional labor management relations.

## The Challenges to the Traditional System

To understand why a third system may be emerging, we must look at some of the challenges that the traditional system is facing. The challenges to the traditional system are coming from environmental changes. In many situations, the employer's bargaining parameters have changed, which in turn impacts labor negotiations and the employer's best alternative to a negotiated agreement (BATNA). Several factors have caused this change: Competition is one key factor; foreign competition and deregulation have created incredible pressures on employers. Labor market conditions is a second element, which bears on how an employer weighs its options and decides whether its best strategy is to work out changes with its current employees and their union representatives or to look for alternatives.

A third element is the decline of unions in all sectors and the pressure from the nonunion sector. Many people assume that there are still industries in which the unions have 100% control. This is not true. I cannot identify an industry in the United States today where there is no significant nonunion sector. Take the transportation industry with its mom-and-pop truckers and Continental Airlines, the steel industry with minimills, and the automobile industry with Japanese transplants that are operating on a nonunion basis. There is a major railroad in Florida that is nonunion. In addition, many of the railroads are selling off their branch lines, which in turn are operated on a nonunion basis. The shipbuilding industry used to be a union stronghold, but not any longer. At the Rhode Island facility of General Dynamics 4000 people are employed on a nonunion basis in a state considered very prounion.

All of these factors are putting pressure on the negotiating environment and on the BATNA of the employer and employees. There is no longer a positive settlement range within which both parties can realize mutual gains; rather, a negative range has been created. In most bargaining situations, when there is a negative range, the buyer (in this case the employer) will say, "Good-bye! I'll deal with someone else in the marketplace." Usually there is a better possibility, which is what is meant by BATNA. However, a premise of labor management relations is that the relationship is a continuing one and there are high disengagement costs.

Employers and unions, therefore, find themselves caught up in a prisoner's dilemma: The parties are negotiating in a negative range in which the terms of trade are no longer acceptable given the alternatives, but the parties are in a fix because disengagement is difficult. A relationship of mutual interdependence persists even though the terms of trade have become unacceptable to one side (the employer).

There are other examples of negotiation situations that fit the paradigm of this prisoner's dilemma. In a divorce situation, the parties have been involved in a continuing relationship and the terms of trade are no longer satisfactory given the alternatives. But because it is so difficult to disengage, some people decide to stay in the negative relationship, while others somehow try to revise their reservation price so that they can continue the partnership.

When there is a negative range, each side must be very careful about what it says to the other side. For example, few employers would say to the rank and file, "We think you are overpaid." That is often the assumption, but it is rarely said. Instead, the employer will focus on its side of the ledger and say, "We have to drop our compensation costs; otherwise, we're not going to stay in business.

We would like to continue to pay you what you have been making, because we think that you are good employees and your productivity is high, but there are new economic circumstances."

## The Employer's BATNA

Let us look at some of the employer's strategies or alternatives to negotiating. I am focusing on the employer once again because this is the side that today often feels the bargain is no longer viable. One frequently used employer strategy is for a company to pull its assets out of its unionized plants. Many companies have expanded on a nonunion basis, for example, Continental Airlines, which is a major nonunion carrier.

Another employer strategy is to subcontract key parts of the business when the nonunionized workers are willing to be employed at 50% to 60% of the scale for unionized employees. TWA put its maintenance work out for bid; Pan American subcontracted all of its food service.

A third employer strategy is to sell portions of the business. Railroads are selling branch lines all over the country. The owner of a branch line is not required under the Railway Labor Act automatically to recognize the union. The new owner has tremendous leverage in deciding whether to recognize the union. Why does it often take a proposed sale to get a revision in the employment contract? One would think that the employees operating trains on branch lines would be willing to renegotiate their contracts to get closer to the employer's BATNA before an employer takes the drastic step of selling it and bringing in a third party.

Part of the problem in a continuing relationship is that considerable *noise* is present in communications. The employees do not know whether to believe the employer when they hear that the company has been losing money for years. "There they go again, saying that we need to make a concession." A lot of mistrust builds up along the way, and one reason that this mistrust develops is that the union does not have access to relevant information because it usually is not involved in the strategic decisions.

Situations also exist in which union leaders recognize that changes have to be made, but the rank and file, who may be isolated, do not accept the need for change. The precedent, traditions, and rituals in any kind of relationship—whether it is a marital or business relationship—make it difficult to say, "Things have really changed. We have to completely reestablish our relationship. We have to go back to the beginning and examine what the alternatives are."

Another strategy that an employer can use is to lower its disengagement costs. If one party has large disengagement costs, it is vulnerable and dependent on the other party, locked into the relationship. More and more, companies are operating during strikes. They say to the union, "We don't care if you strike, because we will respond to the strike by hiring and training replacements." They are developing a BATNA, or market alternative. At this point in labor history, people are willing to cross picket lines because there is not as much solidarity in the labor movement. Employers feel emboldened to use this strategy, and a social technology has been developed on how to do it: train replacements, feed those who are living in the plant and keep their health and morale up. In Rumford, Maine, in the 1980s, the Boise-Cascade plant was on strike and it brought in supervisors from around the country to continue operating the plant.

Also in the 1980s, TWA hired replacements for 4,000 flight attendants. The firing by President Reagan in 1981 of the air traffic controllers encouraged employers, because it said to employers, "If the United States government can fire people who are so critical and weather the heavy costs to the transportation system, then the private sector can do it too."

Employment security is another strategy used by employers. The employer justifies asking for lower wages and reduced fringe benefits by giving job assurances. Another strategy is gain or profit sharing, for which employees give up money at the front end of the contract to get something back later on, if there is good performance. Another strategy is to grandfather the incumbents, by creating a two-tier wage system, with new employees being hired at market rates.

Many believe this is not a moral thing to do. A company in effect will say to its current employees, "We've got a good deal for you. We are not only going to keep your current wages, we are going to increase them and give you job security. What we want in return is the ability to hire new people at lower pay scales, the market rates." This system has been reluctantly accepted by unions. The way they rationalize it is to say, "The people who are coming in at lower wages are still getting paid more than they were before."

American Airlines started this practice in the airlines industry. The union leadership was recommending rejection of the two tier system, but American Airlines went over the heads of the union leadership to convince the rank and file. They ran one of the most professional communication programs I have ever seen, going to union members' homes and showing videos in the offices and stations.

## The Revision of Expectations in Employment

One reason why it is so difficult to renegotiate labor agreements is that the senior employees may say, "Some junior people will get laid off if we don't ratify, but most of us will be okay." Or if the employees are close to retirement, they may vote down the concessions, knowing that the plant will probably close, but they will be able to retire.

Another situation that can occur when a company verges on bankruptcy is that the employees say, "Even if we give them the big concessions that they want, the company won't survive anyway. The situation is so bad that we will just be forestalling the inevitable." Thus, in order for the rank and file to cooperate with the employer, the situation must be such that the concessions have a chance to save jobs.

One strategy that is used by both union leaders and employers to get the employees to confront realities is *decentralization,* contracts are negotiated in the individual plants rather than for the company or industry as a whole. For example, in steel, contracts are no longer negotiated at the level of the steel industry or even the company but, increasingly, at the plant level. In these situations, union members are much closer to the realities of the enterprise because there is greater communication about circumstances.

## Internal Bargaining Within Unions

In *A Behavioral Theory of Labor Negotiation,*[3] Walton and I discussed intraorganizational bargaining, or bargaining within the ranks. Within the union there are many differences across the different levels. There is probably as much bargaining that goes on within the union about a change in pay scales as there is across the table. For example, when Western Airlines was on the brink of bankruptcy a few years ago, management went to the local pilot's union and said, "We need to make a 20% cut. We don't care how you take it. We're going to leave it up to you to figure out how you are going to do it." In this particular situation, the junior pilots held a lot of seats on the negotiating committee, and they decided that the captains, who make $150,000 a year (for flying to Hawaii) would bear most of the cuts and junior pilots, who make $60,000 to $80,000, would not be asked to sacrifice as much.

As soon as word got to the national union headquarters, there was an uproar because the union had adopted a very strong policy about advancement and promotion on the basis of seniority. Typically, pilots move from the copilot seat on a small airplane, to the captain's seat, and then on to the copilot seat of the next larger airplane—right up through the system. In this case, junior pilots were proposing to change the reward structure. In effect, the local union and the employer had agreed to concessions that union headquarters could not accept. The new contract was implemented, however, because at that point in time the national union did not have the power to veto the decision.

A similar dichotomy occurs when the local union is willing to accept concessions, but the national union is prepared to have the plant shut down because they know the business will probably go to other plants. The Teamsters' Jim Hoffa was willing to press for a uniform high scale in the trucking industry, even though some plants were forced out of business.

In many situations today, local unions are trying to save the jobs of their members while the national unions are saying, "When is this going to end?"

## Summary

This quick review of collective bargaining today has underscored the tremendous variety of responses when changes in the environment make existing agreements no longer viable. A variety of strategies, usually initiated by employers, include increasing the costs of remaining with the status quo (forcing an impasse and a strike) and pursuing a BATNA by shifting operations.

But in more cases than not, the parties know they have to work out some kind of change within the current relationship. Companies are either unable or unwilling to resort to drastic alternatives. Unions are aware that times have changed and existing pay scales may not be supportable, or if they are to be made viable, the employees have to be much more flexible and productive.

Thus in a variety of ways, negotiation is the only way to revise the terms and conditions of the employment bargain, and one hopes, in the process the labor management relationship increases its capacity to handle adjustments in the future.

## Notes

1. On the average, union scales are about 15% higher than nonunion ones. In some industries they are dramatically higher. In the transportation sector they are probably 30% to 40% higher. In the automobile industry, they are about 25% higher, although it is not as clear-cut because nonunion companies, such as Nissan and Honda, are paying somewhere between the *area rate* to attract local people and the industry scale, which works out to be about 15% to 20% lower than the union rate.

2. Kochan, Katz, and McKersie (1986).

3. Walton and McKersie (1965).

# 7

# Searching for Mutual Gains in Labor Relations

CHARLES C. HECKSCHER

▶ Although *mutual gains* forms of dispute resolution have spread rapidly through many arenas of social action in the past decade, labor relations has remained notably outside the fold. This is strange, because labor is historically the area that has been most centered on formal bargaining and where the most has been done to study and systematize the process. It has, moreover, generated a great deal of innovation: There is a long history of efforts—many of them apparently successful—to break out of the tradition of confrontation and to move toward problem-centered negotiation. Yet, in the end, these innovations have never made significant inroads and today the general movement is, if anything, in the opposite direction. This is a sobering note in the current symphony of enthusiasm for mutual gains bargaining.

The question that comes to mind, then, is Does the past failure of collective bargaining reforms foreshadow the future of the current negotiation movement? Or do the new techniques have the potential to make the first major improvements in the century-old patterns of labor relations?

# Lessons of the Past

Let me elaborate on the historical record a moment. Twenty-five years ago a group of scholars collected a set of examples of "creative collective bargaining," which outshines what could be assembled today.[1] These included, for example, the union-management Human Relations Committee in basic steel, which sought to overcome a history of bitter strikes through a joint fact-finding and problem-solving process. The committee began in an atmosphere of suspicion, with each side trying to protect the positions that had been so painfully attained in prior bargaining, but over several years of discussion, by all accounts, it evolved to a climate of objectivity and openness. Freed from the pressure of short bargaining deadlines, the parties overcame the need to lock into positions, and they explored new ideas freely. They took on some of the most contentious issues in the labor field—seniority, grievances, wage rates, contracting out, pensions—and developed sophisticated packages that were incorporated into the formal contract. After a few years, they succeeded in implementing the radical idea of *experimental agreements,* which could be revised between contract deadlines.

During this same period there were numerous other impressive attempts to reform collective bargaining, including a committee in the food-processing industry that examined the thorny issue of new technology and job security and a similar joint labor-management effort in the notoriously adversarial long shore industry. All of these went a good ways toward implementing the primary tenets of mutual gains bargaining:

1. They began with agreements in principle to see creative solutions rather than positional compromises.
2. They developed, from the start, shared ground rules different from those of traditional bargaining.
3. They avoided taking early positions while exploring the facts; in several cases the parties found that long cherished "principles" were at odds with their true long-run purposes.
4. They shared information to an unprecedented degree.
5. They took the time to thoroughly explore each other's real interests.
6. And they made space for creative invention by agreeing that ideas proposed in the committee would not be treated as fixed commitments.

Yet none of these efforts survives today. It is hard to trace the course of their decline—there were no dramatic blowups or obvious failures. The steel committee did become a subject of internal debate in the Steelworkers' Union, opposed by rank-and-file militants who feared eroding the power of the strike. A new president who opposed the committee was elected in 1966. Other cases became instances of *successful failures,* by simply fading away despite records of achievement.

This pattern is similar to that of both prior and more recent efforts to change the labor-management relationship. No less a figure than Samuel Gompers, the founder of modern unionism, believed that cooperative relations would evolve from the initial period of conflict. These hopes seemed to be coming to fruition in the 1920s as a wave of novel cooperative agreements, under the name of the *American Plan,* swept across industry. One can trace a continuing line of such efforts, rising during the 1940s and 1960s, falling in the 1930s and 1950s—never completely vanishing but, by the same token, never breaking the dominance of the traditional paradigm.

In the late 1970s and early 1980s, we witnessed yet another wave of hope, driven by the growing perception of a shared competitive challenge. "It's time our adversary system was changed," said Don Ephlin, a vice president of the United Auto Workers (UAW), in 1981. "It's a system that is causing us to run in second place."[2] Ephlin was one of the leaders of a movement called *quality of work life* (QWL), which created problem-solving teams of workers on the shop floor to resolve the day-to-day tensions between workers and management. When the president of the auto workers, Doug Fraser, joined the board of directors at Chrysler, many analysts saw it as a major turning point, bringing an era in which the two sides would share information fully and build commitment to a shared enterprise. At Eastern Airlines the machinists' union entered into an apparently historic compact, which included both board representation and shop floor QWL; impressive reports of cooperation and cost savings began to flow from researchers following this effort.

But, again, this wave seems to have crested. Though the QWL movement achieved much, it has remained limited in scope. Fraser and Lee Iaccoca both declared themselves highly satisfied with the board arrangement, but few others have taken up the example. And cooperation at Eastern, of course, went down in flames; the bitter strike of 1989 became a symbol of the labor movement's attempts to revive its flagging fortunes.

## The Strength of Adversarial Bargaining

Why has confrontational bargaining proved so durable? It is not difficult to build the case for its ineffectiveness. At the broadest level, the countries with the lowest incidence of strikes—Sweden, Germany, Holland, Austria—also happen to be the countries that have achieved the best overall working conditions and protection for employees, as well as considerable success in the international marketplace; both parties seem to win by avoiding pitched battles. Those with the most contentious relations, such as Italy and Britain, have done generally worse. Public opinion clearly favors the growth of cooperation.[3] Union organizers consistently find that the fear of entering a strike is one of the major factors discouraging potential members. What, then, is blocking more cooperation?

The inference one would draw from most writing on negotiation is that the failures have resulted from a lack of *skill*—from an inadequate understanding of the concepts and techniques of mutual gains bargaining. Certainly this argument is persuasive in many cases: The entrenched habits and attitudes of old-line labor leaders are frequent and obvious obstacles to change. Yet it is hard to account in this way for the historical pattern I have described. There have been instances when the skills seem to have been learned, as well as most mortals can learn them, and effectively applied, yet they have failed to sustain themselves. The persistence of the adversarial pattern must have to do, therefore, with more than matters of skill.

Part of the answer to this puzzle can be found by looking at the other side of the picture: at the rewards of traditional bargaining. Despite the apparent self-destructiveness of confrontation, it also has its benefits. Let us take the case, for instance, of Bob White, the leader of the Canadian Auto Workers—until 1985 a part of the United States-based UAW. One can find few popular heroes from the labor movement in the past few decades, but White is undoubtedly one: Taxi drivers in Toronto speak of him with admiration, he has been the subject of a full-length documentary on Canadian national television, and he is often spoken of as a candidate for high political office. The major event that vaulted him to this level of prominence was his victory in the 1984 negotiations with General Motors (GM) of Canada. These negotiations, documented in detail in the extraordinary film *Final Offer,* are a fascinating case study of the paradoxes of collective bargaining.[4]

The film begins with an exploration of working conditions in the auto assembly plants, touching on the age-old themes of monotony and autocracy: These are the daily roots of mistrust and anger in the workplace. But the negotiations, as the key players approach the national bargaining table, have nothing to do with these issues. They quickly center on two key items: GM's desire to give lump-sum bonuses in place of the traditional annual wage increases and its offer of profit sharing. Money has become a proxy for the complex web of frustrations experienced on the job. White quickly locks into the "principle" of continued wage increases; the company counters that the workers and management share an interest in the company's health and that prevents payment of the money up front.

As the dispute develops, there is almost no movement on the basic positions. Instead, there are elaborate tactical maneuvers by which both sides try to line up their bases of power. They fight to a tense standoff until, after a week long strike, the company offers a compromise: They will give White the principle of annual wage increases but will make them significantly lower than they have been in the past.

A classic case, if there ever was one, of positional bargaining: proposal, counterproposal, marshaling of forces, compromise. Gompers would have done it no differently in the earliest days of the labor movement. Now, from an analytic distance, we can easily see that the outcome was far from optimal. It failed to get at many of the major issues. For one thing, the daily working conditions portrayed at the start of the film remain untouched. Still more important, White and his constituents have no way of knowing whether the victory they have won will hold up in the long run. They have neither information nor commitments from the company about the real future of GM's investment in Canada. By conducting an adversarial negotiation, White has *gambled* that the company's threat to pull back from Canada, reducing employment, is a bluff; he may well be wrong, which would be disastrous for all concerned. So we can say that it would have been better for both sides to share information and to construct a solid relationship. That still leaves us the question of why it did not happen.

The center of this case, the key to its unfolding dynamics, is a general, but hidden, theme of collective bargaining: the fact that the leadership, especially on the union side, is tightly constrained by the attitudes of its members. White appears through the story not as a visionary leader marshaling forces toward a strategic horizon, but as a white-water rafter barely staying afloat in a fury of cross currents. His reference point throughout is: What type of agreement is ratifiable? How can we steer between the widespread desire to avoid a strike and the militance constantly stirred up by local dissidents? White pleads for trust from his own executive board, for a little maneuvering room at the table; they, and the membership behind them, refuse to give him much. He may be able to argue them down from 3% to 2.25%, on the grounds that that is the maximum achievable, but he cannot get away with much more.

White is so tightly bound to the membership for two reasons. The first is that their active commitment is essentially his only source of power. The sole significant leverage that he can exert in the dispute is the members' willingness to strike—to take an extremely aggressive action at very high personal cost. He is not working in a situation in which constituent passivity is on his side; he has to manage activism.

The second factor is that he has very few tools for managing this activism. He cannot communicate in detailed and complex ways with his members; there are no forums for education. Unions are unable to meet with members during working hours because of company resistance; they are unable to meet with them outside of working hours because of the general human reluctance to attend meetings. The available means of communication are thin: local presidents have some time to walk the floor and hold brief one-on-one conversations, while the national leader can express points of view in newsletters and through the national media.

Through these thin channels the leadership cannot communicate thick messages. They cannot make arguments, loved by academics, about changing conditions and new opportunities; their most effective, and often only feasible, argument is from habit and familiarity.

They can at best turn the pressure up or down a bit—whip the members into a frenzy of anger or cool them down, but even these appeals, in a volatile situation, may easily go awry or become weapons for internal dissidents. That is why unions tend to be followers of trends, reactors, rather than leaders: they cannot build from attitudes of their members that have been shaped by social events and public interpretations, and at the same time, they do not themselves have effective means to shape attitudes.

What, then, are White's options in this situation? If he had taken a course in mutual gains bargaining, what would he do? Surely he would want to talk about the basic issues of conditions on the assembly line and management-worker relations. Surely he would explore the possibility of giving the company essential cost savings when they were really essential, while retaining standard-of-living increases in normal times, thus creating options for more flexible pay systems. And just as surely, if he did any of these things, he would be pilloried by his constituents, the splits within the union would be exacerbated, and the power to negotiate would vanish.

That is only the union side. Let us go one step further: If White were able somehow to bring his members along, would we then have an opening for mutual gains? Not in this case: Rod Andrews, the company negotiator, was working under tight constituent constraints of his own. Though the Canadian negotiations were nominally independent, Andrews's orders were clearly coming from the U.S. headquarters of GM. It is unlikely that he had sufficient influence in that very hierarchical system to suggest to top management that they begin thinking about some creative options.

These basic constituent pressures are fundamental to labor relations. There are few industrial unions anywhere in the world that are able to get their members out regularly to meetings, or to develop a broadly shared strategy: Their membership is too varied and far-flung for that.[5] And on the management side, the forces of global competition have produced an increasing focus on general strategy and have consequently further diminished the prestige of the labor relations function.[6] Both sides, then, are generally pushed around by their constituents. This is the fundamental barrier to creative bargaining, restricting the scope of invention. The examples of the past show that reform within the bargaining process has not been sufficient to stabilize a new relationship.

## Escaping the Pressures for Confrontation: Charisma, Corporatism, and Involvement

If this basic diagnosis is right, the prospects for mutual gains bargaining in labor relations are grim. My hypothesis is that the reason skill is not enough to bring about change is that there is a structural blockage. A balance is needed between the level of constituent activism required and the richness of mechanisms of discussion and education; but labor unions in contract negotiations have a high requirement for activism and poor mechanisms of communication. That *involvement gap,* as it might be called, is grounded in law, employer policy, tradition, and practical exigencies that are hard to overcome.[7]

These factors distinguish the labor relations field from most other areas of dispute resolution. Public policy disputes, for instance, generally involve constituencies that are relatively passive: all that is needed from them is an annual contribution and perhaps a vote–not personal activism and sacrifice. In private disputes, there are often no major outside constituencies: All parties can be directly brought into the negotiation. But the usual configuration of labor relations creates great pressure from interests outside the negotiating table, making creative bargaining almost impossible to sustain.

One can imagine at least three avenues of escape from this box: to free the union leadership from close scrutiny by the members, to reduce the need for member activism, or to increase the level of education and discussion.

There have been, historically, some instances of the first possibility, in which leaders have been able to bridge the involvement gap by the force of their personal influence or *charisma.* This happens where individuals have been so effective in delivering the goods that they build a large bank of trust with their constituents; they can count on active support without providing detailed justifications. Walter Reuther, the first leader of the auto workers, was one such figure; John L. Lewis of the mine workers was another. Their personal prestige, based on notable bargaining successes, was so great that their members were willing to say, in effect, "If Walter [or John L.] says it's okay, it must be okay for me."

It is not accidental that these leaders were among the most creative bargainers of our time, achieving impressive win-win solutions—some of which set patterns for the rest of industry, others of which still seem ahead of their time. Lewis, for example, encouraged technological innovation in the coal fields, even at the expense of increased unemployment, to maintain and increase wage levels for his members; few other leaders have been able to get away with that. Reuther pioneered the development of employer pension funds that, although bitterly resisted by the auto companies at the time, became a powerful stabilizing force in the society. It is interesting to note that he was also a strong advocate of profit sharing, despite the complexity of this issue and its general unpopularity with workers. Forty years later, Bob White was unable to take such a position in his negotiations with GM; he stayed with the simpler demand, "We want the money up front."[8]

But this charismatic avenue to mutual-gains bargaining is far from ideal. In the first place, it very strongly depends on individuals: The successors to Reuther and Lewis were unable to sustain the level of influence needed for creative bargaining. Second, the process for building the prestige is a costly one: The leaders have to prove their mettle through dramatic adversarial victories before they earn the leeway to try alternatives. Both of these men were masters of confrontation, leading some of the largest strikes in our labor history. Bob White may now have a chance to join their ranks: His success in 1984 may give him the maneuvering room in the future, which he pleaded for, unsuccessfully, at that time (and indeed he has shown himself much more open to innovative proposals since then). But this is at best a long and painful route to change. Finally, even in the best cases the success reached by this path is unstable: Leaders who are given that much latitude by their constituents tend to become increasingly autocratic and out of touch. Reuther's untimely death perhaps forestalled such a fate for him; Lewis, however, became an exemplar of antidemocratic hubris in his later years.

The second route to solving the constituency problem is to reduce the need for member activism. This requires finding sources of power other than the strike, bases for the negotiation that do not require constituents to make high personal commitments to action. The labor movements of Northern Europe have done this by developing much greater political clout than our own and have, therefore, been able to win legislatively what unions here have sought through strikes. Because they have had to ask only for votes rather than the sacrifices of job actions, they have had much more room to maneuver in crafting innovative systems of industrial justice.

This route leads to less personal autocracy than the first, but it produces an elitist version of democracy—a system often called in Europe *corporatist*, in which most issues are settled by negotiations among peak organizations with very little popular involvement. Apart from whatever normative criticisms one might level, this approach has run into practical problems in recent years. The increase in international competition has created pressures that have not been fully resolved in negotiations, which has in turn produced a loss of member trust. Thus there have been, on the one hand, increasing calls for popular involvement and scrutiny and, on the other, a growing apathy and disenchantment with the labor movement. The labor relations systems of Sweden, Norway, and Germany exist today in an uneasy state of tension, holding together their classic corporatist relations with string and baling wire.

The third logical way out is to increase the level of member *involvement* to match the required level of activism, building a more sophisticated consensus than the traditional one around wage increases. This is not easy: Increased discussion can easily lead to fragmentation. (John L. Lewis once said, "Democracy, translated into modern English, [means] labor union inefficiency.") But there are some examples of how it might be done.

## The Involvement Route at Shell-Sarnia

The most extraordinary case of mutual gains relations that I have seen is a Shell chemical refinery in Sarnia, Canada. This plant, which began operations in 1978, is organized in teams: Any one of six teams, with 20 workers each, can run the normal operation on its own. The teams are largely self-governing. Although they began with two management-appointed *coordinators*, the number and responsibilities of these coordinators have been steadily reduced. Teams manage their own work assignments, scheduling, training, and most issues of discipline. Representatives of the teams, along with management and the union, form a review board that oversees most of the governance issues in the plant.

There is a union here: the Energy and Chemical Workers. They conduct contract negotiations on a 3-year cycle, as in the rest of the industry. What is unusual is the outcome: the contract is less than 10 pages long, compared with 65 pages at a neighboring plant. Only the most basic issues of wages and benefits are put into the contract. The rest–including central concerns such as vacation and overtime scheduling, pay progression, hours of work, and the grievance procedure–is left to a more organic and informal document called the *Good Works Practices Handbook*. The handbook can be revised by the review board at any time. There have been no strikes in the life of the plant.

This system includes mutual gains bargaining in a highly developed form. The shift schedule, to take just one example among many, was initially unique in the industry: Based on a 12-hour shift, it allows workers to spend a startling two thirds of their time on days, with more free blocks on weekends than at comparable plants. The idea came out of a long process of investigation and brainstorming by workers early in the life of the plant. Both union officials and management were initially opposed to the plan, which ran against long tradition in the industry, but it turned out to be highly successful by every criterion–increasing operating efficiency as well as employee satisfaction. The same process has been successfully applied to other issues, which have often led to strikes in other contexts: Shift schedules, progression systems, technological innovation, and supervisory roles, to name a few, have undergone major changes in policy as a result of discussions within the teams and the review board.

There is no doubt that these employees are highly skilled at negotiating. But what I want to draw attention to is the context that makes it possible:

1. Virtually total sharing of information: The computer records of the company's operations, including productivity and profit figures, are accessible by all employees.
2. Extensive training: Management provides courses in problem solving and team relations as part of the orientation procedure. In addition, the union organizes periodic discussions and reviews of the plant's development, both informally on the job and formally off site.
3. A flexible work force: The workers were deliberately selected with no prior industry experience; they averaged 30 years of age and had a minimum of 12 years of education. They had few preconceptions either about their jobs or about union-management relations, and they had the conceptual skills to deal with complex issues.
4. Support from the parent institutions: The national union is almost unique in the high level of involvement of its rank-and-file members and has consistently backed the innovations at Sarnia. Shell corporate management has been less sure but has been persuaded at crucial points to keep its hands off the system, even when it conflicted with central directives and procedures.

I might add to this context a relatively stable competitive environment. There have been some reductions in the work force over the decade-long life of the plant, but none that required forced layoffs; the pressure has remained within manageable bounds. We do not know yet how far those bounds can be pushed.

Other instances that approach this level of sophistication reveal many of the same factors. Typically they involve workers with professional training—engineers, teachers, technicians—and unions with highly decentralized structures.[9] This closes the involvement gap from one end, by facilitating increased discussion of complex issues. Often the gap is also closed from the other end by the development of nonstrike tactics—political lobbying or craftlike control of labor markets—that do not demand such a high level of activism from the members.

This third avenue of extended involvement is as yet relatively unexplored. Cases are few and still fragile; there are relatively few unions with the skills of the Energy and Chemical Workers, and not many corporations with the forbearance of Shell. Thus, to return to the theme with which we started, the cases of creative bargaining remain rare, because the context for them has not been set.

## Changing the System: Lessons From Mutual Gains Interventions

That brings me to recent interventions aiming to develop a mutual gains approach to collective bargaining: Are there grounds now for greater optimism than in the past?

The Division of Labor-Management Relations at the U.S. Department of Labor has been, for the last decade or so, encouraging forms of cooperation, especially the QWL efforts referred to earlier. QWL, however, is essentially an activity that occurs around and between contracts, rarely touching the bargaining process itself. Five years ago the division began trying to plug that gap. They brought together a number of practitioners from around the country who had been teaching mutual gains bargaining in various ways; they began developing their own training materials; and in

1987, they funded an effort by the Program on Negotiation at the Harvard Law School to conduct training in three test sites. I have been involved, with Susskind and McKersie, especially in this last activity. It is far too soon for a formal report of results, but some lessons are already emerging.[10]

### The Centrality of Constituencies

We have so far conducted two complete interventions, the first with Michigan Bell and the Communications Workers of America, the second with the University of Cincinnati and the American Association of University Professors. In both cases tensions between the union and management were quite high, but the contexts were very different. Michigan Bell was negotiating with nominal independence but was actually part of a larger holding company, which was conducting simultaneous negotiations with the same union at three other phone companies, presenting a serious constituency problem for management. The union was a relatively traditional, centralized industrial organization. To further complicate the problem, they were seeking to bargain at the regional holding company level and, therefore, treated the negotiations in Michigan as part of a larger strategy. The membership was extremely angry over the previous round of negotiations in 1986 and was demanding that its leaders recover concessions made at that time.

At the University of Cincinnati, by contrast, the negotiations were not tied into other, larger groupings; the issues from the previous strike were less clearly carried over to the current round, and the members were not focused on a clear set of demands at the start. Most important, there was a relatively high level of discussion and involvement of members in bargaining issues, as one would expect in an academic setting. Before agreeing to the intervention, for example, the union demanded that we engage the rank-and-file in a public debate about the merits of the mutual gains approach versus others.

In short, the involvement gap was much smaller in Cincinnati than in Michigan, and the interference of external, distant constituencies much less. It should perhaps not surprise us, therefore, that the Michigan negotiation ended in a bitter strike that lasted for more than 3 weeks, whereas the University of Cincinnati settled its contract with some innovative language. These facts are consistent with a focus on the constituency problem—the macrolevel—as the crucial determinant of success and with the general difficulty of overcoming adversarial relations of the past.

## The Partial Effectiveness of Skills Training

But in these instances, because firsthand experience is available, we can also check the dynamics from the other end—from the microlevel of *skills* training. Could we have done better? And would it have made a difference?

The core of the training was a negotiation simulation, based on the work Susskind has done for many years in nonlabor situations. For Michigan, we designed a game in three parts, each focusing on a key aspect of the mutual gains approach: working through internal disagreements within each side, presenting opening statements that reflected basic interests, and developing packages to meet the other side's interests. The game was played over 2 days by the bargaining committees, composed largely (though not entirely) of people with long experience in collective bargaining. In Cincinnati we used the same game, but the bargaining committee had far less experience.

There are many ways of looking at the new approach and at least as many definitions as practitioners. The existing models tend to be based not on a strong theoretical structure but on a practical sense of what works. Our presentation was no exception. So I will briefly recount not the overall message we thought we were conveying, but the major pieces that seemed to grab these bargainers—especially the experienced ones. This may help us in selecting some solid rocks with which to build a labor relations approach.

Somewhat to my surprise, they seemed astonished and stimulated by the basic distinction between positions and interests—between specific proposals at the table and the motivation behind the proposal. I was surprised because in my experience, bargainers constantly try to work out the other side's true interests and plot strategy around those surmises; the union usually thinks about business conditions and management thinks about the union's politics. But in the simulation they began to realize some of the limitations in their way of thinking about interests:

- They rarely analyzed their own seriousness.
- In thinking about the other side, they tended to look for hidden positions rather than true interests. That is, they generally assumed that the other side had a fixed position that it was hiding; the game was to try to figure it out.
- They never talked *to each other;* conversations were always within their own side.

These distortions made it impossible to develop full understanding of interests, either one's own or the other's. The guesses about each other's true motives were usually accurate in a general sort of way, because these people had after all been dealing with each other for a long time, but they were incomplete. The simulation was exciting to them because it brought new richness to their understanding.

A second key concept in the training was that of inventing: making room for creativity by agreeing that, for at least certain phases of the negotiation, proposals were not binding. This, too, is only a modification of the normal dynamics of bargaining, but one that seemed to have a major impact. What usually happens is that new ideas are tested among the top bargainers in elevators and hallways. We tried, in effect, to expand this free zone of invention to include extended discussions among more members of the committee, thus making it possible to develop and refine ideas much further than before. The parties to the training found this a valuable technique.

These two key microelements—discussing interests and invention without commitment—became in both cases key levers for changing behaviors. Because of these concepts the parties used task forces more widely than they had in the past, involved more people, and spent more time exploring the basic issues before trying to move to specific solutions. For the participants in both negotiations, judging from initial feedback, this process was seen as very constructive.

This is not, however, to say that the skills necessary for mutual gains bargaining were fully developed in the training. Even the two pieces just described needed more practice than we could give, and we left out a lot: We did not even have time to deal in any detail with the techniques of packaging proposals, coming to closure, or dealing with resistance from the other side.

What we achieved in 2 or 3 days, I think, was a flash of insight by many people about the power of new techniques and a commitment by many to try to use them. We know that in the subsequent bargaining the idea of *doing it by the Harvard method* was frequently used as a reference point by both sides. We also know, however, that in both cases the parties were frequently confused about what that method actually was and lacked confidence in their ability to implement it. This problem of skill, which might be overcome by longer and more intense training, undoubtedly played a part in the fact that in Michigan, when the deadline approached, the bargainers fell back more and more on the traditional approaches.[11]

### Prospects for the Future:
### The Developing Context for Mutual Gains

So yes, we could have done better on skill building among the bargainers, but it is not clear it would have made any difference. For it was also evident that the constituencies were a major obstacle to change. In both instances this concern surfaced early in the training and dogged us throughout: The parties, as they came to understand the new concepts, were clearly aware of the potential gap between their skills and approaches and the expectations of those who held the final authority. We were essentially stumped by this issue: All we could do as trainers was to suggest that they work hard at communication. Even within the microdynamics of the training, in other words, the structural issue was felt as a looming concern.

In Michigan, the considerable progress made in the offline task forces simply vanished when the real bargaining began. One key reason seems to be that forces outside the creative process—a top management set on specific cost reductions, a membership equally determined to recoup past losses—asserted themselves at this point and overwhelmed what the fragile committees had sought to accomplish. In Cincinnati, there were similar pressures from the administration and the membership; union officers were angrily accused of excessive cooperation with management in public meetings. But here the ability to integrate these outside forces, to discuss the new information and proposals developed by the committees, was stronger than at Michigan, and it held against the pressures for confrontation.

It is hard to think of practical ways to improve on the management of constituencies. There was no lack of effort, at least on the union side, in either case. In Michigan we began with a *preevent* for more than 90 people from both sides, including all the local presidents and many of the managers with whom they dealt. This 1½-day session included lectures on mutual gains theory, short simulations, and discussion of the parties' past and future relationships. In addition, the two sides had already begun conducting *common interest forums,* at which local presidents met with top management and union officials to discuss the issues of general concern; these forums had at least begun to lay the groundwork for a shared approach. In Cincinnati, as I mentioned before, Susskind participated in a public debate on the merits of the approach, and we also introduced the concepts to an audience of more than 100 in an initial half-day session before working with the bargaining committees.

In both cases, we were weak on the management end. We never had an extensive dialogue with the top decision makers who framed the bargaining agenda. In Michigan, we also failed to make direct contact with the membership. These are flaws that we should try to repair in future efforts.

Nevertheless, we did make considerable efforts, probably as much as can be expected from a training intervention, to deal with the constituency problem. In the case of Michigan, which was the more typical of classic unionism, it was not close to being enough. That case, in short, fits with the experience of a century of attempts at labor management cooperation. Mutual understanding and success in framing creative options is not enough to overcome the forces supporting the adversarial approach.

As we look to the future, we may grow yet more pessimistic. For today management in the core sectors has grown more aggressive than ever in combating unions; open antiunion campaigns and continuation of operations during strikes, nearly unheard of 15 years ago, are now the norm. This is the primary short-term reason why militancy is on the rise among unions. Events such as PATCO or the demise of Eastern Airlines have undermined the relationships of unions and management everywhere. Continued attacks on the very existence of unions will naturally make mutual gains bargaining impossible.

But Cincinnati gives another side of the picture and more reason for hope. There, where the situation was generally favorable to a mutual gains approach, even a brief skill-building intervention was enough to get the ball rolling. The celebration should be muted: The Cincinnati bargainers have, after all, achieved far less at this point than the Human Relations Committee, which ultimately failed. But what may give the case greater significance is that, rather than being a strange and isolated situation, it reflects broad trends that are fundamentally changing the context for collective bargaining.

The economic developments of the past decade have produced some important value shifts. Workers in many industries today believe more than in the past that their interests are bound up with the success of the enterprise, and they have gained considerable sophistication in understanding the pressures of market competition. Furthermore, the sector of the work force within which the Cincinnati group falls—the sector of professional and semiprofessional workers—is growing rapidly, while the clerical and craft workers represented in the Michigan case are stagnant or declining. Finally, a growing number of companies have initiated efforts to involve workers in shop floor decision making, further developing the sense of participation in the total life of the enterprise. The labor movement, which is closely bound to its constituencies, is beginning to reflect these shifts, and as it does, it has started to develop more frequently the mechanisms of decentralized discussion and planning that, I have argued, are crucial to the success of mutual gains bargaining. [12]

These contextual changes may, in the end, have more effect than any of our individual efforts on the dynamics of adversarial collective bargaining. We have found that training sessions cannot *by themselves* overcome an environment that discourages in many ways the open dialogue needed to reach creative solutions to disputes. But they *can* serve as powerful catalysts for change when larger shifts have already laid the groundwork. In an increasing range of cases there is more desire for cooperation than ability to create it; mutual gains techniques have been effective in closing this gap.

## Notes

1. J. J. Healy (1965).
2. Quoted in *Business Week* (1981, September 13).

3. For instance, a 1982 poll of 500 opinion leaders by the Opinion Research Corporation found that 70% favored a shift toward more cooperative labor management relations. And many polls have shown heavy public criticism of the self-interested and adversarial attitudes of unions and companies (Lipset & Schneider, 1983, pp. 171, 173).

4. The film *Final Offer*, by the Canadian Film Board, is available in the United States from California Newsreel.

5. Unions of craft or professional workers sometimes do better because their members are far more tightly bound to a shared community; see, for example, Lipset, Trow, and Coleman (1956) and Walton (1961).

6. At the ultimate level, management's constituents are the shareholders. These are considerably easier to manage than the union members: They can be kept out of the action. If they were aroused they might well put simplistic demands on their agents, requiring short-term cost reduction. But here is no reason that they should be aroused; management's power does not depend on the active support of the shareholders, and indeed, companies have developed many ways to insulate themselves from shareholder demands. This is why the union side is most important in understanding the dynamics of adversarial bargaining. Still, one cannot entirely forget the constituent pressures on management.

7. See Heckscher (1988, chaps. 2-3) for an analysis of these factors.

8. In the United States negotiations, Owen Bieber did accept profit sharing with the auto companies, although he is not what one would call a charismatic leader. But he did not bring this about from a position of strength. Profit sharing was widely seen by the members as a concession to management—a loss for the union—in a period of considerable corporate distress. Bieber has been under constant and powerful attack from his members ever since for the profit sharing and other related policies.

9. For discussions of technical and teacher unions with substantial involvement, see, for example, Walton (1961) and Nicholson, Ursell, and Blyton (1981).

10. The recipient of the grant was the Project on Negotiation in Employment Relations, created at about the same time as part of the Program on Negotiation. Ray Friedman of the Harvard Business School is conducting systematic research that will, in due course, give us better data on this and other issues. Here I am just reporting initial impressions. These preliminary remarks are, moreover, entirely on my own; my colleagues may have different perspectives on what we have learned.

11. There was also, it appeared, less complete commitment to the mutual gains approach in Michigan than in Cincinnati; although most were positive, some key players remained skeptical. In Cincinnati, as in Michigan, there was more traditional bargaining closer to the deadline. But the commitment to pursuing a mutual gains approach remained strong even at that time. Issues that we need to consider further at the microlevel—the actual conduct of the training—include the following. (1) How close the simulation should be to the participants' real experience. In Michigan we developed a game that was a thinly disguised version of their own issues; in Cincinnati it was much more distant. (2) How much personal counseling to provide individuals. We generally avoided this in both cases, although there was somewhat more informal counseling in Cincinnati. This type of issue, however, does not seem crucial in determining the overall success of the effort. In conversations with other practitioners around the country, I have heard of a wide variety of techniques which have produced good results.

12. See Heckscher (1988, chap. 9) for a description of current changes in union structures.

# 8

# Options and Choice for
# Conflict Resolution in the Workplace

MARY P. ROWE

▶ Henry came into my office extremely upset because his supervisor had taken credit for work that Henry had done. Henry said he did not want to *just forget it.* He did not want to leave the department, but he did not see how he could stay. He did not want to make a formal complaint. In short, he felt he had no options. Henry was also afraid of the half dozen other alternatives I suggested to him, including the possibility of a polite, well-crafted letter to his supervisor. However, he finally decided to work with me on a letter and then eventually did send the letter privately to his supervisor. He was astonished that his letter brought an apology, and full credit in public.

Colleen poked her head into my office. *My boss tried to take off my blouse last night in the lab. I stopped in to tell you because I*

AUTHOR'S NOTE: This article was adapted from a lecture about complaints and disputes that arise within institutions. I have been a full-time ombudsman at MIT since 1972 and a consultant to a wide variety of other ombudsmen and other private and public employers. The ideas, examples, and quotes in this article are drawn from that experience and are taken from real cases.

105

*know you want to know about these things and, besides, I just wanted to tell somebody. Charges? A complaint? No, I don't want to make a complaint. He'll never do it again. I really walloped him. I told him if I, or any one else I know, ever has this problem with him again, he'll be missing a piece of himself. I don't want you to do anything about this; what's more . . . you don't need to!*

Sandy came in sadly to talk about a problem with an old friend in the department. Sandy felt the friend might be drinking at lunch, was using poor judgment and might possibly get himself or Sandy into a unsafe situation with high voltage equipment. *I know I should turn him in, but I don't want to call an investigation on him and get him fired.*

## Both Complainants and Complaint Handlers Need Options

People with concerns, and those who complain and are involved in disputes often want more options than they perceive that they have. Employers and others who are responsible for dealing with complaints also have much to gain by offering options. For example, people who believe they have realistic options to solve their problems are much more likely to come forward in timely fashion. I note that those who choose their own options are more likely to be satisfied. In addition, employers may in some cases be protected, if the complainant's choice of an option does not work out well, because the complainant could have chosen a different mode of complaint handling. Despite these arguments, many managers and even some negotiation theorists do not believe that they should provide options, and in practice they and most complainants actually use only one or two ways of complaint resolution.[1]

## Disempowering the Complainant

Decision makers do not instinctively provide options to others about how they may complain or raise a concern. Most people who think about complaint procedures and grievance procedures, at home or at work, imagine only one or two ways to handle a concern or complaint. In fact, in childhood many people learned only two ways to handle conflict: versions of fight or flight. Others seem to think that *experts* should determine the *best* way for complaint-handlers to deal with disputes. Restrictive thinking characterizes the work of many alternative dispute resolution (ADR) theorists as well as the average person's approach to conflict. Some examples of restrictive thinking, and of the all-too-common willingness of decision makers to make decisions about how complainants *ought* to have their complaints handled, are the following.[2]

1. The power orientation: Many people automatically assume that most disputes should be handled, one hopes fairly, by those with more *power*; for example, parents, the relevant supervisor, the CEO. (*Because I'm the parent; that's why! Do it my way or you're fired!*) Many managers, in fact, believe that managers *should* decide the outcome of most workplace disputes and concerns, because it is their responsibility to be a leader and to maintain workplace control.

2. The rights orientation: Many principled people and many political activists think that nearly all disputes should be decided on the basis of justice or the letter of a contract (e.g., union contract). They believe that complaints should be decided on the basis of who is *right*. (*Get the facts and decide the matter fairly.*) While this approach may be appropriate for such problems as larceny, this type of thinking is also commonly applied when the problem is controversial and, in part, a matter of individual perception (i.e., issues of academic credit, sexual harassment, the use of alcohol, and safety). In fact, many managers and academics think of workplace complaint systems *only* in terms of formal, due process, complaint-and-appeal systems. In the extreme form, if a problem cannot be adjudicated fairly, for example, because of a lack of sufficient evidence, a person oriented solely toward this view may take the position that nothing can be done and, therefore, that no complaint exists.

3. The interests orientation: Many ADR practitioners will seek the *interests* of those involved in the dispute and then recommend and/or practice the form of interest-based problem solving with which they are familiar. Mediators tend to think solely or mainly in terms of mediation—and within the context may be *bargainers* or *therapists*;[3] counselors tend to think in terms of therapeutic interventions, communication specialists think about better communication, and organizational theorists think in terms of changing the system to prevent or deal with problems.

In prescriptive research, as negotiation theorists have applied their tools to more and more types of negotiations and conflicts, they have tended to seek *optimal* solutions to problems. For many types of objectively quantifiable problems, this has made excellent sense. My concern is that this type of research, and all three viewpoints above—while extraordinarily useful as advisory tools— tend to focus people's thinking on *singular solutions, rather than ranges of choice.* They also focus on solutions that can be prescribed by those outside the dispute and even outside the system. This is often not as appropriate for complaint handling as it is for other forms of negotiations.

Descriptive research may also lead to stereotyped solutions to problems. For example, some researchers who have observed complaint handling and complaint handlers, correctly note that the ways in which people deal with their disputes are culture specific, and that many complaint handlers deal with disputes in narrowly defined ways. Descriptive researchers in this way may focus quite narrowly on only one type or style of complaint handling, in a way that inadvertently reduces the likelihood that interested managers will learn to think about many different modes of complaint handling.

Complaints and intrainstitutional disputes are not necessarily like commercial or game-theory negotiations, which may have an inherently *best* solution. Also, the specific practices of individual complaint handlers may or may not be as broad as complainants would wish (if they were aware of the choices they were missing). In short, **for a wide range of cases, there may not be any one** *optimal* **way to handle a complaint, other than whatever responsible method is freely chosen, by disputants and the complaint handler, under conditions of choice.** This chapter is about developing options and deliberately providing choices within a complaint system.

## The Value of Options and Choice

*Different People Want to Settle Things in Different Ways.* Different options may be necessary to satisfy the variety of people in a given workplace who believe *complaints should be resolved on the basis of principle,* but who do not share the same principles.

For example, some believe, on principle, that disputes should generally be resolved in an integrative fashion. These people will not be very happy if they are provided only adjudicative, complaint and appeal channels (e.g., *Please don't set up another formal equal opportunity thing for racial harassment; we get singled out enough already.*). People who share this opinion may not complain at all and will prefer to suffer rather than be forced into a polarized situation. The reverse is also true. An exclusively integrative, problem-solving complaint system will not satisfy the feelings of everyone who uses it, for some people will feel that their grievances should be adjudicated as a matter of justice (e.g., *It's time those creeps were stopped. I am going to take them every step of the way if I have to. I'll go to the Supreme Court.*).

*Providing Alternative Modes May Be Necessary to Deal With a Particular Problem.* For example, many complaints cannot be adequately adjudicated in the workplace for lack of sufficient evidence to convict a wrongdoer.[4] A formal process may, therefore, be useless in certain workplace disputes such as harassment, if sufficient evidence of wrongdoing does not exist (e.g., *He only does it behind closed doors; it'd be his word against mine. I don't want to bring a formal complaint; they would say it could not be proved and nothing would happen.*). An adjudicatory process may also be impractical for handling a very complicated web of problems; mediated outcomes may, in such cases, be substantively better because they often include a wider range of topics and feelings. (*Separating the work of the guys on that work team would take an arbitrator 6 weeks. We need to find a way to help them to work out the details themselves, without killing each other or the project.*).

*Choice Itself Is Often Important to Disputants and Complainants.* For example, *I stopped feeling that my hands were tied.* Having choices offers a measure of power and self-esteem and will often be perceived as more fair. Some complainants specifically ask for a *vote* on how something will be handled, instead of, or in addition, to substantive redress. Choice can be itself an *interest,* that can and should be included in interest-based problem solving.

Even in situations for which there appears to be only one responsible option, a complaint handler may be able to provide small choices. For example, suppose a theft must be reported; there seems to be only one responsible option. But there may be some small choices available: Would the complainant prefer to go directly to the security office alone, would she rather have the complaint handler accompany her, or would she rather that the complaint handler go to report the theft? It is especially important to offer some choice if the subject matter is stressful; people cope better with tough problems if they perceive that they have some control over the complaint process, and they are more likely to feel that the process is fair.

*Knowing That There Is a Choice About How to Pursue a Complaint Is Essential to Getting Some People to Complain.* My research[5] indicates that many people do not wish to lose control over their complaints, especially in the beginning while they are thinking things through. For example, many people who come to my office feeling harassed express fear of retaliation and of loss of privacy (e.g., *I know it's important to stop my supervisor from using coke, if only because he's mean as hell. But I can't be the one to complain; I've got a family.*). In addition, they may care about the object of the complaint and may fear being seen as childish or disloyal. Many would ultimately do nothing about their problems if we could not together devise a tailor-made option that satisfied their individual concerns (e.g., *Thank you for letting me wait until after graduation; I just could not have come forward before.*).

*The Complainant's Choice May Be a Better Choice.* This is particularly true when the complainant finds it difficult to identify exactly the factors that are important (e.g., *I don't know why. I just couldn't look her in the face if I didn't try to take it up with her directly one more time before I go to the boss.*).

*The Complainant Who Chooses May Learn Something.* Having a choice of complaint handling modes may encourage complainants to take more responsibility for their lives and to become more effective. Developing and then choosing an option with a skilled complaint handler provides a complainant not just an individual solution, but a method for responsible dispute resolution in the future (*Hey, I came back to see you. You know that year I spent carping at everyone about safety on the plant floor? Well, you know you finally taught me how to negotiate these things. I haven't had a fight about safety, or much of anything else, for 4 years. . . . I just wanted to tell you.*).

*Providing Options May Be Less Costly.* It is important to provide (responsible) options that cost the complainant and the system as little as possible in terms of time, soul, and money. Costly alternatives are often used in situations in which someone mainly *just wants to be heard.* Numerous studies of union grievances have shown that complainants sometimes pursue formal grievances when they think that a grievance is the only available way to express their feelings about dictatorial work relationships. Sometimes people go to court or to government agencies while wishing they had a less costly option (e.g., *I know I may lose this case against that bastard; I know I don't necessarily have a leg to stand on. But he is going to have to listen to me.*). In my experience, the strongest impetus for labor lawsuits against employers is that the plaintiff felt humiliated and could find no other satisfactory way to redress the humiliation. By the same token, sabotage and violence may also be precipitated by humiliation. As Program on Negotiation participant Diane Di Carlo put it, "When social rules provide alternatives, people are less likely to take revenge."

*Providing Choice in How to Deal With a Complaint May Help Protect the Employer.* The complainant that has chosen his or her dispute-processing mode may be better satisfied with the solution. And if he or she is not satisfied, the employer can reasonably plead that the complainant chose the mode himself or herself and, therefore, should take some responsibility for what ensued (e.g., *This company always offers the possibility of formal investigation and adjudication to anyone who feels harassed. When Chris Lee complained, we wrote her a letter offering an investigation. Obviously, this is the option we would have preferred. She refused. She did not permit us to do a fair, prompt and thorough investigation. She absolutely refused to make an open complaint.*

*The only option Lee would agree to was that we develop a training program for that department, which we did immediately.).*

Creating options and choice for complainants will be especially important for the U.S. workplace in the 1990s and beyond. We are moving into an era of extraordinary diversity. The Bureau of Labor Statistics suggests that only about 1 in 10 of net new entrants into the U.S. labor force of the 1990s will be a native-born Anglo (white) male. The rest will be minorities, women, and immigrants, an extremely diverse group of managers and workers compared with the past. It will be especially important to have choices in how to express concerns or pursue grievances in the workplace because individual values will differ greatly.

## Prescriptively, What Are Some of the Choices That an Effective Complaint System Should Provide?

1. **Complaint handlers who will listen and offer respect** to people with concerns and who will help people who are hurt, in grief, confused, angry, aggrieved, or frightened to deal with their feelings. It is essential that this function be offered on a confidential basis, perhaps by employee assistance or ombudsman counselors. Moreover, a complainant should under most circumstances be able to talk and choose *no* further action, if that is what he or she wishes.[6] It may be appropriate to make a referral to a counselor or religious adviser. The option *just to be heard* by the complaint handler may be the appropriate complaint handling mode for the case of Colleen in my opening vignette. Colleen is simply asking for affirmation and that her situation be recorded in the aggregated statistics on sexual harassment. The complaint handler should, if possible, follow up with Colleen to be sure that the harassment has ended. The complaint handler might also agree with Colleen on the importance of bringing in a training program for the whole work unit. However, in most cases of this kind, the complaint handler ought not act without permission.

2. **Any person in the workplace should be able to receive certain types of information** off the record, for example, about how the system works, what fairness is, what salary equity is, and

how to raise a concern. Everyone should also have safe (that is, anonymous or completely confidential) channels to *provide* information to management about unsafe conditions, unethical and illegal practices, and the like. Colleen wants her case recorded for statistical use. Sandy and Henry in my opening vignettes need to know how the system works. Sandy, for example, needs to know about employee assistance, the policies on use of alcohol, and how supervisors and the safety office may be expected to function if and when they hear about Sandy's co-worker. Henry needs to know his employer's policies on assignment of credit and perhaps on fraud.

3. **All employees and managers should be able to find effective, confidential counseling** on how to sort out their complaints and conflicts, how to generate different responsible options for action, and how to negotiate their problems directly if desired.[7] This was an option for Sandy and Henry to consider. For example, Sandy might have learned how to persuade the old friend to seek help and perhaps accompany the old friend to employee assistance while nevertheless insisting on compliance with safety standards. Henry chose to learn to write and send an effective personal letter. Colleen seems to have chosen this option, but can still learn more by talking through what she did (as there are several different ways she could have rejected the harassment).

4. **There should be effective shuttle diplomats and process consultants** as go-betweens and educators, for individuals and groups.[8] It is important to note that this is by far the most common form of *mediation* in the workplace because the assistance of a third party helps people of unequal rank to save face. Henry and Colleen could have asked the complaint handler to talk with their bosses. Sandy could have asked the complaint handler to talk with his co-worker.

5. **Formal mediation should be available,** accompanied by formal written settlements, if desired.[9] This would have been a reasonable option for both Henry and Colleen.

6. **There should be a fair, prompt, and thorough investigation of complaints when appropriate.** A good complaint system can provide formal and informal investigation, with or without written recommendations to a decision maker.[10] Henry might have asked for an investigation by his suprasupervisor. Colleen might have asked for an employee ombudsman (EO) person or her boss's boss to look into her complaint. Sandy's complaint

could trigger a safety inspection and possibly a substance abuse investigation by a specialized staff person or the supervisor.

7. **There should be appropriate, fair process, complaint and appeal channels, with impartial arbitration, peer review, or impartial adjudication.**[11] These options could have been offered to Henry and Colleen, and indeed would likely have been triggered by an investigation. Henry, Colleen, their supervisors, and Sandy's co-worker could appeal a decision they did not like within a formal grievance structure.

8. **There should be effective provision for feedback and systems change,** both as a problem-solving device for specific complaints and to prevent further problems.[12] Colleen's office should offer a program on harassment, Henry's office should train supervisors about work credit, and Sandy's office should train about safety and substance abuse. A good complaint system will provide management the information needed to design effective problem prevention programs.

## How to Provide Options for Complainants

Obviously, an employer wants to take the lead in the design of a complaint handling system, to foster responsible and consistent practice. Potential disputants and potential complaint handlers should be involved in the design process. This may happen naturally in the context of union negotiations or consultive committees, or it may happen ad hoc, through the use of focus groups or by circulating draft proposals to many networks in the workplace.

A grievance channel or a complaint system is often designed around the issue that brought it into existence and, therefore, can be much too narrowly focused. For example, as a result of an organizing campaign, there may be a singular focus on worker versus management grievances. Or a group of concerned employees may generate a great deal of attention to one type of concern such as transfer policy or safety.

This chapter, by contrast, aims to foster choice of complaint-handling options for the whole panorama of real-life workplace disputes. Workplace problems can involve co-workers, peer conflict among managers, or fights among groups. Complaints may arise in *any* area where people feel unjustly treated. In order to make it clear that there truly are options for complaint handling available to everyone within a workplace, *complaint systems should provide all the options discussed above.* Everyone in the organization (managers, employees, union workers, professionals, etc.) should have recourse, with respect to every kind of important concern.

The systems approach also requires having different kinds of people available as complaint handlers. The set of complaint handlers should, within reason, reflect the given work force, and include, for example, African-Americans, females, Asian-Americans, technical people, and so on. This will make it more likely that the work force will believe there are accessible and credible managers, who might offer acceptable ways to raise a concern.

The point is also true with respect to complaint handling skills. Because few complaint handlers are equally good at listening, referring, counseling, mediating, investigating, adjudicating, and systems change, a good system will have a variety of complaint handlers providing a variety of functions. In particular, it often helps to have different people for problem solving and adjudication, since some people are better at integrative solutions and others consistently think distributively and may make better judges.

Finally, a good system will train its employees and its complaint handlers, including all managers, to respect, offer, and pursue the widest possible variety of different options for dealing with disputes and concerns, with as much choice as possible for those who raise concerns. It may not be easy to change the working styles of employees, managers, and complaint handlers, but everyone can learn what his or her own strengths are and can learn at least to respect and offer other options.[13]

*I used to think that my only choices were to put up with the unpaid overtime—shut up—or just quit. Then I thought, well, I could take that slave driver to court or maybe file a formal grievance with corporate* [headquarters]. *Then I thought, I can't stand it any longer, and I began to miss work. Then you pointed out to me that there were several possibilities other than fantasies of revenge or a lawsuit or dropping out. I actually had not considered sending a private letter to my boss, for example, and I certainly had not imagined that you* [the company ombudsman] *would be willing to go see the boss for me.*

*But the best idea was that you would ask human resources to send out a general notice on the overtime rules. The fact that you went to human resources alone, without mentioning me or my boss, really made me feel safer. My boss stopped requiring unpaid overtime and no one knew I was involved. I'm very glad it worked. Who knows? Maybe somebody else's situation got cleared up at the same time.*

## Functions of a Good Complaint System

In sum, a good complaint system will provide *multiple options* for complainants, and as much *choice* as possible among those options. The first three functions of the system will be *available on a confidential basis* if desired. The system will have *men and women and minorities and nonminorities* available as complaint handlers. The system will be *available to everyone* within the workplace, including managers, trainees, employees, and so on and will accept any kind of concern. Necessary functions include:

- *Expressing respect for feelings:* especially rage, fear of retaliation, and grief. Helping people deal with their feelings so they will be able to make good decisions and deal effectively with their problems or complaints.
- *Giving and receiving information* on a one-to-one basis.
- *Helping people help themselves:* confidential counseling with clients, inventing options, listing possible options for the choice of the client, coaching on how the client or group may deal with the problem directly (problem solving, role-playing, anticipating possible outcomes, etc.).
- *Shuttle diplomacy* by a third party, back and forth among those with a problem, to resolve the matter at hand (sometimes called *conciliation* or *caucusing* as one form of mediation).
- *Mediation:* a third party brings together the people with a problem to reach their own settlement; mediation settlements may be formal or informal.
- *Fact-finding or investigation:* this may be done either formally or informally; results may be used or reports made either with or without recommendations from the fact-finder to a decision maker.
- *Decision making, arbitration, or adjudication:* a person or body with power and/or formal authority decides a dispute; this may be structured as part of a formal complaint-and-appeals channel or formal grievance procedure.

- *Systems change:* designing a generic process for a type of problem or complaint; *upward feedback;* making actual changes in policies, procedures, or structures as a result of an inquiry, suggestion, complaint, or grievance.

When all these functions are being performed within an organization, one may speak of a complaint-handling *system.* Without fair, accessible complaint-and-appeals channels, other functions are not likely to work well. Where all functions are working well, the formal grievance channel is not likely to be used heavily. By analogy, a manager who is not able to decide disputes fairly will not be trusted to carry out other functions of a complaint handler. The manager who has all these skills will usually be able to solve most problems without arbitration.

## Appendix: Exercise on "Skills Needed by the Complaint Handler"

This exercise is very simple. The sheet on skills needed (see "Functions of a Good Complaint System," above) is assigned for 1 week or 1 month. The task is for the assignee to notice and keep a journal on the ways in which he or she deals with concerns. In addition, the writer should analyze the complaint handling options chosen by those with whom he or she comes in contact.

The writer should take notice of his or her customary ways of expressing concerns and ask the following questions. Do I seek advice about how to handle my problems? Do I just need to blow off steam, and with whom do I do this? Do I look for mediation services? Do I ask others to be a shuttle diplomat for me? Do I ask for an investigation of my problems? Do I want someone more powerful than I to take care of my complaints? Do I seek a systematic change in the conditions that cause the problem?

By the same token, the writer should notice how others handle complaints and concerns. Do they offer choices to the complainants? Or do they just seem to "know what is best?" Do they appear to listen to the complainer, help to invent options, advise on tailoring an option to the concern at hand? Or do they irritably decide the question before exploring it?

The writer should try to develop insight into his or her normal complaint handling modes with children, colleagues, supervisors, strangers, and so on. It is also useful to analyze the patterns of others, to see how they deal with complaints and concerns.

Obviously, some people will be very much oriented toward justice. Others will problem solve in the face of the most tenacious wrong-doing and in the most serious, win-lose situations. Most people have a variety of skills and can develop and work on new skills. It is useful to reflect on the variety of skills needed in different situations and to provoke discussion as to whether and when certain complaint handling modes appear to be best or necessary.

## Notes

1. See also generally the work of Professor Kolb (Simmons College), and Professor Merry and Professor Silbey (Wellesley College) on the narrow range of conflict resolution modes practiced by mediators whom they have studied. See also the typologies of Myers-Briggs and Chapter 11, this volume, by Professor Williams (Brigham Young University) on negotiating styles.

2. This typology is drawn from the terminology of colleagues at the (Harvard/ MIT/Tufts) Program on Negotiation and Ury, Brett, and Goldberg (1988). It will be noted by negotiations theorists that an orientation on rights is likely to lead to distributive solutions and orientation on power is also most likely to be distributive, although there are a few power-oriented managers who seek integrative solutions. A manager who is oriented toward interests is more likely to seek integrative solutions.

3. See again generally Kolb (1983; also this volume), and Merry and Silbey (1984).

4. For further work on this point see Rowe (1990).

5. Rowe (1990).

6. This possibility is controversial for some types of complaints, for example, harassment. It is in this arena that we see most clearly the extent to which many people would like to be able to make decisions for complainants about how they will be "allowed" to complain. For example, many people think that all harassment complaints should be investigated and adjudicated, whether or not the offended person wishes this to happen. This is a complicated matter, but in most cases I feel that if a complainant knows there are options and refuses investigation and adjudication, and the complaint handler follows up and knows the harassment has ended, the matter should not be pursued. Investigating harassment that is said to have ended should, ordinarily, require permission from the harassed person. There should, of course, not be adverse administrative action, or a record made against the alleged offender, in the absence of a fair investigation. A review of choices actually made by this type of complainant is included in Rowe (1990).

7. See, for example, Rowe (1990).

8. See, for example, Blake and Mouton (1984).

9. See, for example, Ury, Brett, and Goldberg (1988).

10. See, for example, Ewing (1989) Westin and Feliu (1988).

11. Ewing (1989) and Westin and Feliu (1988).

12. There are many good examples of systems change mechanisms in the books cited in this chapter, although each example tends to focus on only one way to produce systems change. Ombuds practitioners typically spend a quarter to a third or more of their time on systems change.

13. See the appendix to this chapter for an exercise that can be used as a diagnostic tool. The exercise provides a framework for analyzing one's own skills as a complainer and a complaint handler and for analyzing the skills and methods of others.

# PART III

# Perspectives on Individual Negotiators

## Introduction

▶ In this section, each of the authors discusses how the issues of individual style, perception and gender affect the process of negotiation. Rather than analyzing outcomes or offering prescriptions, this section contemplates some of the interplays between individuals that make negotiations complex and hard to generalize about.

Rubin, in his chapter, analyzes some ways in which awareness of individual perception can help negotiators to avoid classic pitfalls in negotiation. The awareness of certain biases or tendencies can be a first step toward controlling them and, in turn, transforming a stalled or failed negotiation into a more productive one. He offers suggestions to avoid letting psychological factors get negotiations off track.

Williams reports on his extensive study of lawyers negotiating and on the cooperative and aggressive patterns that he has been able to discern in their negotiating behavior. He analyzes a set of

121

characteristics found in each type of negotiator and offers some suggestions on how a negotiator confronted with such behavior might respond. Based on his descriptive study, he demonstrates what makes an effective, average or ineffective negotiator.

Kolb tackles the interesting question of the role of gender in negotiation. Relying on the theoretical literature and interviews with successful women negotiators, she points out a number of dilemmas that women face in negotiating. Read along with the chapters about psychological factors and effective negotiating styles, the reader may come away with new awareness about how she is perceived, and how to modulate her negotiating style for greater effectiveness.

# 9

# Conflict From a
# Psychological Perspective

JEFFREY Z. RUBIN

▶ In this chapter I talk about conflict from a psychological perspective. Why is it that conflicts escalate? Why do they reach a point of stalemate? And finally, what are some of the ways out of stalemate?

The following characteristics will help define what I mean by a *psychological perspective.* A psychological perspective focuses on perceptions rather than reality. This is not to say that reality is unimportant, but it is what people think about reality rather than reality itself that makes a difference. I define conflict not as divergence of interests but as a perceived divergence of interests.

Second, a psychological perspective focuses on the relationship between the parties. In negotiation, it is the dynamics of the exchange that is really of interest. Psychologists try to understand why it is that people do things. They are more interested in describing and understanding phenomenon than in giving advice. And finally, a psychological perspective relies on empiricism; it asks questions that can be answered through experiments in a contrived or natural environment.

## Conflict Cycle

Many conflicts follow a rhythmic, predictable cycle. I like to think of conflict and its escalation as a play in three acts. In act one, the conflict escalates. Each actor tries to prevail and beat the other into submission, physically and/or psychologically. In act two, a climax is reached. The protagonists run out of steam and we have a stalemate. They have not run out of determination to beat the other, they have simply lost hope of prevailing through coercion. In act three, there is a move toward settlement of the conflict that has escalated in the dramatic production.

Not all conflicts follow this cycle. Some do not get beyond the point of stalemate. Other conflicts are settled by one party dominating the exchange, by one party unilaterally deciding to withdraw or by both parties adopting a pattern of inaction in the hope that allowing time to pass will have an effect on the fate of the conflict.

The following story illustrates act one, the escalation of conflict.

It started out as not much of a fight at all. Joe, aged sixteen, borrowed Dad's car for the night. Joe was supposed to fill the tank up with gas before returning it but he forgot. The next morning Dad was late for an important meeting at work because he had to wait in line unexpectedly for gasoline in the middle of rush hour traffic.

That night, Dad let Joe know the inconvenience caused by his forgetfulness. Joe apologized in an offhand adolescent way, "Oh, sorry Dad," he said, as he looked up from watching a sports program on television.

Things began to heat up. Upset with Joe's lack of concern, Dad remarked on Joe's irresponsible and inconsiderate behavior. Joe rejoined with a few grunts in between sips of Coke and shovelfuls of food. Dad demanded a real apology. When none was forthcoming, he began to chastise his son for being inconsiderate in other situations: leaving his dirty clothing strewn about the house, using up the last of the postage stamps and toilet paper without telling anyone, refusing to help his mother with various kitchen chores and not mowing the lawn.

After taking as much as he could handle, Joe exploded. "Who the hell are you to tell me what to do? I don't see you doing so much around here. When is the last time you did the wash? For that matter, when is the last time you even bothered to smile at anyone? As far as you're concerned I never seem to do anything right. All you do is complain about me and everyone else in the family. You don't care about how other people feel, do you?"

"You don't care about anyone but yourself," responded Dad. "You can forget about using the car."

With mother and sister looking on, father and son continue trading insults and the fight continues to heat up. Joe walks angrily out of the house. Dad sits down and wonders what happened, why he became so angry, and what went wrong between him and his son. (Rubin & Rubin, 1989)

Let us look at some of the characteristics of an escalating exchange. Some of these characteristics will relate directly to the example I have just described and others will not.

## Escalation

First, as conflicts escalate issues tend to proliferate. A fight over a single issue in an escalating exchange is typically transformed into a fight over multiple issues. A simple exchange over the matter of remembering to buy a tank of gas for the car spills over into issues such as washing dishes, taking care of the lawn and so forth.

A second transformation that occurs relates to a shift from a criticism of a specific behavior or action to a focus on personalities. What starts out as criticism of not filling up the car with gasoline is transformed rather quickly in the example into an assault on the other person's character: "You're an irresponsible and inconsiderate person, you're an unsmiling S.O.B. who doesn't think about anything except getting your car filled with gas." This is a particularly important transformation because it occurs very dramatically and often without the awareness of the participants. It is very difficult to move back down the escalatory ladder once the conflict has reached this point.

Witness in the international domain the shooting down of the Korean airline by the Soviets in 1983. President Reagan did not simply condemn the act, but went on to talk about the demonic, satanic Soviet empire. How can the Soviets respond to that exactly? If you are a Soviet citizen and you pick up the newspaper and you read that the president of the United States declares the Soviet Union to be a satanic empire, what do you do?

Incidentally, some interesting research has been done over the last decade by psychologists who have analyzed speeches given by leaders of nations during escalating conflicts, some of which have led to wars. Analysis of these speeches indicates that as conflicts escalate, there is a systematic and predictable shift from complex assertions and criticisms to very simple black-and-white ones: good, bad; right team, wrong team. The more the conflict escalates, the more the polarization occurs. Those interested in this work should take a look at the writings of Tetlock at Berkeley and Suedfeld at the University of British Columbia.

A third transformation that typically occurs is a shift from light to heavy tactics. There are several ways in which this shift can occur. A shift from promises, "if you do what I want I will do something you find rewarding" to threats, "unless you do what I want, I will hurt you." A shift from efforts in persuasion, "there are eight reasons why it is in your interest to change your behavior or point of view" to efforts in coercion. A shift from statements that are contingent in construction, "unless you do the thing I want, I am going to hurt you" to statements that are not contingent, "I will hurt you."

I think that it is reasonable to ask why it is light to heavy rather than heavy to light in an escalating exchange. I can think of at least two reasons why it makes sense for the moves to go from light to heavy rather than the other way around. If I try to get you to do what I want in an escalating exchange by offering you some promise of reward and it fails, I can then move to heavier tactics and say to you and to the world of onlookers, "Well, I tried." I am likely to be seen as weak if, after trying to coerce and intimidate you, I move to lighter tactics.

An example in the international arena occurred when Henry Kissinger negotiated a second settlement between the Israelis and the Egyptians in 1975, after the 1973 war in the Middle East. The Israelis got very tough and refused to budge even when Kissinger threatened that the United States might have to reconsider its policy toward Israel. However, there was congressional support for Israel's stubbornness so Kissinger turned to lighter tactics, promising to pump millions of dollars of economic and military aid into Israel. You can argue that it worked. Israel got back to the bargaining table and concluded an agreement with the Egyptians. But you can also argue that it opened the door to an increasing round of blackmail or influencing efforts that continue to the present day.

A fourth transformation that occurs is a motivational transformation. It begins as an interest in doing as well as one can and shifts to an interest in prevailing, in doing better than the other side. As the conflict escalates, there is a realization that both sides are going to lose and the more they stay in the game, the more they are going to lose. This results in an angry determination that the other side loses even more: "We will both go down the rat hole but I am going to make sure that you go down first and a little bit further than I."

And finally, a fifth transformation is an increase in the number of people involved. What was initially a dispute between two individuals may soon involve friends or relatives. In the example above, the conflict between Joe and his Dad inevitably will involve the mother and sister.

In summary, in act one of an escalating conflict we can have a series of transformations; a proliferation in the number of issues, a shift from criticism of behavior to criticism of character, a shift in tactics from light to heavy, a motivational transformation, and an increase in the number of parties involved.

What is the dynamic, psychological machinery that is driving these transformations? In an escalating conflict the parties get locked into a way of presenting themselves. They have persisted so long in presenting themselves to an adversary as tough and unrelenting that they refuse to back down. They feel that they have too much invested in that presentation to quit. Or they may be locked into perceptions of the other side. They have viewed the other side for so long as a blood-thirsty, merciless adversary that they are unable to abandon that view even if they have been given contradictory information that should disprove the hypothesis.

In an escalating conflict things tend to go up more readily than they come down. In Greek mythology there is the story of Cerberus, a dog with three heads who guards the entrance to Hades. Cerberus has a spiked tail that functions in such a way that you can brush by it on your way into Hades but it will not allow you to get out. This is analogous to what happens in many escalating conflicts.

Consider the example of Joe and his Dad. The next day they apologized to one another and worked out some settlement to the car problem. But a residue of ill feeling has been created that may not go away so quickly.

There are three dynamics that will help explain the transformations. The first is selective perception, changes in how people regard and receive information about the other side in an escalating conflict. The second is self-fulfilling prophesies. These are little bits of psychological machinery that allow attitudes to drive behavior that, in turn, reinforces attitudes and drives the escalation process along. And third, there is overcommitment and entrapment.

## Selective Perception

Let us begin with selective perception. In an escalating conflict we tend to select what we want to see about our adversary and ignore other information. Selective perception allows us to see a glass that is half filled with water as either half full or half empty.

One of the best illustrations of the selective perception phenomenon was an experiment conducted about 35 years ago by social-psychologists, Sherif and Sherif (1969). They studied campers in an American summer camp to try to understand conditions that lead to the escalation of intergroup conflict and circumstances that might make it possible to settle it.

In carrying out the experiment, they deliberately created intergroup conflict among the campers. They began by building several cohesive groups. They encouraged each group to choose its own name, mascot, and color and engaged the groups in competitive sports. In this way they built up the integrity of each group and created a sense of threat from the other groups.

Once they created intergroup conflict, they decided to have a jelly bean hunt. A couple of days after the jelly bean hunt, a picture of a jar of jelly beans was shown to each group. Some groups were told that the jar was filled with the jelly beans collected by their group and they were asked to estimate the number of beans in the jar. Other groups were told that the picture was of the jar of jelly beans found by another group and they were asked to estimate how many jelly beans were in the jar. Interestingly, all the groups were inaccurate. The groups tended to overestimate the number of the jelly beans they thought their group collected and to underestimate the number of jelly beans they thought the other group collected.

In an escalating conflict, we tend to see what we want to see and to distort information to support our expectations. One way we do this is by selectively testing hypotheses. We form a hypothesis about the adversary such as, this person is nasty. Then we gather information to confirm our hypothesis and ignore information that does not support it.

Through selective perception, the perceiver is processing information about the other in a way that tends to feed into, stir up, and strengthen stereotypic views of the other. Through attributional distortion we distort our explanation of other people's behavior in the service of our preconceived notions. We skew our explanations to derogate the other person and to uplift ourselves. We explain our own successes as true skill. Our failures are due to circumstances not under our control. We explain our adversaries' successes as flukes, their failures as true incompetence. If we do something charitable or benevolent it is because we are good kind people. We explain our adversaries' kind behavior as manipulative, ingratiating, not to be trusted, a momentary lapse from their true, evil, and malevolent state.

## Self-Fulfilling Prophecies

In selective perception we have only dealt with perceptions. When behavior is introduced, we have self-fulfilling prophecy, which connects attitudes and behaviors. I have an expectation of you that leads me to behave in a way that produces a response in you that reconfirms my expectation. My prophecy about the kind of person that you are is fulfilled.

Let us say that I think that you are a dangerous person, a person who may endanger me. As a result, I strike out at you and you in turn, strike me back. I am likely to be glad that I did what I did because the blow you gave me shows me that you are a dangerous, crazy person.

I refer to a certain form of self-fulfilling prophecy as the tar baby effect from a Joel Chandler Harris "Uncle Remus" story of many years ago.

Bear and Fox are always trying to catch Rabbit. Fox is clever, Bear is lumbering and foolish and Rabbit is wise and elusive. One of the traps that Fox sets for Rabbit is a tar baby. He decides to fashion a likeness of a rabbit out of tar and set it by the side of the road. He wants to play into, what he correctly anticipates, Rabbit's inherent narcissism. So the tar baby is laid by the side of the road. Rabbit comes along and says to the tar sculpture, "Hi there, nice day isn't it?" The tar baby doesn't respond. "You're not very talkative are you? I said it is a really nice day here, isn't it?" Rabbit gets more and more agitated and upset. "If you are so stuck up that you don't even have the decency to respond to some simple hello, I am going to get really mad and take a slug at you." He hits the tar baby and gets one fist stuck. Then he gets a second fist stuck and eventually is completely entwined in the tar baby.

In this story, the tar baby has not done anything. The rabbit has managed to catch himself up in an intriguing sort of self-fulfilling prophecy.

The following is a similar example of self-fulfilling prophecy. You are at a cocktail party. A person at the party seems aloof and is sitting apart from the rest of the group. Your hypothesis is that the person is unfriendly, arrogant, and stuck up. The fact is that the person is shy, but you do not know this. You say nothing to the person, the person says nothing to you and when you leave at the end of the evening you are convinced that you have been in the presence of a stuck-up pain. This is the most pernicious form of self-fulfilling prophecy because the other person has been completely closed out of the process, and it is, therefore, completely self-fueling. There are many examples of this type of self-fulfilling prophecy in relationships between people and nations.

Fisher likes to say, "There may be reasons to hang up the phone, but never cut the wires." If you cut the wires, you close yourself off from contact with reality, the opportunity to test your hypotheses and confront the other side with your beliefs.

### Entrapment

The third dynamic that drives the transformations in an escalating conflict is overcommitment and entrapment. This is the tendency for people to lock into a particular view of the other and adhere to it.

The following example illustrates an entrapment situation. A decision maker has devoted many resources—money, time and energy—to reaching a certain goal but has not yet been able to accomplish it. The more he or she invests and allocates resources to meet the goal, the greater the conflict because these resources are simultaneously seen as an investment in moving the person to a goal and as an expense.

I first started thinking about the phenomenon of entrapment many years ago when I phoned an airline to get some information. They put me on hold. The longer I waited on hold, the sooner I believed I would get to the point where the person at the other end would give me the information. But, the longer I waited, the more time I was wasting, a reason to get out of the situation immediately and hang up the phone. However, I persisted because I did not want to give up on the time I had already wasted. When I eventually decided to hang up the phone I kept my ear close to the receiver until I put it back on the phone in the hope that at the very last second the person would return on the other end.

This is entrapment but I did not have the insight at the time to understand what was going on. I still get trapped on the telephone but now when I am in a situation like that, I bring along a little work. I prepare to wait and I have something else that I can do. So what was potentially a cost has been transformed into an opportunity.

Passive situations tend to be more entrapping than ones that involve an active allocation of resources. Experimental evidence shows that you are more likely to feel entrapped on the phone in the privacy of your own home than you are on a pay phone. When you are on a pay phone, you are reminded every few minutes that you have to come up with the money necessary to sustain the situation. Whereas in the privacy of your home you remain in the situation continually until you decide to end it. Picture two machines. One machine has a button that when pressed stays on. As soon as you take your finger off, it turns off. This is similar to the pay phone. The other machine has a switch with two positions that you turn on and off. When you turn it on it remains on until you decide to turn it off.

Entrapping situations that involve money typically require action. If your car is not running, it will not run unless you put money into it and get it to a mechanic. A relationship or a job, on the other hand, is more likely to be a passive entrapping situation. It is likely to remain in motion until you choose to bring it to an end. It may be at a standstill, it may be deteriorating, you may be unhappy but the passage of time allows the process to keep on going automatically until you elect to bail out.

People tend to get entrapped when they fail to set limits in advance for the amount of resources that they are willing to devote to a situation. It is not enough to set a limit, one must stick to it. People tend to get trapped because although they set decision rules for themselves, they tend to deviate from the rules they have set. If I flip a coin to see what I am going to do and I do not like the outcome, I decide to make it two out of three. I will then make it three out of five and so on.

People who believe in a just world are good candidates for entrapment. These are people who tend to believe that the world is a place where people deserve what they get and get what they deserve. In other words, that one gets out what one puts in. If you sink time, energy, and money into a project and stick it out long enough, you will get something out of it. But the world is not always a just place. Other people who are good candidates for entrapment are achievers, people who are so goal oriented that they only look forward. Eventually some of these people will turn around and realize that there is a large mountain of cost that they have incurred that they feel compelled to justify. And finally, people who feel the need to save face, to look good in the eyes of others, are good candidates for entrapment. In a gambling game at a cocktail party that starts out with 30 people betting 10 cents, this person will be one of the last 2 people left when the bets reach $4 or $5, as everyone else looks on with their martinis in hand. If you are concerned about not looking foolish in a situation like this, you are likely to persist and remain entrapped.

## Stalemate

Now that I have sufficiently dealt with act one, the escalation of conflict, I will move on to act two when, if you recall, stalemate is reached. At some point in an escalating exchange people simply run out of ammunition. They have not run out of the determination and zeal to beat the other, they simply run out of the hope of accomplishing that objective. At this point, stalemate has been reached, a point of maximum conflict intensity, where things are not likely to get worse. They can only remain where they are or possibly improve.

I think that it is important for practitioners, theorists, and students of negotiation to understand in advance when a point of stalemate is going to be reached. Third-party interventions that work quite well either before or after this point of stalemate may turn out to be a disaster at the point of stalemate. At the point of stalemate, the parties are in a transition from a determination to beat one another but no longer have the resources, to the grudging understanding that it may be possible and even desirable to try to get what one wants through collaboration. It does not mean that the parties like each other, but they begin to accept each other, for the first time, as potential partners and allies rather than purely as adversaries.

The first part of the stalemate process is a bit like two boxers who are slugging it out for a long time. They have not lost their determination to beat the other, but their arms are not letting them. In the second part of this stalemate transition the parties begin to acknowledge the possibility that they can cooperate.

Perhaps the most important issue relating to stalemate is face saving. Although one of the parties understands that it may be necessary to make a concession, he or she does not want to be the first one to do it. An example is a world championship chess match that took place some years ago between Bobby Fisher and Boris Spassky. In one of the games, it was very clear that a draw was going to be reached, but neither player would ask the other for a draw. The game was dragging on and the referee was clearly eager to have it end. The commentator, Shelby Lymon, described the two of them as playing forehead to forehead, studiously avoiding eye contact. Interestingly, at precisely the same moment the two players apparently looked up, glanced at each other, smiled and nodded their heads. The referee eagerly said, "Do I take it that there is a draw?" And so a draw was reached.

What this example shows is that neither side wanted to be in the position in an ongoing exchange of being the first one to ask for something that would suggest in any way that he might be weaker than the other side. People do not want to set a precedent where they look weak or foolish in the eyes of an adversary or in the eyes of their constituents.

I highly recommend that you read Dr. Seuss's *Story of the Zaks.* It is about two Zaks who meet and get stuck in their tracks, one facing north and one facing south, each stubbornly refusing to budge to make room for the other one to pass. They are a bit like Fisher and Spassky, unwilling to get out of the stalemate in any obvious way.

# Deescalation

I will now move on to act three where the conflict deescalates and the dispute is somehow settled. As I mentioned earlier, not all conflicts have an act three.

In discussing disputes, I stay away from the word *resolution*. I am a nitpicker for terminology like many psychologists. If during the course of settlement, resolution is brought about, that is terrific. But I do not count on it, and I do not necessarily aspire to see the resolution of conflict. By resolution I mean a modification of deep-seated behavior, concerns, and attitudes. Often I settle just for a behavioral change if that is all I can get.

### Reducing Conflict

The following is by no means an exhaustive list of ways to reduce conflict, but one that responds to the issues that I have raised in acts one and two. These will focus on, in particular, psychological hooks into the deescalation of conflict.

One way to reverse escalation when there is a problem of selective perception is through techniques that increase individualization. Stereotypic distortion occurs when the parties only see evidence that supports the hypotheses they have developed about the other side, but not evidence that contradicts them. The way out of this is by bringing the parties into greater contact with each other. The best technique that has been found for reducing racial prejudice is what is known as the contact hypothesis. Busing may have some disadvantages, but research shows that it gets people into contact with each other, which is the single most important way of reducing prejudice and stereotypes.

When one brings people into greater contact, each side begins to understand that the other is perhaps just as smart, resourceful, determined, and committed as itself. At the same time, each party may realize that the other side is not analyzing the problem in precisely the same way. Not that the other side is defective or deficient but that he or she may have different assumptions and biases.

President Carter mistakenly assumed in the Iranian hostage crisis that the Iranians were playing the same game that we were. He learned very painfully that the game the Iranians were playing was very different. The United States mistakenly assumed a homogeneity or symmetry of perception that was not there.

A second way of deescalating conflict is to work on communication skills. Listening is more important than talking, and listening between the lines is necessary to understand fully what the other person is saying. Fisher often discusses the issue of listening and communication that relates to separating positions from interests, the difference between what the other person says and what he or she really means and wants.

Third, look for ways of building momentum. This is particularly important in times of stalemate when people are refusing to budge and neither side wants to take that first step. One way of building momentum toward peacemaking is to start with an easy problem. Most conflicts involve a whole bunch of problems. Begin by taking one that is workable. Next, get each side to make irreversible commitments that each acknowledges it will keep. Entrapment can be used in a positive sense to build commitments to projects and relationships that we value. More attention must be given in negotiation to figuring out ways of building commitments that each side views as irreversible. The more the sides have stuck to a commitment and the more they have invested in it, is what Fisher and Ury (1981) and others refer to as the transformation from face-to-face to side-by-side problem analysis (see, generally, *Getting to Yes*). It is a realization by the parties not only that there is a basis for competition and an adversarial relationship but that there is also a basis for collaboration and joint problem solving.

Let us return to the Sherifs' (1969) research on intergroup conflict among campers. They tried several ways to settle the conflict, none of which worked. Bringing the leaders of each group together did not work. Bringing the groups to the table to talk did not work; they just ended up throwing watermelon pieces at each other. What did work was introducing a superordinate goal, a goal that transcended the conflict. This is a fourth technique. In this instance, they sent the groups out on a camp trip and then arranged for the truck to run out of gasoline. The only way they could get gasoline was to use a rope, the same rope that the Sherifs poetically used in a game of tug of war, tie it to the truck and pull it to a place where they could get gasoline. No group had enough boys in it to pull the truck by themselves so they had to do it together. They also arranged for the water supply to break down. The only way to get a water supply to the camp was for the groups to work together to build a ditch. These are tasks that introduced goals and a basis for cooperation that transcended the conflict.

A similar type of problem recently confronted the Jordanians and the Israelis. In the Gulf of Aqaba, which borders the two countries, there was a problem with mosquitoes. The Jordanians and the Israelis were each spraying to get rid of the mosquitoes and sending the problem back and forth across the gulf. This was a problem of joint interest or joint concern.

Fifth, be firm on goals but flexible on means. It is a good idea to let the other side know what you want, but it is important to be flexible about ways of getting there. Negotiators who are rigid when it comes to both goals and means and refuse to be inventive along the way, fail.

Sixth, consider the wisdom of *the rule of change.* When you are stuck in stalemate in act two, doing things differently from the way they are currently being done may have benefits. It may get things going and build momentum when all hope has been lost. If two sides have been brought together and instead of using the opportunity to communicate, they yell and scream at each other, then it may be better to separate for a while. If the two sides have been separated for a long time and they are not making progress, then maybe the time has come to bring them together. If the two sides are tackling a multiissue problem by taking on one issue at a time and are unable to make any progress, then it might make sense to change things around and tackle all the issues at once. If on the other hand, they have been tackling all the issues at once, then maybe the time has come to follow Fisher's general advice to fractionate the conflict into smaller component parts and take on one issue at the time (see, generally, *Getting to Yes*, 1988). The point is that it is often helpful to part from what is currently being done and simply do something different.

Seventh, search for face-saving arrangements. People are much more likely to move toward settlement if arrangements can be found that make it possible for concessions to be made without losing face. This can be done through third-party negotiation. Or it can be done through front- and back-channel communication, an example of which took place during the Iranian hostage crisis when an Argentinean businessman and a French lawyer successfully managed, behind the scenes, to broker an agreement between the Americans and the Iranians. Or when Robert Kennedy and his Soviet counterpart were able to work out an agreement in Washington restaurants to end the Cuban missile crisis in 1962, when it appeared in public that we were heading toward the brink of a nuclear confrontation.

The above are examples of techniques that have been successfully used to deescalate actual conflicts. By introducing such techniques early in a conflict, it is possible to reduce its chance of escalating into a crisis. Contact with the other side, communication, building momentum toward peace, creating superordinate goals, flexibility, changing the immediate setting, and face saving can all be used to direct the parties toward problem solving.

# 10

# Her Place at the Table: Gender and Negotiation

DEBORAH M. KOLB

> *"I didn't know it was your table," said Alice at the Mad Hatter's Tea Party*
>
> *Alice in Wonderland*

▶ In this chapter I discuss feminist theories of development and social organization and how they relate to the resolution of conflict in negotiation. I will be covering two main themes: a woman's voice in negotiation and her place at the table.

## Her Voice in Negotiation

A central agenda of recent feminist studies across the social sciences has been to heed the often "unheard" voices of women. They maintain that women's experience is often treated as a variant, typically an inferior variant, of a dominant male model. Recent scholarship has tried to right the record. What has emerged is a conception of an alternative way of making sense of the world and of acting within it.

Existing research and our own experiences suggest that the voices of women are often hushed in formal negotiation. Conflict and competition are important in formal negotiation, and therefore, it may not be a comfortable place for many women. In reaction to this unnatural setting, some women may try to emulate (and do so quite successfully) a culturally dominant style. Other women find that their strengths and skills are impaired in this conflict setting. Later on, I will discuss the ways in which women experience conflict and how this may impact their behavior and how they are perceived in a negotiation.

There is a certain irony in trying to articulate a woman's voice in negotiation. Negotiation is often put forth as an alternative to violence and adversarial proceedings. Some people argue that it reflects a feminine view of interaction; that it is better to talk than to fight and, rather than pit parties against one another in a win lose contest, all parties' interests and needs should be considered and met. If this is true, why is it necessary to articulate the women's voice in negotiation?

There are at least three reasons. First, there are significant differences in the ways men and women approach negotiation and the styles they use in search for an agreement. In every training situation in which we have been engaged, women ask us to talk about gender issues. This leads us to believe that at least some women experience gender as a factor in negotiation. Research on this topic yields contradictory conclusions, but this may have more to do with the setting of the research (usually the laboratory) and the questions the researchers pose.

Second, there is evidence in real, as opposed to simulated, negotiations, that women do not fare very well. For example, in divorce mediation, women receive settlements that are economically inferior when compared with the settlements they receive in adjudication. In salary negotiations, men receive higher raises than women. If negotiation were a woman's place, we would expect women to excel and not to be disadvantaged.

There is a third reason to focus on a woman's voice in negotiation. The advice given by principled negotiation advocates is to focus on interests, rather than positions and to invent options for mutual gain. This entails separating people from problems and using objective criteria. It emphasizes a rationalized and objective approach to negotiation that may be different from the subjective and embedded feminine approach. Technical and rationalized analysis increasingly dominates negotiation.

Articulating alternative voices has become increasingly important in negotiation. Popular theories of negotiation imply that all conflicts can be formulated in a similar way and that all parties, despite differences in experience and status, can achieve the same results. The prescriptive voice of principled or joint-gain negotiation, while there is much to applaud in its perspective, has a tendency to drown out alternative ways of seeing and doing things. We need to consider the structure and context of negotiations in more nuanced ways.

There are four themes that are important in understanding the ways in which women may frame and conduct negotiations. These themes are a relational view of others, an embedded view of agency, an understanding of control through empowerment, and problem solving through dialogue. While these themes suggest some of the ways women may define their place in negotiated settings, variations in class, race, culture, family makeup, and social setting also affect gender differences.

## A Relational View of Others

Women view things in terms of relationships, and this fact affects significant aspects of their social lives. They are oriented toward nurturance and affiliation and make meaning through interconnection. Women never had to repudiate identification with a caretaking mother to define their own sexual identity in adolescence. Instead of separation and individuation as a primary motive for action, women conceive of action within the context of affiliation and relatedness to others.

The studies by Miller,[1] Chodorow,[2] and Gilligan[3] suggest that boys differ from girls in that they define themselves through their relationships. Gilligan points out that girls consistently show a sensitivity to others' needs and include others' points of view in their judgments on moral dilemmas. Keller describes women as living "in a domain between one and two" where they are not cast in opposition to others but rather see themselves in positions of mutual aid and support.

What women expect from interactions is a grounding for emotional connection, empathy, shared experiences and mutual sensitivity, and responsibility. In this two-way interactional model, to understand is as important as being understood and empowerment is as important as being empowered.

In negotiation, there are two major ways in which this relational view is expressed. As a negotiating party, a woman conceives of her interests within the context of her responsibilities and commitments. She is always aware of how her actions in one context impact other parts of her life and people who are important to her.

The second way in which this relational view is expressed has to do with relational ordering. Relational ordering means creating a climate in which people can come to know each other, share (or not share) values and learn of each other's modes of interacting. To women, expressing emotions and feelings and learning how others experience situations are as important as the substance of the discourse. In this context, separating people from the problem *is* the problem. Negotiation conducted in a woman's voice will often start from a different point and run a different course.

### Embedded View of Agency

Women understand events contextually, both in terms of their impact on important ongoing relationships and as evolving situations with a past and a future. Men stereotypically focus on individual achievement and activities that are defined in terms of task and structure. This is known as a self-contained concept of agency. Women, on the other hand, have an embedded form of agency in which boundaries between themselves and others and between a task and its surroundings are overlapping and blurred. Because women operate from an embedded sense of agency, any negotiation must be understood against the background from which it emerges. It is not experienced as a separate game with its own set of rules but as part of an extended context. Because of this, it is possible that women may be slow to recognize that a negotiation is occurring unless it is specifically separated from the background against which it occurs. The following is an example from one of my students that illustrates this point:

> When I was working in real estate, there was an occasion when I gave a listing to an associate without a prior agreement as to the split arrangement. I trusted my associate. We had worked together for a long time and I assumed that he would realize my input and include me in the split. He did not and I had to go to management to get my share.

At the same time, background understandings are likely to be imported into a negotiation setting. In a prisoner's dilemma game that we ran with our women students, the relationships the women had with each other spilled over into the game and led to cooperative outcomes.

### Control Through Empowerment

Power is often conceived as the ability to exert control over others through the use of strength, authority, or expertise to obtain an outcome on one's own terms. Conceiving of power in this way leads to a division between those who are powerful and those who are powerless. Power gained at the expense of others may feel alien to some women. Some people see this form of power as being incongruent with female roles. Because women may feel that assertiveness can lead away from connection, they tend to emphasize the needs of others so as to allow them to feel powerful. Women's behavior, therefore, often appears to be passive, inactive, or depressed.

There is a continuing debate about the place of power in negotiation. Some, such as Fisher argue that it is possible to mobilize power in ways that contribute to better outcomes. Others suggest that such a view denies the economic and political context in which negotiation occurs.

Feminist researchers have proposed an alternative model of interaction that stresses *power with* or *power from emerging interaction* rather than dominion, mastery, or *power over*. This alternative model emphasizes mutual empowerment rather than competition. It overrides the active/passive dichotomy and calls for interaction among all participants in the relationship to build connection and understanding and enhance everyone's power. It allows all parties to speak their interests and transcend the individualized and personalized notion of acquiring, using and benefiting from power. Mutual empowerment is often thought of as naive. However, particularly in situations in which there is an ongoing and valued relationship, it is often a much preferred model.

## Problem Solving Through Dialogue

Dialogue is central to a woman's model of problem solving. Women frame, consider, and resolve problems through communication and interaction with others. This kind of communication is different from persuasion, argument, and debate. According to Surrey,[4] women seek to engage the other in a joint exploration of ideas whereby understanding is progressively clarified through interaction. There is an expectation that the other will play the part of an active listener and contribute to the developing movement of ideas.

Women distinguish between two types of talk. One is *really talking,* which requires careful listening and shared interactions. Half-baked or emergent ideas grow as both participants draw deeply from their experiences and analytical abilities. In *didactic talk* the participants do not share ideas. Studies of women in management roles suggest that women reveal more about their attitudes, beliefs, and concerns than men in similar positions. This can contribute to productive dialogue.

In the strategic-planning model of negotiation, the parties try to analyze and second-guess the possible interests and positions of the other. While it is possible to plan and strategize about one's role prior to an interaction, a woman's strength may be in her ability to adapt and grow as she learns more about situations through involvement. Just as conflicts build up over time, women see conflict resolution as evolutionary. Problem solving through dialogue entails a special kind of joining and openness in negotiation and leads to newly emerging understanding. The parties learn about the problem together and have a high regard for each others' interests.

This framework for negotiation is very different from the "dance" of positions. It is also different in some respects from joint gain negotiation. Joint gain negotiation involves a search for a set of agreements that satisfy interests which the parties are seen to value differently. First, there is the identification of differences and then the creative exploration of options that will satisfy them. What is implied in this model is a view that goals and interests are relatively fixed and potentially known by the parties. Here, the secret to reaching an agreement is to design a process where goals and interests can be discovered and incorporated into an agreement.

In problem solving through dialogue, the process is less structured. Goals emerge from mutual inquiry. Those involved must be flexible and adaptive rather than controlling in response to uncertainty. The process can lead to new understandings of problems and possible solutions.

## Her Place at the Table

We rarely hear the woman's voice in formal, public negotiation, and when it is there, it tends to be muted and easily overwhelmed. This may occur because the formal negotiating table may be an alien place for many women. Negotiations are settings for conflict resolution and conflict runs counter to a woman's qualities and values. Attitude studies consistently show that women are more peaceful and rejecting of violence than men. Conflict is associated with aggressiveness, which is a stereotypical masculine attribute. When women or girls act aggressively it is interpreted differently from aggressive actions of men or boys. Women (similar to other groups who are subordinate) lack the expertise in dealing openly with conflict because behavior and feelings associated with it have often been suppressed. Women are socialized to believe that conflict with men or those in authority is wrong, and they feel vulnerable in the face of it. In their private lives, conflict often takes on personal and emotional overtones.

For all these reasons, many women may experience conflict situations as ones in which they have few options and limited ability to affect outcomes. In bargaining situations, many women may find that their natural problem-solving skills are mitigated by their feelings about place. There are several reasons for this. Some women fear possible hostility or acrimonious relations and tend to emphasize harmony over other interests, including their own. Other women become anxious and find that their presentation style and their ability to communicate are impaired. Some women, through socialization and professional experience, have adopted the dominant negotiating style only to find that others' stereotypes and perceptions of them undermine their behavior and performance.

## Preserving Harmony

One of my students recently described herself as "incorrigibly integrative." By *integrative* she meant that it was important to her to ensure that all parties were happy even if it meant downplaying her own interests. Studies of negotiation suggest that a woman's preference for harmony may dominate other interests. Watson and Kasten[5] have observed that female negotiating pairs can avoid discussing the main point of a conflict and yet still believe that they have negotiated effectively if their interaction was pleasant. In studies of managers, it is clear that women, relative to men, have a lower tolerance for antagonistic situations and do what they can to smooth over differences even if it means making sacrifices.

There is evidence that empathy, considered to be a particular strength of women, leads them to behavior that promotes harmony. Empathy is the capacity to participate in another's experience through shared thought and feeling. It can be advantageous in negotiation because it can enable one to learn about a negotiating partner's interests and intentions. Although research has generally supported the assumption that women are more empathetic than men, there is also some evidence that the opposite is true.

There are several explanations for why women may be less empathetic than men in negotiation. One is that empathy may lead to exploitation. In negotiation, learning of another's interests is carried out to benefit one's own position, sometimes at the expense of the other. If women are highly responsive to how what they do might impact their relationships, they may be reluctant to exploit what information they acquire.

Second, if a negotiating table is not a natural place for a woman, her ability to empathize may be impaired. I have some evidence from my students that in bilateral negotiating situations, where parties are pitted against one another, women had difficulty in placing themselves in the role of the other. In group decision making, women students distinguished themselves in listening to, understanding, and responding to each other. Yet in the bilateral negotiation role plays, the students claimed that anxiety interfered with their ability to listen and impaired their performance. Concern over their own next response led them to miss clues revealing issues of importance to their opponents. They also experienced difficulty in eliciting information because they were reluctant to probe and persuade. They assessed their opponents' interests based only on information that was volunteered.

Third, it has been suggested that in empathizing with others, women may undervalue their own interests and not develop self-empathy. Studies suggest that in a variety of group settings, women listen more and speak less. This may limit their opportunities to satisfy their own interests. The dilemma is for women to resolve their conflict between compassion for others and their own autonomy. They must overcome a tendency only to be responsive.

Comments from my students support these findings. One of my students gave the following example:

> In real life I find it easier to negotiate for others. While supervising two editors this fall, I fought tooth and nail for reasonable schedules, appropriate workloads, and fair performance evaluations. Interestingly enough, I fared better when I represented their interests than when I represented my own!

The ability to take the role of the other in negotiation, to ascertain interests and needs, is an important skill in negotiation. However, it may be a double-edged sword.

### Styles of Talk

The essence of negotiation is strategic communication. Parties want to learn about the alternatives available to and the interests of the other. At the same time, they want to communicate it in ways that further their own aims whether it is to clarify their interests or hide them, depending on strategy.

Women speak differently. Their distinctive communication style that serves them well in other contexts may be a liability in negotiation. Krieger[6] notes that the female pattern of communication involves deference, rational thinking in argument, and indirection. The male pattern of communication typically involves linear or legalistic argument, depersonalization, and a more directional style. While women speak with more qualifiers to show flexibility and an opportunity for discussion, men use confident, self-enhancing terms. In negotiation, female patterns of communication may be read as weakness or lack of clarity and may get in the way of focusing on the real issues in the conflict. The women in our class had difficulty putting their wants into words and tended, instead, to wait for information that was volunteered.

Because women's speech is more conforming and less powerful it does not signal influence. Women talk less and are easily interrupted while they, in turn, are less likely to interrupt. In mixed groups they adopt a deferential posture and are less likely to advocate their positions openly. At the same time, there is a tendency to be too revealing and to talk too much about their attitudes, beliefs, and concerns.

One of my students described her deferential efforts to negotiate with the mayor for AIDS resources:

> My strategy was to seek incremental progress to ensure that appropriate steps were taken to address the educational and service needs presented by the AIDS epidemic and to eliminate discrimination against gay people. Given the environment of the mayor's office, I believe now that I weakened my position by being too reasonable for too long. My strategy initially had been to demonstrate that I would not waste the mayor's time with trivialities, thereby establishing the understanding that when I pressured him, he should understand that it was a serious issue. I look back now on how polite, calm, and respectful I was with him in communicating the urgency of the AIDS epidemic and in pushing funding and program proposals. It is a horrible and laughable memory, for I failed to make him uncomfortable enough to warrant his attention. My subtlety was a liability when it came to "persuading" the mayor to take action where he was resistant. My negotiation style didn't change, even though I watched the mayor for 2 years and seldom saw him take action on anything unless he was pinned to the wall. I should have been far less deferential. I would risk approaching him more directly, for I made it too easy for him to dismiss me. I was liked and relatively well respected, but as a negotiator these qualities don't go far. To risk being more of a kick-ass would have served me better, and the mayor as well, by getting things attended to before they reached crisis proportions.

The process of negotiation, as it is customarily enacted, calls for parties to be clear and communicate directly and authoritatively about their goals, feelings, interests, and problems. A deferential, self-effacing, and qualified style may be a significant detriment. Women must become more knowledgeable and experienced with negotiation skills and more adept in an alternative style of communication at the negotiation table.

## Expectations at the Table

When men and women come to the table to negotiate, they bring with them expectations and outlooks that shape the way they see the other and the credibility and legitimacy accorded their actions. When women come to the table to negotiate, they often evoke certain stereotypes about feminine behavior that can affect how they are seen by their negotiating partners. The stereotypes are familiar. A woman is expected to act passive, compliant, nonaggressive, noncompetitive, accommodating, and attend to the socioemotional needs of those present. If she displays these characteristics through her behavior, then she reinforces some of these stereotypes and may find her effectiveness impaired. However, and this is often the situation with professional women, she may act in ways that contradict these stereotypes. That is, she is aggressive and competitive in pursuing her interests. The question is: Can she pull it off?

Existing research is not encouraging. It suggests that it is not so easy for women, particularly for those in management, to act forcefully and competitively without inviting criticism and questions about both her femininity and ability. They are seen as a threat to the accustomed social order. When men and women are rated on their performance in decision making and negotiating tasks, women are seen as less influential and receive less credit for what influence they may have exerted. As mediators, they are judged less effective even when the outcomes they achieve are superior.

Women are expected to do the emotional work in a group. In negotiation contexts, they often carry the burden for attending to relationships and the emotional needs of those involved. While such a burden might be consistent with a voice she might like to speak in, these expectations frequently constrain her ability to maneuver for herself or those she represents. Women must learn how to use their strengths and manage the dual impressions of femininity and strategic resolve. These are important negotiating tactics for women.

## Conclusions

I have developed two themes that in some sense stand in contradiction to each other. The first, arguing from existing feminist literature, describes what a woman's voice in negotiation might sound like. If given the opportunity and setting, women might create an alternative structure and process in public negotiation. Women do not always speak in what I have described to be the woman's voice. Variations in class, race, culture, and social setting certainly affect how they approach negotiation. It may, therefore, be more appropriate to speak of alternative voices. An alternative voice can open up possibilities in negotiation, not just to change the kinds of strategies we employ, but to transform our understanding of the process. In situations where trust, openness, and long-term relationships are critical, this voice is likely to be heard and be influential.

The second theme relates to the typical negotiation situation where the voice is not only hushed but the speaker is open to compromise or exploitation. Gender has been a variable in hundreds of negotiating experiments, and yields a picture that is contradictory at best. How an individual acts in a setting has to do with her sense of place and how she defines the situation in which she finds herself. To the degree that negotiation signals conflict and competing interests, a situation often at odds with the voice she speaks, women may experience anxiety and fraudulence in that place. These feelings compounded by her demeanor and style of communication may impact and sometimes impair her efficacy at the bargaining table.

Our dual focus on voice and place suggests some new ways to pursue the gender issue in negotiation as a topic of research and training.

How can we document the fact that an alternative voice—based on a relational view of others, an embedded view of agency, a focus on empowerment, and problem solving through dialogue—is decipherable? Comparisons of homogeneous gender groups is not the best way to study the alternative voice. In such laboratory studies, women may be especially susceptible to cues. Also, most studies take place in a cultural context (professional schools, business and legal negotiations) in which *the* voice dominates. The alternative voice must be studied in a context where it can be heard such as all female organizations (e.g., law firms and consulting practices). We need to learn more about how negotiation in these settings is conducted.

Her place at the table, however, can be studied in more traditional settings. What we want to understand more fully is how men and women experience the process of negotiation. We want to know not just what they do but how they think and feel about what they do, how this is related to outcomes, and how those involved think and feel about the outcomes and process they used to get there. This will form the basis for studying variations among men and women.

Education and training are quite complicated. On the one hand, it is important to know and articulate the voice we, as women, tend to bring to negotiation. It is part of the interpretive lens through which we understand what will happen at the table. What it is and how it is likely to be heard should become part of any analysis we carry out in preparation for negotiation. It is obviously important to realize that speaking the voice has its time and place. We need to help people become better at recognizing it. At the same time, we must be realistic about expectations that are placed on us as women at the table and develop ways to anticipate and manage these expectations. Appreciating some of the ways our style might impede our success, we need to experiment with a variety of presentation modes. There is much we can learn from experience and from those who have successfully managed to find their place at the table and come to speak with a voice that is their own.

## Notes

1. Miller (1983).
2. Chodorow (1978).
3. Gilligan (1982).
4. Surrey (1987).
5. Watson and Kasten (undated paper).
6. Krieger (1987, October).

# 11

# Style and Effectiveness in Negotiation

## GERALD R. WILLIAMS

▶ Should alternative dispute resolution be taught in a prescriptive or descriptive manner? A prescriptive approach says, "This is how it ought to be done." A descriptive approach says, "I have examined large numbers of experienced dispute resolvers and this is how they do it; here are the characteristics and patterns of highly effective negotiators."

Roger Fisher is one of the best examples of someone who takes the prescriptive approach; I am at the opposite end of the spectrum. I have always believed the most important information for a negotiator is an accurate description of how experienced negotiators operate. What are the patterns, the traits, the characteristics of effective and ineffective negotiators? If you have an understanding of the patterns of behavior of effective and ineffective negotiators, then your own experience, intuition, judgment, and instincts come into play and help you adjust to particular negotiating situations.

My message is "I can't give you a prescription; I won't presume to tell you what you ought to do; but I can give you a detailed report on the negotiating patterns of highly effective negotiators, and also the patterns of ineffective negotiators. Then I hope you will go out and apply that knowledge in your own individual ways."

To my mind, the prescriptive and descriptive approaches are highly complementary and we benefit most from a combination of the two. It seems to me that any course in negotiation ought to include them both and should perhaps begin with a description of negotiating patterns and end with our best prescription for improving on the state of the art.

## The Brigham Young University Study of Lawyers' Behavior

Let us focus on describing the negotiating patterns of experienced lawyers. The first two chapters of my book *Legal Negotiation and Settlement* (Williams, 1983) give a formal description of our findings. An appendix at the back my book describes the research methodology of the Brigham Young University study. Very briefly, in 1972 I joined with three behavioral scientists to study the negotiating characteristics of lawyers. We were fortunate to receive a grant from the Law and Social Sciences Division of the National Science Foundation. Over a period of 3 years, we used a variety of methods to learn as much as possible about lawyers and negotiators. We studied about 350 to 400 lawyer/negotiators in Denver and a comparable number in Phoenix. I will describe the results of this research below, but before doing so, there is a threshold question that deserves our attention: Do negotiating patterns or skills really make a difference in the outcome of particular cases? The best way to answer this question is to find a group of experienced negotiators, pair them up one on one, and have them negotiate the same case to a conclusion, and then compare the outcomes.

And that is exactly what we did. In cooperation with the Drake Law School and the bar association in Des Moines, Iowa, we asked experienced lawyers if they would volunteer to participate in this experiment. We were not sure whether lawyers would agree to this, because we informed them that if they volunteered, they were giving us permission to publish the results with their names attached. In other words, their reputation was on the line.

**TABLE 11.1**  Des Moines Personal Injury Case: Outcomes by Experienced
Attorneys on Identical Facts

| Pair Number | Plaintiff's Opening Demand (dollars) | Defendant's Opening Offer (dollars) | Agreed Settlement (dollars) |
|---|---|---|---|
| 1 | 32,000 | 10,000 | 18,000 |
| 2 | 50,000 | 25,000 | no agreement |
| 3 | 100,000 | | 56,875 |
| 4 | 110,000 | 3,000 | 25,120 |
| 5 | 657,000 | 32,150 | 95,000 |
| 6 | 100,000 | 5,000 | 25,000 |
| 7 | 475,000 | 15,000 | no agreement |
| 8 | 210,000 | 17,000 | 57,000 |
| 9 | 180,000 | 40,000 | 80,000 |
| 10 | | | 15,000 |
| 11 | 350,000 | 48,500 | 61,000 |
| 12 | 87,500 | 15,000 | 30,000 |
| 13 | 175,000 | 50,000 | no agreement |
| 14 | 97,000 | 10,000 | 57,000 |
| Average settlement | | | 47,318 |

Remarkably, 40 lawyers agreed to participate. We assigned half of
them the role of plaintiffs, half the role of defendants, provided them
with the facts, and gave them 2 weeks to prepare. Then we had them
come together on a Saturday morning to negotiate a solution if they
could. Of the 20 pairs of attorneys, only 14 pairs were willing to give
us the results with their names, so I can only report what happened
with them. I assume, although it is pure conjecture, that the other 6
outcomes may have been more extreme.

Table 11.1 lists the plaintiff's opening demand, the defendant's
opening offer, and the agreed settlement (if any) for the 14 pairs
of negotiators. They went out, negotiated and returned, each pair
of attorneys handed me a piece of paper and I wrote their names
and outcome on the board. As indicated by the table, the first pair
settled for $18,000. The second pair could not agree; they are going
to trial. The third pair settled at $56,875. As I recorded these
outcomes on the chalkboard, tension in the room began to mount.
People were looking at each other, and they were wondering about
their own competence. The next pair settled at $25,120; then
$95,000; then $25,000. Out of 14 pairs of experienced attorneys,

working with identical facts, we had a low of $15,000; a high of $95,000; and an average of about $47,000. Everyone else was scattered somewhat randomly between the extremes.

I was feeling very nervous and began wondering if we could make sense of this apparent chaos. You can imagine what happened. Up went the hand of the plaintiff's lawyer who settled for $15,000, the lowest outcome of any negotiator in the room. He explained that this was a case of doubtful liability and to get $1,000 or $2,000 would be a victory, $10,000 to $12,000 would be stealing and he had gotten $15,000. "That," he said, "is the most that you can get on these facts." Up went another hand. We know whose hand it was. It was the defense lawyer's who had just paid $95,000 to settle this case. The lawyer explained that this case has a potential $0.5-million liability and to negotiate it down to $400,000 or $300,000 would be a moral victory, and he had gotten it down to $95,000. That was the true bottom value of this case. We all chuckled sort of nervously, believing as a matter of etiquette we ought to let the two worst negotiators in the room defend themselves. But that was not the whole story. Other hands went up—the person who got $56,000 or $25,000 or $80,000—every lawyer in the room wanted to tell us about their outcome.

It was one of those times when there is mass confusion and hysteria and you are afraid of the situation because you cannot learn from it. It slowly began to dawn on us what was happening: Every lawyer in that room believed he or she had wondered what God would have done in similar circumstances. They each believed their outcome was the single best outcome. Since that day, I have felt much more humble about my ability to tell what a case is worth. This experience, and many others like it, suggests that negotiating skills really do make a difference, and it is well worth our time to learn as much as we can about the patterns and characteristics of highly effective negotiators.

## The Process

Outcomes are concrete, specific, measurable, and quantifiable, but experiences like the one in Des Moines convince me that they do not teach us very much about negotiation, because they are too variable. Rather than worry too much about outcomes, it is better to focus our attention on the process. After all, once you have your outcome, it is too late to do anything about it. So I recommend becoming an expert not on outcomes, but rather on the process by which they are arrived at.

Initially, most people assume that negotiating behavior is too unpredictable. In my experience, that is not true. Negotiating behavior tends to fall into patterns that can be recognized and responded to by astute observers. Process is more important to pay attention to than outcome. The predictive power of knowing what experienced negotiators do is not to be underestimated.

## Characteristics of Effective and Ineffective Negotiators

The most important goal of our negotiation research project was to learn the characteristics of highly effective negotiators. We selected attorneys as our subjects not only because three of the researchers were law school professors but because attorneys as a whole are experienced negotiators, since they regularly negotiate in their daily work.

But not everyone agrees on the definition of *effective.* In working with lawyers around the country, we found the most frequent definition was this: Effective negotiators are *the ones who get the most money for their clients.* But immediately someone else would chime in and say no, effective negotiators are *the ones whose clients are most satisfied,* on the theory that you might obtain a very high dollar outcome, but if your client is not satisfied, what good have you done? Then the next person would interrupt and say no, effective negotiators are *the ones where both sides are the most satisfied,* in the belief that agreements in which both sides are satisfied will be self-enforcing; they will not come unraveled over time. Finally, there were a few lawyers who thought the most effective negotiators were *the ones who came closest to totally destroying the other side.*

Obviously, in studying the characteristics of effective negotiators, it would make a lot of difference which one of these definitions was being used. Rather than impose our own definition or preferences, we were determined to keep these possibilities open,

so we could learn from experienced negotiators how they themselves define *effectiveness.*

Our solution was to keep all of these possibilities open, and see
what we could learn from the experience of many hundreds of
experienced legal negotiators. We mailed a questionnaire to a
random sample of 1,000 attorneys in the Denver metropolitan area,
asking this question: Think of an attorney against whom you have
negotiated, who was so effective as a negotiator that you would
hire that person to represent you if you were involved in a similar
case in the future. The questionnaire then asked them to describe
briefly the case or transaction and then to describe that person by
answering the items in the questionnaire, which contained about
130 different items relating to negotiator traits, behavior, strategy,
and motivation. We also asked for descriptions of "average" and
"ineffective" negotiators.

We received a total of 351 completed questionnaires, giving us
that number of very richly detailed descriptions of negotiators who
were considered effective by their peers. In our review of the
literature, we had hypothesized that the results would show that
cooperative approaches to negotiation were more effective than
"tough" or combative approaches. Our initial analysis of the completed questionnaires seemed to confirm this hypothesis; then we
ran the usual descriptive statistics of the lawyer responses, and the
resulting profile of effective negotiators was overwhelmingly "cooperative" in its makeup. We reported this outcome at a conference
on law and the behavioral sciences in 1974, where several re-
spected behavioral scientists took issue with our general conclusion. Prompted by their critique, we realized that standard statistical analysis focuses on characteristics of the group as a whole; it
does not attempt to differentiate among subgroups that may exist
within the data. With the help of consulting statisticians, we
discovered a method, called Q-Analysis,[1] that allowed us to search
for statistically significant subgroups among effective negotiators.

This resulted in a major breakthrough that proved our critics
were right: Effective negotiators were not *all* cooperative in their
approach. Rather, they represented three distinct approaches to
negotiation, each with a different set of negotiating characteristics.
When we performed this analysis on the average and ineffective

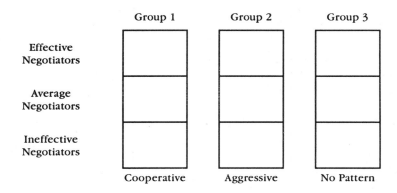

**Figure 11.1.** Patterns of negotiation among attorneys in Denver.

negotiators, we found that they each contained three significantly different subgroups. The results are shown in Figure 11.1. When we studied their characteristics, it was apparent that attorneys in Group 1 were basically *cooperative* in their approach to negotiation and that attorneys in Group 2 were basically *aggressive* in their approach. Attorneys in Group 3 did not represent a discernible pattern.[2]

When readily identifiable patterns emerge from questionnaire data like this, there are two possibilities. Either you are very lucky or there is a flaw in your research design. My three social scientific colleagues felt it was better to be cautious about this, so we did what any of you would do in similar circumstances: We went back to the federal government, we got more money, and we replicated the study in a different metropolitan area, this time Phoenix, Arizona. We restructured the language and location of the questions on effectiveness, so that the same patterns could not be produced unless they were actually present among attorneys in Phoenix. Remarkably, the replication produced the same patterns as in Denver. My colleagues tell me that from a social scientific point of view, these patterns are very solid. Our methodology in Phoenix also gave us information on the numbers of attorneys that fall into each category, as you can see in Figure 11.2.

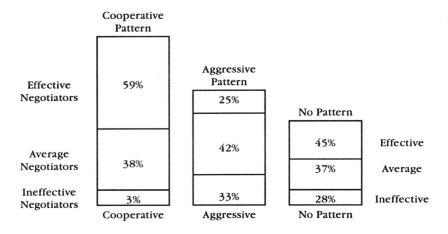

**Figure 11.2.** Negotiating patterns of experienced attorneys.

## Aggressive and Cooperative Patterns of Effective and Ineffective Negotiators

In my opinion, the discovery of these two patterns among effective, average, and ineffective negotiators is the single most important product of our research. Among other things, it sheds new light on the perennial question among negotiation theorists: Which is the most effective strategy, toughness or cooperation? As you can see from Figure 11.2, neither approach can claim a monopoly on effectiveness. A cooperative negotiator might be effective, or average, or ineffective; likewise for the aggressive negotiator. So it is a mistake to assume that if you are cooperative (or if you are aggressive), you will be effective. Effectiveness as a negotiator depends not on which approach you adopt but on *what you do within that particular strategy.* Both have the potential to be used effectively.

At this point, the most important task is to learn as much as we can about the qualities or characteristics of the negotiators in each pattern, as shown in Figures 11.3 and 11.4.

Let us begin by looking at Figure 11.3, which shows descriptions of effective negotiators of both types. Each individual item is important, and I do not know any other single exercise that would be more

Cooperative Objectives
1. Conduct self ethically
2. Maximize settlement
3. Get a fair settlement

Aggressive Objectives
1. Maximize settlement for client
2. Obtain profitable fee for self
3. Outdo or outmaneuver opponent

Cooperative Traits
1. Trustworthy
   Ethical
   Fair
2. Courteous
   Personable
   Tactful
   Sincere
3. Fair minded
4. Realistic opening position
5. Does not use threats
6. Willing to share information
7. Probes opponent's position

Aggressive Traits
1. Dominating
   Forceful
   Attacking
2. Plans timing and sequence of
   actions (strategy)
   Rigid
   Uncooperative
3. Carefully observes opponent
4. Unrealistic opening position
5. Uses threats
6. Reveals information gradually
7. Willing to stretch the facts

Traits Shared by Both Types of Effective Negotiators
1. Prepared on the facts
2. Prepared on the law
3. Observes the customs and courtesies of the bar
4. Takes satisfaction in using legal skills
5. Effective trial attorney
6. Self-controlled

**Figure 11.3.** Effective legal negotiators.

beneficial to you in terms of developing as a negotiator than to learn the characteristics so well that they become second nature to you.

One set of comparisons is too important to skip, and that has to do with the *objectives* of the negotiators in each pattern. In the questionnaire, we asked attorneys to tell us what their opponents' *objectives* or motives were, what their goals were, and what they were trying to accomplish. The results are very instructive.

Look in the upper left-hand corner of Figure 11.3 (Cooperative Objectives). The highest-rated objective of negotiators who fell in the effective cooperative category is to "Conduct themselves ethically." The second-highest objective was "Maximize" the settlement for their clients, which is, after all, an ethical duty of lawyers. But for effective cooperative attorneys, the word *maximize* is modified by item number three, "Get a fair settlement." We find

| COOPERATIVE STYLE | AGGRESSIVE STYLE |
|---|---|
| Cooperative Objectives<br>  Same as Effective Cooperatives | Aggressive Objectives<br>  Same as Effective Aggressives |
| Cooperative Traits<br>  1. Trustworthy<br>     Ethical<br>     Fair<br>  2. Trustful<br>  3. Courteous<br>     Personable<br>     Sociable<br>     Friendly<br>  4. Gentle<br>     Obliging<br>     Patient<br>     Forgiving<br>  5. Intelligent<br>  6. Dignified<br>  7. Self-controlled | Aggressive Traits<br>  1. Irritating<br>  2. Unreasonable opening position<br>     Bluffs<br>     Uses take it or leave it<br>     Withholds information<br>     Attacking<br>     Argumentative<br>     Quarrelsome<br>     Demanding<br>     Aggressive<br>  3. Rigid<br>     Egotistical<br>     Headstrong<br>  4. Arrogant<br>     Disinterested in others' needs<br>     Intolerant<br>     Hostile |

Traits Shared by Both Types of Ineffective Negotiators
None

**Figure 11.4.** Ineffective legal negotiators.

that cooperative attorneys want to get a good outcome, but they are also concerned with fairness. They are *self-monitors* who do not want to go beyond what would be fair to both sides.

By comparison, look at the upper right-hand corner of Figure 11.3, which shows the objectives of the effective aggressive negotiators: Their highest-rated motive is to "Maximize the settlement for the client," then to "obtain a profitable fee" for themselves. This interests me, because another part of the questionnaire asked if they were greedy. They were rated as *not* greedy but very interested in making a lot of money for themselves. Now there is a thin line between greed and a thirst for riches, and somehow effective aggressive negotiators manage to stay on the high side of that line.

But the most telling objective for effective aggressives is item number three: "Outdo or outmaneuver the opponent." Do you see the patterns emerging here? If you think about the terms win-win and win-lose negotiating, it seems that effective cooperatives epitomize the spirit of win-win negotiating; they want to get a good outcome for their client, but they want the other side to also feel that it got a good outcome as well. Cooperatives are quintessential win-win negotiators.

On the other hand, effective aggressive negotiators see it completely differently. Their attitude is this: "If all you want me to do is go around making everybody feel good about themselves, you don't need me. . . . It's not worth getting up in the morning for; it's not a serious objective." So they are win-lose negotiators; they want a clear winner and a clear loser; if the score is still tied, then the game's not over yet; you have to go into overtime.

Let me ask this question: Which is the better approach? In my opinion, they both have a place in the world of negotiation. As our study shows, experienced negotiators value both; both can be effective. So in general, our task is to accept the reality that both approaches are valid and both have their place. Of course, there is one more nagging issue, and it is this: Are they both equally effective in every situation? Or are there situations in which one of them will be less effective (or even crushingly so) and times when the reverse would be true? All of my experience tells me there are differences in this respect, and that an important task for every negotiator is to learn to recognize these patterns, to understand how they operate, to know when they are likely to be productive and when counterproductive, and most important, perhaps, how to deal with opponents in each of the patterns.

Turning to Figure 11.4, a couple of things bear mentioning. One is that their objectives, as rated by their opponents, are identical to the objectives of their effective counterparts, so they are trying to accomplish the same thing. The only variable is how they go about it. It is what you do, not what you are trying to do, that becomes important.

The second point is to look for the defects in the ineffective cooperative negotiator's approach, because people who are interested in dispute resolution tend to be cooperative, although this is not universally so. I suppose all of us wake up in a cold sweat occasionally thinking, "I'm a marshmallow." Let us look at what makes marshmallows.

Look at cluster number one: ineffective cooperatives are trust-worthy, ethical, and fair. There is no weakness in any of these characteristics because they are true for effective cooperatives as well. If you, like me, aspire always to be ethical, trustworthy, and fair, we ought to stand up and shout "hurrah!" We can be these things and still be effective, although they cannot protect us against being ineffective.

Cluster two, ineffective cooperatives are trustful. Therein lies a key to the overwhelming defect in ineffective cooperative negoti-ators. It is one thing to be trustworthy and to have people take you at your word no matter what, but it is quite another thing to be as trustful of the other side as you would like them to be of you. In every videotape we have made that has a cooperative versus an aggressive negotiator, trustfulness is the fatal weakness of the ineffective cooperative. In the dictionary, synonyms for *trustful* include words like *gullible, naive, easily exploited,* and so on.

Cluster three, ineffective cooperatives are courteous, person-able, sociable, and friendly. There is nothing wrong with these. They are also true of effective cooperatives.

Cluster four gives us another handle on ineffective cooperatives: They are gentle, obliging, patient, and forgiving. They never can be stirred up. It seems that no matter what happens, they are going to be polite and courteous, forgive you for what you do and try to get along with you.

Number five, they are intelligent. It is not out of brute stupidity that they do what they do.

Number six, they are dignified, as they give it all away. Number seven, they are self-controlled. Self-control also turns out to be a very important quality for effective negotiators of both types, so we will return to it.

Ineffective cooperatives are, in a manner of speaking, marshmal-lows. They are Casper or Casperina Milquetoast. I will admit that I was born and raised a Milquetoast. My mother would tear her hair out and say, "Gerry, I don't know the key to success in life, but I know the key to failure. And that is trying to please all of the people all of the time." It is the need to be loved and the belief that you have to be "nice" in order to be loved. No one can resist you if you are nice. This is the internal logic and personality dilemma of cooperatives.

The need-to-be-loved problem has never entered the consciousness of ineffective aggressives. Lawyers have a phrase for them: insufferably obnoxious. If you have dealt with somebody who is insufferably obnoxious, you know what it means. If you are normally a calm person who never raises his voice and 30 seconds into a telephone conversation, you are screaming into the mouthpiece, you know you are dealing with an aggressive, ineffective person. You do not know what to do except shout back, because they are so outrageously irrational. They bring that out in a person.

One reason that ineffective aggressive negotiators are so obnoxious or irritating (the highest rated characteristic laid out in cluster two) is that they make unreasonable opening demands or offers, even more extreme than their effective counterparts, and it is a pure bluff. They are affirmatively unprepared on the law and unprepared on the facts. With this in mind, it is easy to see why they are so irritating. As you see in cluster two, they adopt an unreasonable opening position and it is a bluff.

They use a take-it-or-leave-it strategy. When you ask them "What have you got that makes this worth $5 million?" rather than tell you, they withhold information. Instead of giving you information, they attack you for being stupid enough to ask. They are attacking, argumentative, quarrelsome, demanding, and aggressive.

In the third cluster, they are seen as rigid, egotistical and headstrong. Now you begin to appreciate why effective negotiators get such a high rating on self-control. It requires a lot of self-control to deal with obnoxious opponents without losing your head.

Finally, the fourth cluster. Someone suggested that these symptoms border on a clinical condition; they are arrogant, disinterested in the needs of others, intolerant, and affirmatively hostile.

How many negotiators fit this description? According to our numbers, 8% of the practicing bar is insufferably obnoxious, at least when it comes to negotiating strategy. Judging from reactions of groups of businesspeople to these results, it appears the 8% figure is not too far off for other occupational groups as well.

This is a snapshot of the characteristics of cooperative and aggressive negotiators. Of course snapshots are static; they freeze the action into a single moment in time. The best way to expand on our understanding of these patterns is to watch them in action, see how they unfold over time, and correlate the static descriptions with particular sequences of action in actual negotiations.

Based on the percentages of cooperative and aggressive negotiators we found in our research, in one-on-one negotiation, there are three possible combinations of patterns:

1. Cooperative negotiator versus cooperative negotiator
2. Cooperative negotiator versus aggressive negotiator
3. Aggressive negotiator versus aggressive negotiator

It is possible to predict some general tendencies for each combination. The first combination, cooperative versus cooperative, is the most stable; if the problem can be solved, they will solve it. This is their common goal. The third combination, aggressive versus aggressive, is intriguing. In a way, you might expect a brawl. But this often is not the case; although there is a higher risk of breakdown and the negotiation will take longer and consume more resources, the negotiators do speak the same language and do understand one another. They are also perfectly capable of cooperating with one another if they are convinced that is the better way to proceed. So this is not a bad combination either. Now what about the second combination, cooperative versus aggressive? In my opinion, this combination is at the root of the majority of problems in negotiation, because these two negotiators do not speak the same language; they do not understand one another. They are operating on contrary assumptions.

Let us pursue this one step farther. As you can see from the empirical descriptions in Figure 11.3, cooperative negotiators are trustworthy, ethical, and fair; they want a fair outcome; they adopt realistic positions; they avoid the use of threats; they disclose the facts early; and they value the prospect of agreement. In other words, cooperatives are problem solvers. How do they solve problems? On the merits; their instinct is to lay the facts out on the table. If I am a cooperative negotiator and I lay out my facts, and if you are cooperative, and you lay out your facts, then the two of us, as objective, fair-minded adults, can solve any problem. That is how cooperatives see their task. Against other cooperatives, this works very well. And since 65% of the negotiators in our study are basically cooperative, a cooperative will face another cooperative about 66% of the time.

But aggressive negotiators do not see themselves primarily as problem solvers, at least not in the same sense as cooperatives. They are warriors. Their strategy assumes the other side is an enemy to be attacked and defeated and their strategy is well adapted to that end. They are dominating, forceful, and attacking; they adopt more extreme positions; they use threats; they are reluctant to reveal information; and they seek a victory over the other side.

Which is the better strategy? Of course, we all prefer our own. Cooperatives feel their way is better; aggressives have no doubt it is their own. In my opinion, they are both wrong, because when you need a problem solver or a healer nothing else will quite do, and when you really need a warrior, it is also true that nothing else will do. We cannot escape the reality that they are *both* legitimate and, in their time, indispensable. The question is not: Which strategy should I invariably use? but rather: How can I develop sufficiently as a negotiator that I can appropriately invoke one or the other, depending on the requirements of the situation? I have come to believe that a fully developed negotiator should be capable of appropriately adopting either one in the proper circumstances.

In Figures 11.5 and 11.6, I have taken the descriptions of effective cooperative and effective aggressive negotiators and made lists showing how the patterns look when both sides remain true to their pattern in a negotiation against their opposite type. Surprising as it may seem, these two lists are good predictors of what will happen in initial encounters between cooperative and aggressive negotiators. The quality of the process and the outcome will depend on the ability of the two negotiators to diagnose the problem and appropriately adjust to compensate for it.

Highlighting some of the items in the figures, we see that the typical pattern that occurs when an aggressive and a cooperative attorney negotiate against each other is that the aggressive negotiator looks more capable, and makes the negotiation a lot more interesting to watch. As you can see at the top of Figure 11.5, aggressives make high opening demands. Why doesn't it undermine their credibility? Of course, in many instances it does, but effective aggressives are smarter than that; they tend to be more subtle. They do not make all their demands at once. Instead, they test the waters and see how much they can get away with. Their

A. Typical pattern against a trustful cooperative
  1. Made high demands (escalating over time)
  2. Stretch the facts (increasing over time)
  3. Outmaneuver the opponent (to look foolish, to lose)
  4. Use intimidation
  5. Make no concessions

B. Typical objectives of aggressive negotiators
  1. Intimidate the opponent
     Question: Why intimidate?
        Answer #1: Against cooperative opponent, maximize own gain and maximize
        opponent's losses
        Answer #2: Against aggressive opponent, reduce likelihood of exploitation
        and attack

C. Weaknesses or risks of the aggressive approach
  1. Creates tension, mistrust, and misunderstanding
  2. Fewer settlements (more cases go to trial)
  3. Lower joint outcome (lower joint gains)
  4. If taken too far, often provokes costly retaliation

**Figure 11.5.** The aggressive negotiator.

demands often begin reasonably, then escalate over time. If they made those outrageous demands up front, they would be laughed at because they have not yet learned how much they can get away with. It would expose their hand.

Aggressive negotiators tend to move slowly and cautiously, and they are outrageous only in proportion to how much trust is placed in them. Stretching the facts is a real dilemma. Most people, all cooperatives included, feel it is unethical to stretch the facts. In my experience, effective aggressives feel the same way, but they define their terms much differently, which gives them far more leeway than cooperatives feel appropriate.

Aggressives seem to find satisfaction or meaning in outmaneuvering their opponents. Even though the aggressive in the *Cottonburger* videotape[3] does not crack a smile, you can see that he enjoys or takes satisfaction in his ability to take unanswered swipes against his opponent and you see him systematically and repeatedly doing it. To win by forcing the other party to look foolish and to get a miserable outcome or no outcome at all is often part of their agenda. They use intimidation, which comes in many varieties.

A. Typical pattern of cooperatives (against strong aggressives)
   1. Make fair, objective statement of facts
   2. Make reasonable demands
   3. Make repeated unilateral concessions
   4. Ignore intimidation and bluffing by opponent
   5. Accept opponent's factual representations without question

B. Objectives of cooperative negotiators
   1. Establish cooperative, trusting atmosphere
   2. Induce aggressive attorney to reciprocate, based on what I call the cooperative assumption:
      1. *If* I am fair and trustworthy and
      2. *If* I make unilateral concessions,
      3. *Then* the other side will feel an irresistible moral obligation to reciprocate

C. Weaknesses or risks of the cooperative approach
   1. Risk of exploitation (if aggressive fails to reciprocate)
   2. Risk of later overreacting to aggressive's unfairness

**Figure 11.6.** The cooperative negotiator.

They try not to make any concessions. In this negotiation, the aggressive makes none at all.

Why do aggressives do what they do? Why do they operate in this way, and why do they continue their attack against an opponent who is clearly being cooperative? I can imagine two objectives. One, against a cooperative opponent, they believe it serves their purposes in two ways: It maximizes their own gains and it minimizes their opponents' gains. Axelrod's book *Evolution of Cooperation*[4] really repudiates their belief in all except pure zero-sum situations. But it appears that something in the aggressives' worldview leads them to a contrary opinion. Second, and especially evident in foreign policy, aggressives recognize that one way to avoid being too soft is always to be hard negotiators; that way, they are never in danger of being too trusting. This saves them from the more difficult task of figuring when and whom to trust.

The following characteristics held true for all cooperatives negotiating against aggressive opponents. The first was that they tend to make a fair, objective statement of the facts. Cooperatives do not build in a fudge factor; they do not start at one position and then move toward another one just for the effect. They think that the way to solve a problem is on the merits. They are eager to lay out all the facts as soon as they are given the opportunity. This gives an enormous advantage to aggressives who play the opposite strategy.

Second, cooperatives tend to make very reasonable demands, consistent with a fair statement of the facts. They tend to stay very close to what they really hope to get or to what their client is expecting.

Third, cooperatives tend to make repeated unilateral concessions; not reciprocated concessions, but unilateral concessions. They seem to want to rely on the principle of reciprocity. I'll come back to that in a moment.

Continuing down the list, cooperatives tend to ignore the intimidation and bluffing and huffing and puffing of their opponent. To a cooperative, smoke tactics are irrelevant: "So what if the other side doesn't trust my client. . . . We are mature objective adults. That doesn't get in our way." But to the aggressive opponent, this is a sign of weakness and vulnerability in their opponent, and they feel emboldened to increase their attack, to go for the jugular.

Fifth, cooperatives tend to accept their opponents' factual representations as the unquestionable truth.

Cooperatives' underlying goal and their number one objective (based on the data) is to establish a cooperative, trusting atmosphere in which common interest and values are shared: "If there is a problem to solve, we can solve it. I trust you, you can trust me."

Putting these several items together, it is easy to see why you would negotiate this way against a cooperative opponent, but why would you behave this way against an aggressive opponent? Psychologists tell us that a very effective way to influence another's behavior is to *model* it; and it seems that cooperative negotiators in this situation are modeling the very behavior they wish to see in their opponents. Sociologists and anthropologists would probably say that cooperatives are invoking the principle of reciprocity, or mutual exchange, which is found in every human society. Cast in this light, cooperatives who follow this pattern of behavior against an aggressive opponent are relying on an unwritten, unspoken, and perhaps unconscious assumption along these lines:

> If I am fair and trustworthy, and if I make repeated unilateral concessions, then at some point in the negotiation process, the other side will

recognize my good faith and will feel an irresistible moral obligation to reciprocate with concessions of comparable value.

This assumption is what makes cooperative negotiators so vulnerable to exploitation. And it shows why I feel the tit-for-tat (of being nice, provocable, forgiving, and clear to the other side) strategy is an important step in the right direction. It is not, by any means, a complete solution, but it teaches cooperatives to be alert for aggressiveness and the need to do something about it.

## Videotape of the *Cottonburger* Negotiation

According to an old proverb, what we hear, we forget; what we see, we remember; what we do, we master. Applied to the study of negotiation, it is not enough merely to hear about the patterns of cooperative and aggressive negotiators. To arrive at a common understanding of the vocabulary of cooperation and aggressiveness, and to gain an appreciation of how visible these patterns are when you watch for them, we need to see and discuss these patterns as they occur naturally among experienced negotiators.

As part of our research effort, we asked attorneys for the names of people they considered to be effective negotiators, then we contacted them and asked if they would be willing to come to Provo, Utah, and let us videotape them as they negotiated a case or transaction. We prepared the fact situations for use in these negotiations. Our goal was to learn what experienced negotiators actually do, and we gave them no instructions about how to negotiate. We said nothing about cooperation or aggressiveness or any other strategy. Our only instruction was this: Negotiate on these facts just as you would if a real client were involved. In our first attempt, we videotaped six negotiations. By random chance, two of the six involved a cooperative negotiator against an aggressive opponent. The facts involved a new technology that allowed a high protein meat substitute to be made from cotton seed. Although it may sound farfetched, it is based on an actual technology.

We also wanted to avoid a situation I have seen many times before, where the two negotiators get together and decide in advance what they are going to do, so we did not permit them to talk with one another until they were brought to the negotiating table and the cameras were running. Because they had no opportunity to feel each other out beforehand, they were forced to rely on their own assumptions. As a result, the negotiating dynamics are more dramatic than they would be in real life, because in real life the negotiators would not proceed until they had learned more about each other.

I say this because the two negotiators in the *Cottonburger* tape have solid reputations as exceptionally effective negotiators in their respective communities; I am certain they fully deserve those reputations. In the appropriate situation, I would be honored to be represented by either one. If negotiators of this high caliber can have a temporary blind spot in a spontaneous negotiation on videotape, so can you and I. So my advice is this: if anyone ever asks you to negotiate on videotape in a situation like this, you should absolutely refuse, because it is impossible to show your full abilities in this distorted setting. You cannot learn enough about one another while in front of a camera to do justice to the situation.

To appreciate what happens in this negotiation, you need to know the underlying facts. Briefly, the case involves the sale of cottonburger.

Cottonburger is a pseudonym for an actual technology that was developed by a European scientist, a high-protein meat substitute made from cotton seed, which was very cheap at the time. It was developed by a scientist we have named Dr. Schwartz of Switzerland. His goal is to make cottonburger available on a nonprofit basis in the protein-deficient developing nations—a very humanitarian goal. He plans to start in India and Nigeria, which at the time were the countries of greatest need. To do this, he needs to generate some income. His only sales to date have been in Europe, to elementary-level schools at 3 cents a pound. There is no prospect of other sales in Europe. The salespeople have beaten the pavement and no one seems to be interested. He has 100,000 pounds on hand in Europe in warehouses that need to be sold or they will have to be destroyed.

Because he is not making money in Europe, the U.S. market really becomes the key to his being able to carry his plan forward. The profits in the U.S. market are crucial. He does not have the know-how to produce it or market it himself in the United States, so he must find a good U.S. producer and distributor. He has found the right person, he believes, in a Mr. Jones of Chicago. As reflected in their correspondence to date and his instructions to his attorney, he is willing to offer the following terms and conditions: to grant an exclusive distributorship as an inducement to the distributor; to receive 12 cents a pound; to protect the enzyme formula from being stolen, he needs some protection built into the contract; to come to the United States for 3 months or so to help set up production; wants to work half-time on his own product, which is a kind of ice cream, and he wants access to a good laboratory to work on that; and finally, would like three lab assistants available to help him. It turns out that an aggressive negotiator is representing him. Schwartz knows that Jones has very conservative political views but this is not a problem for him and he deems it irrelevant.

Jones is a Chicago-based distributor of meat products. As reflected in Jones's correspondence with Schwartz and instructions to his attorney, these are the particulars: he wants to test market cottonburger in the United States; he needs 50,000 pounds to run the test; he is offering 5 cents a pound, which is 2 cents over break even for Schwartz, plus he will pay the shipping costs; he wants Dr. Schwartz to come to the United States to help set up production of cottonburger, and feels Schwartz should stay 8 to 10 months; he is offering to pay $1,500 per month, plus travel expenses; it is essential for Jones to have exclusive rights to distribute cottonburger in the United States, and he and Schwartz have already agreed to that.

There is a complicating factor, however. Jones would like to "steal" the formula and go into production independent of Schwartz. Although it might sound artificial, we built this complication into the facts to see how an experienced negotiator would deal with it. Of course, if Jones had this intention, he would not reveal it to counsel, so we put the information in the file as if by mistake. Then, we tried to give Jones a persona that would somewhat excuse his low standards in this matter.

As fate would have it, the person assigned to represent Jones is a true cooperative negotiator, and as you might suppose, cooperatives do not like to leave ethical dilemmas unresolved. His first duty, of course, would be to work this problem through with his client. But since this was a simulation and there was no actual client, what could he do? As is seen on the videotape, his solution is simply to inform the lawyer on the other side that Jones wants to learn to make the formula. His opponent, who is a tough-minded aggressive, hears the warning and proceeds to protect his client by building clauses into the proposed contract to prevent discovery of the formula and to prevent any unauthorized sales of cottonburger if the formula were discovered.

All that remains for these attorneys to do is work out the details of the issues given to them in their instructions. They both have general authority to resolve the issues anywhere within the parameters given there. We gave the negotiators absolutely no instructions about how to negotiate; we merely asked them to negotiate just as they would if they represented these two parties on these facts.

When you watch the *Cottonburger* videotape, you can observe how literally the behavior of the two negotiators is also anticipated by our research findings about cooperative and aggressive patterns. Compare the factual assertions of both negotiators with the facts they were given by their clients. This will give you a feeling for what it means when we say that cooperative negotiators are willing to share information and that aggressive negotiators reveal information only gradually and are willing to stretch the facts. In the videotape, viewers notice how, in this initial encounter between two skilled negotiators, they both made inaccurate initial assumptions about the other, and neither of them is able, under the pressure of a one-time negotiation on videotape, to diagnose and confront the problem. If this can happen to negotiators as experienced and highly regarded as these two, then no one is immune. It can happen to us all. In my opinion, when negotiating against our opposite pattern, we also tend to make unfounded assumptions about the other that undercut our effectiveness with the negotiation process. A major challenge for negotiators of both types is to become much more conscious of their own patterns and assumptions, to be consistently more attentive to discerning their opponents' patterns, and to develop the ability to make continuous, appropriate adjustments to correct for these factors.

## Conclusion

I will conclude with two final observations. In my opinion, the most important single statement by the aggressive negotiator in *Cottonburger* is this:

Let me indicate what I think are the essential items of any contract we're going to reach, without saying that if you reject all of them, or any one of them, that we can't continue to search this. I want to put this into a context of the kind of an arrangement that Jones can live with and still protect Schwartz's interest.

What is the aggressive negotiator saying here? Recall from the empirical data reported in Figure 11.3 that cooperative negotiators want to be fair. There is an internal, personal sense that I want to get a good outcome for my client, but within the limits of what would be fair to the other side as well. Cooperative negotiators are self-monitors; they feel a responsibility to keep their demands within the limits of fairness or good faith. By contrast, as the aggressive's statement clearly implies, aggressive negotiators have a completely different attitude. If I am an aggressive negotiator, I do not know all of the other side's facts, and since the other side is represented by able counsel, why should I try to impose limits? My task is to push the other side as far as it will go; it is up to them to stop me if I go too far. So aggressive negotiators are not self-monitors; their strategy is to go as far as they can, and to shift the responsibility onto the other side to stop them when it hurts too much. In his statement, the aggressive feels he has adequately warned his opponent that he's playing by aggressive rules. But, in my opinion, the cooperative opponent fails to hear this warning, and continues to rely on the assumption that his opponent is monitoring his demands and keeping them within good faith limits of fairness. Otherwise, he would respond in a very different way to the escalating demands of his aggressive opponent.

The most important statement by the cooperative attorney came somewhat later in the negotiation, when the aggressive negotiator had laid out virtually all of his demands. There was a pause, and after a few seconds, the cooperative looked up at him and said, "Does that pretty well cover your points?"

This phrase offers a valuable insight into the cooperative's perception of the negotiation to this point. When he asks, "Does that pretty well cover your points," he seems to be assuming that the escalating points or demands by the aggressive attorney are made in good faith, and that they would have come out the same way regardless of how he, the cooperative, reacted as he heard them.

He does not see that his failure to react to the increasingly extreme demands creates an almost irresistible invitation to the aggressive attorney to continue escalating them. The cooperative attorney interprets his task relatively passively up to this point, receiving information about the good faith interests and needs of the other side. But unfortunately, his opponent interprets this as weakness, and as an opportunity to get a better deal for his client by escalating his demands to extreme proportions.

There is a temptation to say "It couldn't happen to me" rather than to grapple with the implications of these two inconsistent patterns. In my experience, no one is immune from the tensions created by the conflicting motives and strategies of these two dominant negotiating patterns, and we will all become more effective in proportion to our ability to appropriately respond to them.[5]

## Notes

1. For a description of the Q-Analysis, see Williams (1983, pp. 138-139).

2. There is a good reason for this. Actually, in each category, the Q-Analysis produced five or six distinct groups of negotiators, but only the first two groups had significant numbers of attorneys, so for convenience in discussing the results, I have been presenting the information as if Groups 3, 4, 5, and 6 were a single "third" group.

3. *Cottonburger,* made by Williams, is a videotape between an aggressive and a cooperative negotiator and is approximately one-half hour long. It can be purchased through the Program of Negotiation's Case Clearinghouse (see Appendix II). There are also teaching notes available and accompanying text for classroom use. If you are using this chapter in a course, the students can be instructed to see the video and read the chapter afterward.

4. Axelrod (1984).

5. My current research suggests cooperative and aggressive patterns are components or subcategories of two larger roles or functions in society and that we must look to those larger functions for a more complete understanding of the significance of these strategies and their appropriate use on behalf of clients. The results of this research will soon be published.

# PART IV

# Appendices

# APPENDIX I

# Sample Curriculum on Negotiation and Dispute Resolution

The following is an outline of the curriculum for the seminar that I taught and from which I created the book. I designed the course to be approximately one-third lecture and discussion led by the main instructor, one-third lectures by guest lecturers, and one-third experiential exercises and simulations including two all-day classes. Weekly seminar sessions run 2½ hours for a full semester.

The course was designed and taught by me in its first 3 years as a window on the field of dispute resolution techniques and theories currently being worked on by practitioners and academics chiefly from the Boston area. Each year, the guest lecturers varied, although over the past 7 years, some guests have spoken more than once. The topics covered by guest lecturers also change annually, but are designed with a balance between different perspectives.

The course aims to teach a range of effective negotiation and dispute resolution practices. Its goal is to have students become aware of their own and others' behavior in negotiation and the effect or response that their communication has on others. The skills taught in the course include reversing roles and seeing the other side's perspective, creating mutually acceptable options, and using external standards to evaluate agreements. The participants are both graduate students and professionals (lawyers, psychotherapists, urban planners, businesspeople, etc.) who wish to improve their negotiating and dispute resolution skills.

All students are required to keep a journal that reflects on their real-world negotiations and relates to the readings, lectures and discussions in the course. Where possible, students are urged to write in it daily, and then turn in their journals at midterm and the end of the semester. In addition, two sets of questions, based on the course for that year, are developed by the students and instructor at midterm and at the end of the term and answered by each student. Examples of such questions follow the sample curriculum below.

The following texts are assigned to be read in advance of the course, if possible. While specific readings are assigned during the semester, reading the four books in their entirety is strongly recommended. The books are:

Fisher and Ury (1981), *Getting to Yes*
Raiffa (1982), *The Art and Science of Negotiation*

In addition, two other books should be read for background. These are:

Pruitt and Rubin (1986), *Social Conflict: Escalation, Stalemate and and Settlement*
Susskind and Cruikshank (1987), *Breaking the Impasse*

Exercises are handed out in class as are copies of particular articles. (A sample exercise is contained as an appendix to Rowe's chapter in this volume.) Finally, the additional articles are assigned for the relevant session. All exercises are available through Harvard Program on Negotiation (see Appendix II).

## Session I. Overview of Seminar

"Window-on-the-field" integrative approach; mapping of sessions, readings, and goals of the workshop sessions.

### Exercise

"Pepulator"

### Readings (to be read after first class meeting)

Fisher and Ury (1981), *Getting to Yes* (reread)
Hofstadter (1983), "Metamagical Themas"
White (1985), "Review of *Getting to Yes*"
McCarthy (1985), "The Role of Power and Principle in *Getting to Yes*"
Fisher (1985), "Beyond YES"
Bazerman (1987), "Six Years Later: Where Negotiation Is Now and Where It Should Go"

During the first all-day workshop and the second one at midterm, the class is exposed to different dispute resolution techniques including negotiation, mediation, facilitation, and collaborative problem solving.

## Saturday Workshop I

9:15-12:00    *Positions Versus Interests:* An analysis of principled negotiation and its techniques in contrast to positional bargaining and other theories of horse trading
Exercise: "Sally Swansong" and debriefing
12:00- 1:00    Lunch and preparation for exercise
1:00- 5:00    Exercise: "Harborco" and debriefing

### Readings

Raiffa (1982, pp. 137-147), *The Art and Science of Negotiation* (reread)
Schelling (1960), "Essay on Bargaining"
Lewicki and Litterer (1985, chap. 5), "Strategies and Tactics of Integrative Bargaining"

# II. Alternative Dispute Resolution and the Legal System

### Readings

Sander (1985), "Alternatives Inside and Outside the Courts: The Forgotten Forums"
Goldberg, Green, and Sander (1985, chap.1), "The Disputing Universe"
Zack (1980), "Understanding Grievance Arbitration in the Public Sector"
Bazerman and Farber (1984), "Analyzing the Decision Making Processes of Third Parties"

# III. Mediated Negotiation and Public Disputes

### Readings

Susskind and Cruikshank (1987, chaps.) "Introduction" and "Assisted Negotiation"

# IV. The Issue of Gender in Negotiation

*Guest Lecturer*

Jeffrey Rubin

*Readings*

Rubin and Brown (1985), "Bargainers as Individuals"
Pruitt and Rubin (1986) *Social Conflict: Escalation, Stalemate and Settlement Random House* (look through generally)

# V. Ways of Disputing, an Ombuds Perspective

*Guest Lecturer*

Mary Rowe

*Readings*

Rowe (1987), "The Corporate Ombudsman: An Overview and Analysis"
Questions to be handed out

# VI. Mediation

*Exercise*

"Neighborhood Care"

*Video*

*Mediation*

*Readings*

Bercovitch (1984), "Uniform or Diverse Interventions"

Journals and answers to questions are due. Students should also submit any questions that they would like to discuss at the midterm discussion on this date.

# VII. Mid-Course Discussion: What are the Common and Conflict Themes and Issues So Far?

## Readings

Lewicki and Litterer (1985, chap.), "Planning and Preparation"

Fisher (1983), "Negotiating Power"

Lax and Sebenius (1986, chaps.), "Creating and Claiming Value" and "The Manager's Dilemma"

Raiffa (1982, pp. 119-130), *The Art and Science of Negotiation* (reread)

Schelling (1960, chap.), "An Essay on Bargaining" (reread)

# VIII. Intra-organizational Conflict

## Guest Lecturer

Deborah Kolb

## Readings

Kolb (1987), "Out of Sight"

## Saturday Workshop II

| | |
|---|---|
| 9:15-12:30 | Facilitation and Collaborative Problem Solving Exercise: "Dirty Stuff" |
| 12:30- 1:30 | Lunch |
| 1:30- 5:00 | Video on union negotiation, *Final Offer* |

## Reading

Heckscher (1988, chaps.), "Introduction" and "Multilateral Negotiation"

# IX. Community Mediation

## Readings

Goldberg, Green, and Sander (1985), "Neighborhood Justice Centers"

Davis (1987), "Justice Without Judges" (just skim)

## X. Competitive and Cooperative Negotiating Styles

*Video*

*Cottonburger*

*Readings*

Williams (1983, chap.), "The Dynamics of Cooperative and Competitive
   Negotiation"

## XI. Intercultural Factors in Negotiation

*Readings*

Casse (1980), *Training for the Cross-Cultural Mind*

Journals and answers to questions due. Questions for discussion should
be submitted.

## XII. Wrap-up and Synthesis of Course

*Readings*

Pruitt and Rubin (1986), *Social Conflict*
Susskind and Cruikshank (1987), *Breaking the Impasse*
Others to be handed out in class

## Sample Questions

Please answer one question in each set (for a total of three questions).
Your exam should be typewritten, double-spaced, and stapled. Each response should be about 1,000 words in length.

### Question 1

a. What three (and only three) key lessons about negotiations have you
   learned this semester? Or, stated differently, what three points of
   advice would you give to your best friend facing a negotiation? Be as

specific as possible (such as particular techniques, different kinds of knowledge, etc.) Describe these lessons in "plain English" (assume your friend has not and will not have time to read *Getting to Yes*) and explain why they are important.

Or

b. What are the limitations of negotiation as a dispute resolution method? That is, are there types of disputes, situations, or conditions under which negotiations, principled or otherwise, should be avoided? Explain how one should judge whether negotiations ought to be undertaken, giving illustrative examples as appropriate.

## Question 2

a. How do you think an outside "helper" can assist in a negotiation? In your answer, consider the range of third-party roles you have read about, tried, and discussed this semester. Be as specific as possible, using illustrative examples that draw on your own experience in work or your field of study.

Or

b. Do you believe gender is a significant factor in negotiations? If yes, how does gender affect negotiations (illustrate with examples)? What can a negotiator do to mitigate or eliminate any negative impacts of gender differences (from the perspective of either a male or female)? If no, what factors are significant in negotiations?

## Question 3 (Everyone Must Answer This Question)

a. What have you learned about yourself with respect to negotiations? How will this information affect the way you deal with conflict and disputes in the future in your professional and/or personal life?

## Course Description

The Seminar in Negotiation and Dispute Resolution is the core component in the Specialization that the Program on Negotiation (PON) has offered since 1985. The Specialization offers encouragement and support to graduate students committed to developing a special expertise in negotiation and dispute resolution to apply in fields such as human resources management, international peacemaking, managerial negotiations, competitive decision making, family conflicts, or environmental and public policymaking.

The specialization program includes:

- The above curriculum in negotiation and dispute resolution and a one semester course in mediation offered in collaboration with Radcliffe College (also open to nonspecialization students and midcareer professionals).
- Four additional, elective courses in negotiation and dispute resolution, subject to approval by PON staff.
- A 300-hour internship with selected public and private dispute resolution agencies and organizations.

Students enrolled in the specialization program work with PON staff to design an individualized curriculum that balances study in theory with training in the skills of negotiation and dispute resolution. The specialization does not confer a degree or certification. Specialization staff are available for consultation on coursework, internship possibilities, and career opportunities.

The Specialization was designed to complement graduate study, and participants are largely enrolled in degree-granting programs at Boston-area institutions. However, professionals or students from outside the Boston area may pursue the Specialization as a "special student" without concurrent enrollment in a nearby graduate degree program.

# APPENDIX II

# Case Clearinghouse Materials

The Program on Negotiation has a Case Clearinghouse that provides teaching materials for those interested in developing programs within their own organizations.

Simulations, role-plays, videotapes, and teaching notes are available at cost and can be obtained by calling or writing the Case Clearinghouse:

> Program on Negotiation at Harvard Law School
> Pound Hall 513
> Cambridge, MA 02138
> (617) 495-1684

For more specific curriculum questions or issues about systems design for organizations, write the editor:

> Lavinia Hall, Esq.
> c/o Program on Negotiation at Harvard Law School

# Bibliography

Abel, R. L. (Ed.). (1982a). *The politics of informal justice. Vol. 1: The American experience.* New York: Academic Press.

Abel, R. L. (Ed.). (1982b). *The politics of informal justice. Vol. 2: Comparative studies.* New York: Academic Press.

Alger, C., & Stohl, M. (Eds.). (1988). *A just peace through transformation: Cultural, economic, and political foundations for change.* Boulder, CO: Westview.

Allison, G. T., Carnesale, A., & Nye, J. S., Jr. (Eds.). (1985). *Hawks, doves and owls: An agenda for avoiding nuclear war.* New York: Norton.

Allison, G. T., Ury, W. L., & Allyn, B. J. (1989). *Windows of opportunity: From cold war to peaceful competition in U.S.-Soviet relations.* Cambridge, MA: Ballinger.

Argyris, C. (1970). *Intervention theory and method: A behavioral science view.* Reading, MA: Addison-Wesley.

EDITOR'S NOTE: This bibliography was originally compiled by staff of the Harvard Program on Negotiation. I have added to it many of the authors' references in this volume. It was developed as a resource list for those interested in dispute resolution and so contains more than is directly referenced in this book.

Assefa, H. (1987). *Mediation of civil wars: Approaches and strategies—The Sudan conflict.* Boulder, CO: Westview.

Assefa, H., & Wahrhaftig, P. (1988). *Extremist groups and conflict resolution: The MOVE crisis in Philadelphia.* New York: Praeger.

Auerbacn, J. (1983). *Justice without law?* New York: Oxford University Press.

Axelrod, R. (1984). *The evolution of cooperation.* New York: Basic Books.

Bacharacn, S. B., & Lawler, E. J. (1980). *Power and politics in organizations: The social psychology of conflict, coalitions, and bargaining.* San Francisco: Jossey-Bass.

Bacharach, S. B., & Lawler, E. J. (1981). *Bargaining: Power, tactics, and outcomes.* San Francisco: Jossey-Bass.

Bacow, L. S. (1980). *Bargaining for job safety and health.* Cambridge: MIT Press.

Bacow, L. S., & Wheeler, M. (1984). *Environmental dispute resolution.* New York: Plenum.

Bartos, O. J. (1974). *Process and outcome of negotiations.* New York: Columbia University Press.

Bazerman, M. H. (1986). *Judgment in managerial decision making.* New York: Wiley.

Bazerman, M. H. (1987). Six years later: Where negotiation is now and where it should go. *National Institute for Dispute Resolution Forum.*

Bazerman, M. H., & Farber, R. (1984). *Analyzing the decision making process of third parties.* Unpublished paper, Massachusetts Institute of Technology.

Bazerman, M. H., & Lewicki, R. J. (Eds.). (1983). *Negotiating in organizations.* Beverly Hills, CA: Sage.

Beckman, N. (1977). *Negotiations.* Lexington, MA: Lexington Books.

Bellman, H. S., Sampson, C., & Cormick, G. W. (1982). *Using mediation when siting hazardous waste management facilities. A handbook.* Washington DC: Environmental Protection Agency, Office of Solid Waste.

Bellow, G., & Moulton, B. (1981). *The lawyering process: Negotiation.* Mineola, NY: Foundation.

Ben-Dor, G., & Dewitt, D. B. (Eds.). (1987). *Conflict management in the Middle East.* Lexington, MA: Lexington Books.

Bercovitch, J. (1984). *Social conflicts and third parties: Strategies of conflict resolution.* Boulder, CO: Westview.

Bingham, G. (1986). *Resolving environmental disputes: A decade of experience.* Washington, DC: The Conservation Foundation.

Binnendijk, H. (Ed.). (1987). *National negotiating styles.* Washington, DC: U.S. Department of State, Center for the Study of Foreign Affairs.

Blake, R., & Mouton, J. S. (1984). *Solving costly organizational conflict.* San Francisco, CA: Jossey-Bass.

Blaker, M. (1977). *Japanese international negotiating style.* New York: Columbia University Press.

Blau, P. M. (1964). *Exchange and power in social life.* New York: John Wiley.

Boulding, E. (1988). *Building a global civic culture: Education for an interdependent world.* New York: Teachers College Press.

Boulding, K. E. (1962). *Conflict and defense: A general theory.* New York: Harper & Row.

Brand, N. (1987). *Labor arbitration: The strategy of persuasion.* New York: Practicing Law Review.

Brock, J. (1982). *Bargaining beyond impasse: Joint resolution of public sector labor disputes.* Dover, MA: Auburn House.

Brockner, J., & Rubin, J. Z. (1985). *Entrapment in escalating conflicts: A social psychological analysis.* New York: Springer-Verlag.

Brooks, E., & Odiorne, G. S. (1984). *Managing by negotiations.* New York: Van Nostrand Reinhold.

Burton, J. W. (1962). *Peace theory: Preconditions of disarmament.* New York: Knopf.

Burton, J. W. (1984). *Global conflict: The domestic sources of international crises.* UK: Wheatsheaf Books.

Burton, J. W. (1987). *Resolving deep-rooted conflict: A handbook.* Lanham, MD: University Press of America.

Carlson, D., & Comstock, C. (Eds.). (1986). *Citizen summitry: Keeping the peace when it matters too much to be left to politicians.* Los Angeles: Tarcher.

Carlson, D., & Comstock, C. (Eds.). (1987). *Securing our planet: How to succeed when threats are too risky and there's really no defense.* Los Angeles: Tarcher.

Carpenter, S. L., & Kennedy, W. J. D. (1988). *Managing public disputes: A practical guide to handling conflict and reaching agreements.* San Francisco: Jossey-Bass.

Casse, P. (1980). *Training for the cross-cultural mind.* The Society for Intercultural Education, Training and Research (SIETAR). Washington, DC.

Casse, P., & Deol, S. (1985). *Managing intercultural negotiations: Guidelines for trainers and negotiators.* Washington, DC: Sietar International.

Chamberlain, N. W. (1951). *Collective bargaining.* New York: McGraw-Hill.

Cheatham, A. (1988). *Annotated bibliography of conflict resolution in schools.* Amherst, MA: National Association for Mediation in Education.

Chodorow, N. (1978). *The reproduction of mothering.* Berkeley: University of California Press.

Clarke, L. (1989). *Acceptable risk? Making decisions in a toxic environment.* Berkeley: University of California Press.

Clarke, S. H., Donnelly, L. F., & Grove, S. A. (1987). *A court-ordered arbitration in North Carolina: An evaluation of its effects.* Chapel Hill, NC: Institute of Government, Publications Office.

Coddington, A. (1968). *Theories of the bargaining process.* London: Allen & Unwin.

Cohen, H. (1980). *You can negotiate anything.* Secaucus, NJ: Stuart.

Cole, R. E. (1989). *Strategies for learning: Small-group activities in American, Japanese, and Swedish industry.* Berkeley: University of California Press.

Coleman, J. S. (1957). *Community conflict.* New York: The Free Press.

Collison, W. (1988). *Conflict reduction: Turning conflict to cooperation.* Dubuque, IA: Kendall Hunt.

Colosi, T. R., & Berkeley, A. E. (1986). *Collective bargaining: How it works and why: A manual of theory and practice.* New York: American Arbitration Association.

Conybeare, J. A. (1987). *Trade wars: The theory and practice of international commercial rivalry.* New York: Columbia University Press.

Coogler, O. J. (1978). *Structured mediation in divorce settlements: A handbook for marital mediators.* Lexington, MA: Lexington Books.

Cook, R. F., Roehl, J. A., & Sheppard, D. J. (1980). *Neighborhood justice centers field test: Final evaluation report.* Washington, DC: U.S. Department of Justice.

Coombs, C. H., & Avrunin, G. S. (1988). *The structure of conflict.* Hillsdale, NJ: Lawrence Erlbaum.

Coser, L. (1956). *The function of social conflict.* New York: The Free Press.

Coulson, R. (1983). *Fighting fair: Family mediation will work for you.* New York: The Free Press.

Coulson, R. (1986). *Arbitration in the schools.* New York: American Arbitration Association.

Coulson, R. (1987a). *Alcohol, drugs, and arbitration.* New York: American Arbitration Association.

Coulson, R. (1987b). *Business mediation: What you need to know.* New York: American Arbitration Association.

Cross, J. G. (1968). *The Economics of bargaining.* New York: Basic Books.

Cutrona, C. (Ed.). (1986). *Bringing the dispute resolution community together.* Washington, DC: Society of Professionals in Dispute Resolution.

Czempiel, E. O., & Krell, G. (Eds.). (1989). *The future of European arms control.* Boulder, CO: Westview.

Dahrendorf, R. (1959). *Class and conflict in industrial society.* Stanford, CA: Stanford University Press.

Davidow, J. (1984). *A peace in southern Africa: The Lancaster House conference on Rhodesia.* Boulder, CO: Westview Press.

Davis, A. (1987). *Justice without judges.* Massachusetts State District Court Publication, Dorchester.

Deutsch, M. (1973). *The resolution of conflict: Constructive and destructive processes.* New Haven, CT: Yale University Press.

Doherty, R. E. (1984). *Labor relations primer: An introduction to collective bargaining through documents.* Ithaca, NY: ILR Press.

Douglas, A. (1962). *Industrial peacemaking.* New York: Columbia University Press.

Druckman, D. (Ed.). (1977). *Negotiations: Social-psychological perspectives.* Beverly Hills, CA: Sage.

Dunlop, J. (1984). *Dispute resolution: Negotiation and consensus building.* Dover, MA: Auburn House.

Dunlop, J., & Healy, J. J. (1955). *Collective bargaining: Principles and cases.* Homewood, IL: Irwin Press.

Edwards, H. (1986). Alternative dispute resolution: Panacea or anathema. *Harvard Law Review, 99,* 668.

Edwards, H. T., & White, J. J. (1977). *The lawyer as negotiator: Problems, readings and materials.* St. Paul, MN: West.

Elkouri, F., & Elkouri, E. A. (1985). *How arbitration works* (4th ed.). Washington, DC: Bureau of National Affairs.

Emond, P. (Ed.). (1989). *Commercial dispute resolution: Alternatives to litigation.* Aurora, Ont.: Law Books.

Erickson, S. K., & Erickson, M. S. M. (1988). *Family mediation casebook: Theory and process.* New York: Brunner/Mazel.

Felstiner, W., Abel, R., & Sarat, A. (1980-1981). The emergence and transformation of disputes: Naming, blaming, claiming. *Law and Society Review, 15,* 631.

Filley, A. C. (1975). *Interpersonal conflict resolution.* Glenview, IL: Scott, Foresman.

Fisher, G. (1980). *International negotiation: A cross-cultural perspective.* Chicago: Intercultural Press.

Fisher, R. (Ed.). (1964). *International conflict and behavioral science: The Craigville papers.* New York: Basic Books.

Fisher, R. (1969). *International conflict for beginners.* New York: Harper & Row.

Fisher, R. (1972). *Dear Israelis, dear Arabs: A working approach to peace.* New York: Harper & Row.

Fisher, R. (1978). *Points of choice: International crises and the role of the law.* Oxford, UK: Oxford University Press.

Fisher, R. (1981). *Improving compliance with international law.* Charlottesville: University of Virginia Press.

Fisher, R. (1985, January). Beyond yes. *Negotiation Journal 1*(1).

Fisher, R., & Brown, S. (1988). *Getting together: Building relationships as we negotiate.* Boston, MA: Houghton Mifflin.

Fisher, R., & Ury, W. L. (1978). *International mediation: A working guide—Ideas for the practitioner.* Cambridge, MA: Harvard Negotiation Project Publication.

Fisher, R., & Ury, W. L. (1981). *Getting to yes: Negotiating agreement without giving in.* Boston: Houghton Mifflin.

Folberg, J. (Ed.). (1984). *Joint custody and shared parenting.* Washington, DC: Bureau of National Affairs.

Folberg, J., & Milne, A. (Eds.). (1988). *Divorce mediation: Theory and practice.* New York: Guilford.

Folberg, J., & Taylor, A. (1984). *Mediation: A comprehensive guide to resolving conflict without litigation.* San Francisco: Jossey-Bass.

Fouraker, L. E., & Siegel, S. (1963). *Bargaining behavior.* New York: McGraw-Hill.

Fraser, N. M., & Hipel, K. W. (1984). *Conflict analysis, models and resolutions.* New York: Elsevier Science.

Galanter, M. (1984). Worlds of deals: Using negotiation to teach about leagal process. *Journal of Legal Education, 34,* 268.

Gershenfeld, W. J. (Ed.). (1986). *Arbitration 1985: Law and practice.* Washington, DC: Bureau of National Affairs.

Gershenfeld, W. J. (Ed.). (1987). *Arbitration 1986: Current and expanding roles.* Washington, DC: The Bureau of National Affairs.

Gilligan, C. (1982). *In a different voice: Psychological theory and women's development.* Boston, MA: Harvard University Press.

Glendon, M. A. (1989). *The transformation of family law.* Chicago: University of Chicago Press.

Gold, C. (1986). *Labor management committees: Confrontation, cooptation, or cooperation.* Ithaca, NY: ILR Press.

Goldberg, S. B., Green, E., & Sander, F. E. A. (1985). The disputing universe. *Dispute Resolution.* Boston: Little, Brown.

Goldberg, S. B., Sander, F. E. A., & Rogers, N. (1992). *Dispute resolution.* Boston: Little, Brown.

Goldmann, R. B. (Ed.). (1980). *Roundtable justice: Case studies in conflict resolution: Reports to the Ford Foundation.* Boulder, CO: Westview.

Gray, B. (1989). *Collaborating: Finding common ground for multiparty problems.* San Francisco: Jossey-Bass.

Green, E. (1982). *The CPR mini-trial handbook 1982. Corporate dispute management.* New York: Matthew Bender.

Grossman, M. M. (1984). *The question of arbitrability: Challenges to the arbitrator's jurisdiction.* Ithaca, NY: ILR Press.

Gruenberg, G. W. (Ed.). (1989). *Arbitration 1988: Emerging issues for the 1990's.* Washington, DC: BNA Books.

Gruenberg, G. W. (Ed.). (1990). *Arbitration 1989: The arbitrator's discretion during and after the hearing.* Washington, DC: BNA Books.

Gulliver, P. H. (1979). *Disputes and negotiations: A cross cultural perspective.* New York: Academic Press.

Harsanyi, J. C. (1977). *Rational behavior and bargaining equilibrium in games and social situations.* Cambridge, UK: Cambridge University Press.

Haydock, R. S. (1984). *Negotiation practice.* New York: John Wiley.

Haynes, J. M. (1981). *Divorce mediation: A practical guide for therapists and counselors.* New York: Springer.

Haynes, J. M., & Haynes, G. L. (1989). *Mediating divorce: Casebook of strategies for successful family negotiations.* San Francisco: Jossey-Bass.

Healy, J. J. (Ed.) (1965). *Creative collective bargaining: Meeting today's challenges to labor-management relations.* Englewood Cliffs, NJ: Prentice Hall.

Heckscher, C. (1988). *The new unionism: Employee involvement in the changing world.* New York: Basic Books.

Heitler, S. M. (1990). *From conflict to resolution: Strategies for diagnosis and treatment of distressed individuals, couples, and families.* New York: Norton.

Henrikson, A. (1986). *Negotiating world order: Artisanship and architecture of global diplomacy.* Wilmington, DE: Scholarly Resources.

Himes, J. S. (1980). *Conflict and conflict management.* Athens: University of Georgia Press.

Hofstadter, D. (1983, April). Metamagical themas. *Scientific American.*

Hollins, H. B., Powers, A. L., & Sommer, M. (1989). *The conquest of war: Alternative strategies for global security.* Boulder, CO: Westview.

Horowitz, D. L. (1985). *Ethnic groups in conflict.* Berkeley: University of California Press.

Ikle, F. C. (1964). *How nations negotiate.* New York: Harper & Row.

Intriligator, M., & Jacobsen, H. A. (Eds.). (1988). *East-West conflict: Elite perceptions and political options.* Boulder, CO: Westview.

Isard, W., & Smith, C. (1982). *Conflict analysis and practical conflict management procedures: An introduction to peace science.* Cambridge, MA: Ballinger.

Jandt, F., & Gillette, P. (1985). *Win-win negotiating: Turning conflict into agreement.* New York: John Wiley.

Janis, I. L. (1982). *Victims of groupthink* (2nd ed.). Boston: Houghton Mifflin.

Jervis, R. (1976). *Perception and misperception in international politics.* Princeton, NJ: Princeton University Press.

Kagel, S. (1986). *Anatomy of a labor arbitration.* Washington, DC: BNA Books.

Kagel, S., & Kelly, K. (1989). *The anatomy of mediation: What makes it work.* Washington, DC: BNA Books.

Kahn, L. S. (1988). *Peacemaking: A systems approach to conflict management.* Lanham, MD: University Press of America.

Kanowitz, L. (1985). *Alternative dispute resolution: Cases and materials.* St. Paul, MN: West.

Katz, S. N. (Ed.). (1987). *Negotiating to settlement in divorce.* Clifton, NJ: Prentice Hall Law & Business.

Katz, N. H., & Lawyer, J. W. (1985). *Communication and conflict resolution skills.* Dubuque, IA: Kendall/Hunt.

Keller, E. F. (1980). How gender matters, or why it's so hard for us to count past two. *New Ideas in Psychology.*

Kellerman, B., & Rubin, J. Z. (Eds.). (1988). *Leadership and negotiation in the Middle East.* New York: Praeger.

Kelly, M. A. (1987). *Labor and industrial relations: Terms, laws, court decisions, and arbitration standards.* Baltimore, MD: Johns Hopkins University.

Klingel, S., & Martin, A. (Eds.). (1988). *A fighting chance: New strategies to save jobs and reduce costs.* Ithaca, NY: ILR Press.

Knebel, F., & Clay, G. S. (1987). *Before you sue: How to get justice without going to court.* New York: Morrow.

Kochan, T. A. (1980). *Collective bargaining and industrial relations.* Homewood, IL: Irwin.

Kochan, T. A., et al. (1979). *Dispute resolution under fact-finding and arbitration.* New York: American Arbitration Association.

Kochan, T. A., Katz, H. C., & McKersie, R. B. (1986). *The transformation of American industrial relations.* New York: Basic Books.

Kolb, D. M. (1983). *The mediators.* Cambridge: MIT Press.

Kranitz, M. A. (1987). *Getting apart together: The couple's guide to a fair divorce or separation.* San Luis Obispo, CA: Impact.

Kremenyuk, V. A. (Ed.). (1991). *International negotiation: Analysis, approaches, issues.* San Francisco: Jossey-Bass.

Kressel, K. (1972). *Labor mediation: An exploratory survey.* Albany, NY: Association of Labor Mediation Agencies.

Kressel, K. (1985). *The process of divorce: How professionals and couples negotiate settlements.* New York: Basic Books.

Kressel, K., Pruitt, D., & Associates. (1989). *Mediation research: The process and effectiveness of third-party intervention.* San Francisco: Jossey-Bass.

Krieger, S. (1987, October). Organizational theory: Implications of recent feminist research (ways women organize). Organizational Behavior and Industrial Relations Colloquim, School of Business Administration, University of California, Berkeley.

Kriesberg, L. (1982). *Social conflicts* (2nd ed.). Englewood Cliffs, NJ: Prentice Hall.

Lakos, A. (1989). *International negotiations: A bibliography.* Boulder, CO: Westview.

Lax, D. A., & Sebenius, J. K. (1986). *The manager as negotiator: Bargaining for cooperation and competitive gain.* New York: The Free Press.

LeBow, R. N. (1987). *Nuclear crisis management: A dangerous illusion.* Ithaca, NY: Cornell University Press.

Lemmon, J. (1985). *Family mediation practice.* New York: The Free Press.

Levin, E., & Grody, D. (1987). *Evidence in arbitration.* Washington, DC: BNA Books.

Lewicki, R. J., & Litterer, J. A. (1985a). *Negotiation.* Homewood, IL: Irwin.

Lewicki, R. J., & Litterer, J. A. (1985b). *Negotiation: Readings, exercises and cases.* Homewood, IL: Irwin.

Lewicki, R. J., Sheppard, B. H., & Bazerman, M. (Eds). (1986). *Research in negotiation in organizations.* Greenwich, CT: JAI Press.

Lewis, J. L. (1960, November 1). Address before the 43rd Consecutive Constitutional Convention of the United Mineworkers of America. *United Mineworkers' Journal,* pp. 12-15.

Lieberman, J. K. (1981). *The litigious society.* New York: Basic Books.

Lind, E. A., & Tyler, T. R. (1988). *The social psychology of procedural justice.* New York: Plenum.

Lipset, S. M., & Schneider, W. (1983, August-September). Confidence in confidence measures. *Public Opinion,* pp. 42-44.

Lipset, S. M., Trow, M. A., & Coleman, J. S. (1956). *Union democracy: The internal politics of the International Typographical Union.* Glencoe, IL: Free Press.

Lovenheim, P. (1989). *Mediate, don't litigate.* New York: McGraw- Hill.

Luce, R. D., & Raiffa, H. (1957). *Games and decisions: Introduction and critical survey.* New York: John Wiley.

Mack, A., & Keal, P. (1988). *Security and arms control in the North Pacific.* Sydney: Allen & Unwin.

Maggiolo, W. A. (1986). *Techniques of mediation.* New York: Oceana.

Marks, J. B., Johnson, E., Jr., & Szanton, P. L. (1984). *Dispute resolution in America: Processes in evolution.* Washington, DC: National Institute for Dispute Resolution.

Massey, P. A., & Bureau of National Affairs Editorial Staff. (Eds.). (1987). *Grievance guide.* Washington, DC: Bureau of National Affairs.

Matthews, R. (Ed.). (1988). *Informal justice?* London: Sage.

Matzmanian, D. A., Stanley-Jones, M., & Green, M. J. (1988). *Breaking political gridlock: California's experiment in public-private cooperation for hazardous waste policy.* Claremont: California Institute of Public Affairs.

Mautner-Markhof, F. (1989). *Processes of international negotiations.* Boulder, CO: Westview.

Mayle, P. D. (1987). *Eureka summit: Agreement in principle and the big three at Tehran, 1943.* Newark: University of Delaware Press.

Maynard, D. W. (1984). *Inside plea bargaining: The language of negotiation.* New York: Plenum.

McCall, J. B., & Warrington, M. B. (1989). *Marketing by agreement: A cross-cultural approach to business negotiations.* London: John Wiley.

McCarthy, J. (Ed.). (1980). *Resolving conflicts in higher education.* San Francisco: Jossey-Bass.

McCarthy, W. (1985, January). The role of power and principle in getting to yes. *Negotiation Journal 1*(1).

McGillis, D., & Mullan, J. (1977). *Neighborhood justice centers: An analysis of potential models.* Washington, DC: U.S. Government Printing Office.

McKelvey, J. T. (Ed.). (1988). *Cleared for takeoff: Airline labor relations since deregulation.* Ithaca, NY: ILR Press.

McKersie, R. B., & Hunter, L. C. (1973). *Pay, productivity and collective bargaining.* London: Macmillan.

Merry, S., & Silbey, S. (1984). What do plaintiffs want: Reexamining the concept of dispute. *The Justice System Journal, 9,* 151-179.

Miller, J. B. (1983). The construction of anger in women and men. Work in Progress No. 83-01 Stone Center Working Paper Series, Wellesley, MA.

Moore, C. W. (1986). *The mediation process: Practical strategies for resolving conflicts.* San Francisco: Jossey-Bass.

Morley, I., & Stephenson, G. (1977). *The social psychology of bargaining.* London: Allen & Unwin.

Morrison, W. F. (1986). *The pre-negotiation planning book.* New York: John Wiley.

Murray, J. S., Rau, A. S., & Sherman, E. A. (1989). *Processes of dispute resolution: The role of lawyers.* Westbury, NY: Foundation.

Nader, L. (Ed.). (1980). *No access to law: Alternatives to the American judicial system.* New York: Academic Press.

Nader, L., & Todd, H. F. (1978). *The disputing process: Law in ten societies.* New York: Columbia University Press.

Neumann, D. (1989). *Divorce mediation: How to cut the cost and stress of divorce.* New York: Holt.

Nicholson, N., Ursell, G., & Blyton, P. (1981). *The dynamics of white-collar unionism: A study of local union participation.* New York: Academic Press.

Nierenberg, G. I. (1973). *Fundamentals of negotiating.* New York: Hawthorne Books.

Nierenberg, G. I. (1986). *The complete negotiator.* New York: Nierenberg & Zeif.

Nieuwmeijer, L. (1988). *Negotiation: Methodology and training.* Pinetown, South Africa: Owen Burgess.

Nordlinger, E. A. (1972). *Conflict regulation in divided societies.* Cambridge, MA: Harvard University Press.

North, R. C. (1990). *War, peace, and survival: Global politics and conceptual synthesis.* Boulder, CO: Westview.

Olson, M., Jr. (1965). *The logic of collective action: Public goods and the theory of groups.* Cambridge, MA: Harvard University Press.

Palenski, J. E., & Launer, H. M. (Eds.). (1986). *Mediation: Context and challenges.* Springfield, IL: Charles C Thomas.

Patchen, M. (1988). *Resolving disputes between nations: Coercion or conciliation?* Durham, NC: Duke University Press.

Peters, E. (1955). *Strategy and tactics in labor negotiations.* New London, CT: National Foremen's Institute.

Porter, J. N., & Taplin, R. (1987). *Conflict and conflict resolution: A sociological introduction with updated bibliography and theory section.* Lanham, MD: University Press of America.

Provine, D. M. (1986). *Settlement strategies for federal district judges.* Washington, DC: Federal Judicial Center.

Pruitt, D. G. (1981). *Negotiation behavior.* New York: Academic Press.

Pruitt, D. G., & Rubin, J. Z. (1986). *Social conflict: Escalation, stalemate, and settlement.* New York: Random House.

Pruitt, D. G., & Snyder, R. C. (Eds.). (1969). *Theory and research on the causes of war.* Englewood Cliffs, NJ: Prentice Hall.

Quandt, W. B. (1986). *Camp David: Peacemaking and politics.* Washington, DC: Brookings Institution.

Rahim, M. A. (1988). *Managing conflict in organizations.* New York: Praeger.

Raiffa, H. (1982). *The art and science of negotiation.* Cambridge, MA: Belknap.

Rapoport, A. (1964). *Strategy and conscience.* New York: Harper & Row.

Rapoport, A. (1966). *Two-person game theory: The essential ideas.* Ann Arbor: University of Michigan Press.

Rapoport, A. (1967). *Fights, games, and debates.* Ann Arbor: University of Michigan Press.

Rapoport, A. (1970). *N-person game theory: Concepts and applications.* Ann Arbor: University of Michigan Press.

Rapoport, A., & Chammah, A. M. (1965). *Prisoner's dilemma.* Ann Arbor: University of Michigan Press.

Riker, W. H. (1962). *The theory of political coalitions.* New Haven, CT: Yale University Press.

Riskin, L. L., & Westbrook, J. E. (1987). *Dispute resolution and lawyers.* St. Paul, MN: West.

Rogers, N. H., & McEwen, C. A. (1989). *Mediation: Law, policy, practice.* New York: Lawyers Cooperative.

Rogers, N. H., & Salem, R. A. (1987). *A student's guide to mediation and the law.* New York: Matthew Bender.

Roth, A. (1979). *Axiomatic models of bargaining.* Berlin: Springer-Verlag.

Rowe, M. (1987). The corporate ombudsman: An overview and analysis. *Negotiation Journal, 3,* 127.

Rowe, M. (1990). People who feel harrassed need a complaint system with both formal and informal options. *Negotiation Journal, 6*(2): 161-172.

Rubin, J. Z. (Ed.). (1981). *Dynamics of third party intervention: Kissinger in the Middle East.* New York: Praeger.

Rubin, J. Z., & Brown, B. R. (1975). *The social psychology of bargaining and negotiation.* New York: Academic Press.

Rubin, J. Z., & Rubin, C. (1989). *When families fight: How to handle conflict with those you love.* New York: Ballantine Books.

Rubinstein, R. A., & Foster, M. L. (Eds.). (1988). *The social dynamics of peace and conflict: Culture in international society.* Boulder, CO: Westview.

Rubinstein, S. P. (Ed.). (1987). *Participative systems at work: Creating quality and employment security.* New York: Human Sciences.

Sampath, D. K. (1989). *Tiruporur file: An Indian experiment.* Madras, India: Tamil Nadu State Legal Aid & Advice Board.

Salacuse, J. W. (1991). *Making global deals: Negotiating in the international marketplace.* Boston: Houghton Mifflin.

Sander, F. E. A. (1984). *Mediation: A select annotated bibliography.* Washington, DC: American Bar Association Special Committee on Dispute Resolution.

Sander, F. E. A. (1985). *Alternatives inside and outside the courts: The forgotten forums.* Harvard Law School, Cambridge, MA.

Sander, F. E. A., & Snyder, F. E. (1979). *Alternative methods of dispute settlement: A selected bibliography.* Washington, DC: American Bar Association.

Sandole, D., & Sandole-Staroste, I. (Eds.). (1987). *Conflict management and problem solving: Interpersonal to international applications.* New York: New York University Press.

Saunders, H. H. (1985). *The other walls: The politics of Arab- Israeli peace process.* Washington, DC: American Institute Enterprise.

Schelling, T. C. (1960). *The strategy of conflict.* Cambridge, MA: Harvard University Press.

Schelling, T. C. (1961). Essay on bargaining. In *The Strategy of Conflict.* Cambridge, MA: Harvard University Press.

Schelling, T. C. (1966). *Arms and influence.* New Haven, CT: Yale University Press.

Schelling, T. C. (1978). *Micromotives and macrobehavior.* New York: Norton.

Schelling, T. C. (1984). *Choice and consequence: Perspectives of an errant economist.* Cambridge, MA: Harvard University Press.

Schindler, C., & Lapid, G. G. (1989). *The great turning: Personal peace, global victory.* Santa Fe, NM: Bear.

Schniedewind, N., & Davidson, E. (1987). *Cooperative learning, cooperative lives: A sourcebook of learning activities for building a peaceful world.* Dubuque, IA: Brown Publishing and Roa Media.

Scott, B. (1981). *The skills of negotiating.* UK: Gower.

Sebenius, J. K. (1984). *Negotiating the law of the sea: Lessons in the art and science of reaching agreement.* Cambridge, MA: Harvard University Press.

Sherif, M., & Sherif, C. W. (1969). *Social psychology.* New York: Harper & Row.

Shostak, A. B., & Skocik, D. (1986). *The air controllers' controversy: Lessons from the PATCO strike.* New York: Human Sciences.

Siegel, S., & Fouraker, L. E. (1960). *Bargaining and group decision-making: Experiments on bilateral monopoly.* New York: McGraw-Hill.

Simkin, W. E., & Fidandis, A. (1986). *Mediation and the dynamics of collective bargaining* (2nd ed.). Washington, DC: Bureau of National Affairs.

Singer, L. (1990). *Settling disputes: Conflict resolution in business, families and the legal system.* Boulder, CO: Westview.

Smith, C. G. (Ed.). (1971). *Conflict resolution: Contributions of the behavioral sciences.* Notre Dame, IN: University of Notre Dame Press.

Smoke, R. (1987). *Paths to peace: Exploring the feasibility of sustainable peace* (with W. Harman). Boulder, CO: Westview.

Snyder, G. H., & Diesing, P. (1977). *Conflict among nations.* Princeton, NJ: Princeton University Press.

Staudohar, P. D. (1986). *The sports industry and collective bargaining.* Ithaca, NY: ILR Press.

Stein, J. G. (Ed.). (1989). *Getting to the table: The processes of international prenegotiation.* Baltimore, MD: Johns Hopkins University Press.

Stevens, C. M. (1963). *Strategy and collective bargaining negotiation.* New York: McGraw-Hill.

Strauss, A. (1978). *Negotiations: Varieties, contexts, processes, and social order.* San Francisco: Jossey-Bass.

Stulberg, J. B. (1987). *Taking charge/managing conflict.* Lexington, MA: Lexington Books.

Surrey, J. L. (1987). Relationship and empowerment. Work in Progress No. 30 Stone Center Working Paper Series, Wellesley, MA.

Susskind, L., Bacow, L. S., & Wheeler, M. (Eds.). (1983). *Resolving environmental regulatory disputes.* Cambridge, MA: Schenkman Books.

Susskind, L., & Cruikshank, J. (1987). *Breaking the impasse: Consensual approaches to resolving public disputes.* New York: Basic Books.

Susskind, L., Elliott, M., & Associates. (1983). *Paternalism, conflict, and coproduction: Learning from citizen action and citizen participation in Western Europe.* New York: Plenum.

Susskind, L., Richardson, J.R., & Hildebrand, K. J. (1978). *Resolving environmental disputes: Approaches to intervention, negotiation, and conflict resolution.* Cambridge, MA: MIT.

Swingle, P. (Ed.). (1970). *The structure of conflict.* New York: Academic Press.

Tannis, E. G. (1989). *Alternative dispute resolution that works!* North York, Ont: Captus Press.

Teger, A. I., Cary, M. S., Hillis, J., & Katcher, A. (1980). *Too much invested to quit.* New York: Pergamon.

Thakur, R. (Ed.). (1988). *International conflict resolution.* Boulder, CO: Westview.

Thibaut, J. W., & Walker, L. (1975). *Procedural justice: A psychological analysis.* Hillsdale, NJ: Lawrence Erlbaum.

Touval, S. (1982). *The peace brokers: Mediators in the Arab-Israeli conflict, 1948-1979.* Princeton, NJ: Princeton University Press.

Touval, S., & Zartman, I. W. (Eds.). (1985a). *International mediation in theory and practice.* Boulder, CO: Westview.

Touval, S., & Zartman, I. W. (Eds.). (1985b). *The man in the middle: International mediation in theory and practice.* Boulder, CO: Westview.

Ury, W. L. (1985). *Beyond the hotline: How crisis can prevent nuclear war.* Boston: Houghton Mifflin.

Ury, W. L., Brett, J. M., & Goldberg, S. B. (1988). *Getting disputes resolved: Designing systems to cut the costs of conflict.* San Francisco: Jossey-Bass.

Vermont Law School Dispute Resolution Project. (1984a). *Removing the barriers to the use of alternative methods of dispute resolution.* South Royalton: Vermont Law School.

Vermont Law School Dispute Resolution Project. (1984b). *A study of the barriers to the use of alternative methods of dispute resolution.* South Royalton: Vermont Law School.

Vermont Law School Dispute Resolution Project. (1987). *The role of mediation in divorce proceedings: A comparative perspective.* South Royalton: Vermont Law School.

Von Neumann, J., & Morganstern, O. (1944). *Theory of games and economic behavior.* Princeton, NJ: Princeton University Press.

Wall, J. A., Jr. (1985). *Negotiation: Theory and practice.* Glenview, IL: Scott, Foreman.

Wallensteen, P. (Ed.). (1988). *Peace research: Achievements and challenges.* Boulder, CO: Westview.

Walton, R. E. (1961). *The impact of the Professional Engineering Union.* Boston: Division of Research, Graduate School of Business Administration, Harvard University.

Walton, R. E. (1969). *Interpersonal peacemaking: Confrontation and third party consultation.* Reading, MA: Addison-Wesley.

Walton, R. E. (1987). *Managing conflict: Interpersonal dialogue.* Reading, MA: Addison-Wesley.

Walton, R. E., & McKersie, R. B. (1965). *A behavioral theory of labor negotiations: An analysis of a social interaction system.* New York: McGraw-Hill.

Warschaw, T. (1980). *Winning by negotiation.* New York: McGraw-Hill.

Watson, C., & Kasten, B. (n.d.). Separate strengths? How women and men negotiate. Center for Negotiation and Conflict Resolution at Rutgers University, NJ.

Wehr, P. (1979). *Conflict regulation.* Boulder, CO: Westview.

Weithorn, L. A. (Ed.). (1987). *Psychology and child custody determination: Knowledge, roles and expertise.* Lincoln: University of Nebraska Press.

Westin, A. F., & Feliu, A. G. (1988). *Resolving employment disputes without litigation.* Washington, DC: BNA Books.

Whelan, J. G. (1990). *The Moscow summit, 1988: Reagan and Gorbachev in negotiation.* Boulder, CO: Westview.

White, R. K. (1968). *Nobody wanted war: Misperception in Vietnam and other wars.* Garden City, NY: Doubleday/Anchor.

White, R. K. (1984). *Fearful warriors: A psychological profile of U.S.-Soviet relations*. New York: The Free Press.

White, R. K. (1985, January). Review of getting to yes. *Negotiation Journal 1*(1).

White, R. K. (Ed.). (1986). *Psychology and the prevention of nuclear war: A book of readings*. New York: New York University Press.

Wilkins, A. L. (1989). *Developing corporate character: How to successfully change an organization without destroying it*. San Francisco: Jossey-Bass.

Wilkinson, J. H. (Ed.). (1990). *Donovan Leisure Newton & Irvine ADR practice book*. Colorado Springs, CO: Wiley Law Publications.

Williams, G. R. (1983). *Legal negotiation and settlement*. St. Paul, MN: West.

Winham, G. R. (1986). *International trade and Tokyo round negotiation*. Princeton, NJ: Princeton University Press.

Winham, G. R. (1988). *Trading with Canada: The Canada-U.S. free trade agreement*. New York: Priority Press.

Wondolleck, J. M. (1988). *Public lands conflict and resolution: Managing national forest disputes*. New York: Plenum Press.

Woodhouse, T. (Ed.). (1988). *The international peace directory*. Plymouth, UK: Northcote House.

Young, O. R. (1967). *The intermediaries: Third parties in international crises*. Princeton, NJ: Princeton University Press.

Young, O. R. (Ed.). (1975). *Bargaining: Formal theories of negotiation*. Urbana: University of Illinois Press.

Zack, A. (1980). *Understanding grievance arbitration in the public sector*. Washington, DC: Department of Labor.

Zack, A., & Bloch, R. I. (1983). *Labor agreement in negotiations and arbitration*. Washington, DC: Bureau of National Affairs.

Zack, A. M. (Ed.). (1984). *Arbitration in practice*. Ithaca, NY: ILR Press.

Zargoria, S. (1988). *The ombudsman: How good governments handle citizens' grievances*. Cabin John, MD: Seven Locks Press.

Zartman, I. W. (1976). *The 50% solution: How to bargain successfully with hijackers, strikers, bosses, oil magnate, Arabs, Russians, and other worthy opponents in the modern world*. Garden City, NY: Anchor Press.

Zartman, I. W. (Ed.). (1978). *The negotiation process: Theories and applications*. Beverly Hills, CA: Sage.

Zartman, I. W., & Berman, M. R. (1982). *The practical negotiator*. New Haven, CT: Yale University Press.

Zimny, M., Dolson, W., & Barreca, C. (Eds.). (1990). *Labor arbitration: A practical guide for advocates*. Washington, DC: BNA Books.

# Index

Abel, Richard, 43
Accordion planning approach, 33
Adjudication:
   final offer arbitration, 49
   gender-related outcome differences, 139
   multidoor courthouse, 58-59
   process spectrum, 46
   workplace complaint systems, 116
Adversarial bargaining, 89-92
Advocacy groups, 30
Aggressive negotiation style, 157-169
Airlines, 80-84, 88-89
Air traffic controllers, 82
Alternative dispute resolution (ADR), 43
   categorical referral, 52-54
   court-annexed arbitration, 53-54
   dangers of, 50

hybrid mechanisms, 48-50
individual referral, 54-57
legal education, 45, 59
multidoor courthouse, 58-59
prescriptive and descriptive approaches, 151
restrictive thinking in, 107
sample curriculum, 179
sanctions and incentives, 57-58
American Airlines, 83
American Association of University Professors, 98
American Plan, 88 AMPO exercise, 24-27
Arb-med, 49-50
Arbitration, 14
   court-annexed, 53-54
   fact-finder function, 48-49

final offer, 49
management training, 22-23
medarb, 49-50
workplace complaint systems, 116
Associated Metropolitan Police Organization (AMPO), 24-27
Attributional distortion, 129
Auctions, 8, 17-18
Axelrod, R., 167

BATNA, 24, 44, 66
labor relations, 79-83
negotiating power in, 9-11
Bibliography, 186-198
Bidding situations, 8, 17-18
Bieber, Owen, 104n8
Bipartisan committee, 64
Brigham Young University exercise, 152-154
Bureau of Land Management, 39

Camden sewage district case, 72-75
Canadian Auto workers, 89-93
Carter, Jimmy, 21-22
Case Clearinghouse, 185
Case evaluation, 51
Categorical referral, 52-54
Charisma, 93-94
Child custody cases, 52
Choice, 108-112. See also Options
Chrysler, 88
Clean Air Act, 62, 69
Coercion, 126
Collaborative problem-solving, 28-29
commitment in, 37
concentric rings of involvement, 36-37
educational problems, 37
key decision-maker participation, 34-35
planning, 33
problem identification, 36
representation issues, 35-36
resistances to, 31-32
social trends, 30-31
urban development case, 38-39

Collective bargaining, 78, 86-88. See also Labor relations
Commitment:
collaborative processes, 37
entrapment, 130-132, 135
negotiation power of, 10
Common interest forums, 102
Communication:
conflict deescalation, 135
labor negotiations, 81
negotiation power and, 6-7
union members, 91
women's styles, 143-144, 146-148
Communications Workers of America, 98
Complaint resolution, 105-106
complainant disempowerment, 106-108
effective system functions, 116-117
minority representation, 115-116
options for, 108-116
skills exercises, 117-118
systems approach, 115
Concentric rings of involvement, 36-37
Concessions, unilateral, 168-169
Confidential information, 16, 49
Conflict, psychological perspectives of. See Psychological perspectives
Conflict cycle, 124
deescalation, 134-137
escalation, 125-132
stalemate, 132-134
Conflict resolution. See Alternative dispute resolution; Complaint resolution; Legal negotiation; Public dispute resolution; specific methods and problems
Consensus-based approaches, 29-30
planning process, 33
public policy negotiation, 63-67
Contact hypothesis, 134
Continental Airlines, 80, 81
Contingent contract, 24
Cooperative agreements, 88
Cooperative negotiation style, 157-169, 182
Corporatism, 95
Cottonburger simulation, 169-174
Counseling, 113

Court-annexed arbitration, 53-54
Creativity, 28, 100
Cuban missile crisis, 137

Decentralization, 83, 97
Deescalation, 134-137
Dialogue, 143-144
Dispute pyramid, 43-45
Dispute resolution. *See* Alternative dispute resolution; Complaint resolution; Public dispute resolution; *specific methods and problems*
Distributive bargaining, 15-17, 61
Divorce mediation, 139

Eastern Airlines, 88-89
Education and training:
    alternative dispute resolution (ADR), 45, 59
    Case Clearinghouse, 185
    collaborative problem-solving, 37
    complaint handler skills, 117-118
    inventing in, 100
    labor negotiation, 96, 99-101
    limitations, 103
    manager negotiation skills, 22-23
    mutual gains approach, 99
    prescriptive and descriptive approaches, 151
    problem-solving tools, 28-29
    sample curriculum, 177-184
Edwards, H., 50
Egypt, 126
Empathy, 145-146
Employee ombudsman, 113
Employer-employee relations. *See* Labor relations
Employment security, 82
Empowerment:
    choices and, 109
    feminist views, 142-143
Entrapment, 130-132, 135
Environmental issues, 18, 39
    regulatory negotiation, 67, 69, 72
Environmental Protection Agency (EPA), 62, 67-73

Ephlin, Don, 88
Escalation, 125-128
    deescalation, 134-137
    entrapment, 130-132
    selective perception, 128-129
    self-fulfilling prophecy, 129-130
    stalemate, 132-134
Ethical issues:
    effective legal negotiation, 159
    third-party negotiators, 46-47, 55
*Evolution of Cooperation* (Axelrod), 167
Expectations, 128-129, 148-149
Experimental agreements, 87

Face-saving, 133, 137
Facilitation, 14, 29
Fact finding, 48-49
    consensus for, 74
    negotiated rule-making, 70
    special master, 54
    workplace complaint systems, 116
Fair division Steinhaus procedure, 20
*The Federal Register,* 67
Feelings, 116
Felstiner, Bill, 43
Feminist perspectives, 138. *See also* Gender and negotiation
Final offer(s), 11, 49
*Final Offer* (Canadian Film Board), 90
Fisher, Bobby, 133
Fraser, Doug, 88
Funding, 69-70
Future value, 23-24

Galanter, M., 48
Games theory, 17, 108
Gender and negotiation:
    agency concepts, 141-142
    dialogue emphasis, 143-144
    empathetic behavior, 145-146
    expectations, 148-149
    power concepts, 142-143
    preserving harmony, 145
    relational viewpoints, 140-141
    sample curriculum, 180
    styles of talk, 146-148

women's voice, 138-144, 149
General Dynamics, 80
General Motors of Canada, 90, 92
Gompers, Samuel, 88
Grievance options, 111. *See also* Complaint resolution; Labor relations

Harassment, 105-106, 109, 114
Harvard Program on Negotiation, viii, 183-184
    Case Clearinghouse, 185
    sample curriculum, 179-183
    training projects, 98
Historic preservation, 35
Hussein, Saddam, 10

Iacocca, Lee, 88
Individualization, 134
Individual referral, 54-57
Industrial relations. *See* Labor relations
Information:
    third-party negotiator functions, 16, 49
    worker access, 112-113
Interests:
    choice as, 109
    common interest forums, 102
    complaint resolution problems, 107
    labor negotiations, 99-100
    mediation and, 47-48
    negotiator understanding of, 7-8
    stakeholder analysis, 35
Intergroup conflict, 128, 135
International conflicts, 125-126, 136-137
Involvement, 36-37, 93
Iranian hostage crisis, 137
Iraq, 10
Israel, 126, 136

Joint gains. *See* Mutual gains
Jordan, 136

Kennedy, John F., 6
Kennedy, Robert, 137

Key decision-maker participation, 34-35
Kissinger, Henry, 126
Kuwait, 10

Labor markets, 79
Labor relations, 77-85
    adversarial bargaining strengths, 89-92
    Canadian Auto Workers, 89-93
    charismatic influences, 93-94
    collective bargaining reform, 86-88
    constituent pressures, 92
    decentralization, 83
    employer's BATNA, 79-83
    future prospects, 101-103
    grievance options, 111
    mutual gains bargaining, 86, 92, 95-101
    political power and, 94-95
    positions and interests in, 99-100
    Shell-Sarnia refinery, 95-97
    scorable game exercise, 24-27
    traditional system problems, 79-81
    training, 96, 97, 99-101
    union internal bargaining, 83-84
Land use planning, 39
Leadership problems, 30, 31-32
Legal negotiation:
    aggressive and cooperative patterns, 157-169
    Brigham Young University study, 152-154
    *Cottonburger* simulation, 169-174
    court-annexed arbitration, 53-54
    dispute pyramid, 43-45
    effective and ineffective negotiators, 155-157
    ethical conduct, 159
    hybrid mechanisms, 48-50
    individual referral, 54-57
    minitrials, 54, 55-56
    neutral experts, 54, 55
    overcoming obstacles to, 51-52
    process spectrum, 46-47
    *See also* Alternative dispute resolution
*Legal Negotiation and Settlement*
    (Williams), 152

Legitimacy standards, 8-9
Lewis, J. L., 93-94
Listening, 7, 135, 146
Litigotiation, 48

Malpractice claims, 52-53
Management-union partnership, 79, 101
Med-arb, 49-50
Mediation, 14, 29
    categorical referral, 52-54
    ethical problems, 46-47, 55
    fact-finder function, 48-49
    gender-related outcome differences, 139
    individual referral, 54
    management training, 22-23
    Michigan program, 57
    multidoor courthouse, 58-59
    political clout, 22
    process spectrum, 46
    rights versus interests in, 47-48
    sample curriculum, 180
    scorable negotiation exercise, 25-29
    state offices for, 76
    workplace complaint system, 113, 116
Mediation-arbitration, 49-50
Medical malpractice, 52-53
Merger cases, 23
Michigan Bell, 98
Michigan mediation program, 57
Minitrials, 54, 55-56
Minorities, 115, 116
Multidoor courthouse, 58-59
Mutual gains, 26-27
    charismatic approach, 94
    collective bargaining reforms, 86-88
    future prospects, 101-103
    labor negotiations, 92
    public dispute negotiation, 61
    Shell-Sarnia refinery, 95-97
    skills training, 99-101

National Institute for Dispute Resolution, x
Natural Resources Defense Council, 69
Negotiated rule-making, 67-72

Negotiation effectiveness, 155-157
    aggressive and cooperative patterns, 157-169
    *Cottonburger* simulation, 169-174
Negotiation power, 4-12
Negotiation process, 1, 46, 154-155
Negotiation skill, 4
    case outcomes and, 152-154
    complaint handlers, 117-118
    process and, 154-155
    *See also* Education and training
Neutral analysis, 18-21
Neutral experts, 54, 55
Newark redevelopment, 38-39

Obnoxious negotiating style, 163
Options:
    in effective complaint systems, 112-114
    lack of, 106-108
    providing, 114-116
    value of, 108-112

Panama Canal Negotiations, 21-22
Perceived injurious experiences (PIES), 43
Personality problems:
    conflict escalation, 125
    negotiator training for, 15
    obnoxious attorneys, 163
Philatelist auction, 8, 18
Planning process, 33
Political power, 22, 94-95
Postsettlement-settlement, 17
Power:
    choices and, 109
    complaint resolution problems, 107
    feminist views, 142-143
    lateralization of, 30-31
    negotiation power, 4-12
Prejudice, 134
Prenegotiation stage, 71
Prisoner's dilemma, 80, 142
Problem-solving:
    educational problems, 28-29
    industrial training, 96

women's approach, 143-144
*See also* Collaborative problem-solving
Process, 1, 46-47, 154-155
Profit sharing, 82, 94, 104n8
Program on Negotiation. *See* Harvard Program on Negotiation
Promotion, 84
Property division, 19-21
Psychological perspectives, 123
   conflict cycle, 124
   deescalation, 134-137
   escalation, 125-132
   stalemate, 132-134
Public dispute resolution, 61-63
   Camden sewage district case, 72-75
   consensus-building, 63-67
   funding, 69-70
   legislated solutions, 62
   regulatory negotiation, 67-72
   state mediation offices, 76

Q-Analysis, 156
Quality of work life, 88, 97

Racial prejudice, 134
Radioactive waste, 72
Railroads, 80, 81
Reciprocity, 168-169
Redevelopment, 38-39
Regulatory negotiation, 67-72
Relational viewpoints, 140-141
Representation, 35-36
Reuther, Walter, 93
Rights, 47, 107
Rules manipulation, 17-18

Sarat, Austin, 43
Sarnia Shell refinery, 95-97
Sealed-bid auction, 8, 17-18
Selective perception, 128-129, 134
Self-control, 162, 163
Self-fulfilling prophecy, 129-130
Self-monitoring, 160, 173
Seniority, 84
Settlements. *See* Legal negotiation

Seuss, Dr., 133-134
Sexual harassment, 105-106, 109, 114
Shareholders, 104n6
Shell, 95-97
Sherif, C., 128, 135
Sherif, M., 128, 135
Simulations:
   *Cottonburger* case, 169-174
   labor negotiations, 24-27
   mutual gains approach, 99
   settlement outcome study, 152-154
Skills. *See* Education and training; Negotiation skill
Social Security negotiations, 64-65
Spassky, Boris, 133
Special master, 54, 73
Stakeholder analysis, 35
Stalemate, 132-135
Standards, 8-9
State mediation offices, 76
Steering committee, 36
Steinhaus procedure, 20
Stereotypes, 134, 148
*Story of the Zaks*, 133-134
Strategic analysis, 18
Strategic planning negotiation model, 143
Strikes, 82, 91, 102
Subcontracting, 81
Summary jury trials, 54, 55-57
Systems approach, 115

Tar baby story, 129-130
Teams, 95-97
Technical assistance, 70
Third-party intervention, 14-15
   distributive bargaining, 15-16
   ethical problems, 46-47
   face-saving arrangement, 137
   information function, 16
   integrative bargaining, 15, 16-17
   labor negotiation exercise, 24-27
   management training, 22-23
   neutral analysis, 18-21
   process spectrum, 46
   public compensation, 70
   stalemated situations, 133
   *See also* Mediation

Training. *See* Education and training
Transportation industry, 80-84
Trust, 6

Unilateral concessions, 168-169
Unions:
bargaining power, 91-92
charismatic influences, 93-94
collective bargaining reform, 86-88
communication problems, 91
constituent pressures, 91-93, 102
decentralization, 97
decline of, 79-80, 102
internal bargaining, 83-84, 88
management partnership, 79, 101
member involvement, 95-97

political clout, 94-95
traditional roles, 78
*See also* Labor relations
United Auto Workers (UAW), 88-89

Valuation, 19-21, 23-24

Walk-away alternatives. *See* BATNA
Western Airlines, 84
White, Bob, 89-93
Win-lose decision-making, 29
Women negotiators. *See* Gender and
negotiation
Women's voice, 138-144, 149
Working relationships, 6-7, 71

# About the Authors

**Roger Fisher** is the Director of the Harvard Negotiation Project and the Williston Professor Emeritus of Law at Harvard Law School, where he has taught since 1958. Before coming to Harvard, he practiced law in Washington, D.C., specializing in the settlement of public international disputes. He has taught and written extensively on international law and international conflict and, for more than a decade, has devoted himself to understanding and improving the process by which people, organizations, and governments negotiate. He is the co-author of both *Getting to YES: Negotiating Agreement Without Giving In* and *Getting Together: Building Relationships as We Negotiate* and is the founder of the Harvard Negotiation Project, a research organization dedicated to improving the theory and practice of dispute resolution. Through the consulting firm of Conflict Management, Inc. (and the nonprofit

Conflict Management Group), he has taught and advised corporate executives, labor leaders, attorneys, diplomats, and military and government officials on negotiation strategy. In 1991-1992, he led negotiation workshops in The Republic of South Africa, Malaysia, Colombia, Canada, and Greece.

**Lavinia Hall** is a mediator and consultant on negotiation and dispute resolution. An attorney by training, she works as a neutral on public and private sector issues. She works to resolve disputes, design systems to handle conflict, and help parties to be more effective negotiators.

For more than 15 years as a facilitator, she has developed processes to help groups achieve consensus. She is particularly interested in helping to achieve mutual gains within cross-cultural and indigenous peoples' debates and in employment relations. She uses processes ranging from facilitated policy dialogues to minitrials. The issues she has worked on include joint employer-employee initiatives, environmental cleanups, negotiated bankruptcies and reorganizations, long-range efforts on Native American and government relations, conflict resolution in school systems, and designing systems to resolve mass toxic tort claims.

She has conducted mutual gains negotiation training for thousands of people in corporations, government agencies, and other organizations in the United States and Canada. She is the editor of *Changing Tactics: Negotiating for Mutual Gains* and the author of numerous articles on business mediation, mutual gains negotiation, and the teaching of dispute resolution.

Before starting her own practice, she was a senior mediator with Endispute, Inc. at Harvard Law School's Program on Negotiation, she was Director of Curriculum and the Cross-disciplinary Specialization in Negotiation and Dispute Resolution. She has also practiced law and worked for state government. She holds a B.A. from Bennington College, an M.A. in Linguistics from New York University and a J.D. from New York Law School.

**Charles C. Heckscher** received a Ph.D. in sociology from Harvard University and worked for 4 years for the Communication Workers' union, helping to establish joint worker participation projects with AT&T. In 1988, he published a book on employee representation in the changing corporate environment. His current research explores whether a new form of organization—a "postbureaucratic" system—is developing from the current period of corporate restructuring. He is focusing particularly on the role of middle managers and "knowledge workers" in the change process. He has also been active in promoting new labor management relations, changes in union strategies, and the improvement of mechanisms of voice.

**Deborah M. Kolb** is Professor of Management at the Simmons College Graduate School of Management and Executive Director of the Program on Negotiation at Harvard Law School. She is also Co-Director of the Employment Relations Project in the Program on Negotiation.

She is an authority on mediation and other forms of institutional and organizational dispute resolution and conflict management. She is currently carrying out field research on ways that informal dispute handling processes enhance the capacity of people in organizations to deal with differences. She is the Principal Investigator for the Building Theory from Practice Project in the Program on Negotiation, a project that brings scholars together who are studying the practice of successful mediators. The book *When Talk Works: Profiles of Master Mediators* will be published in late 1992.

Her teaching and professional practice focus on negotiation and conflict resolution in the management of organizations. Among other firms, she has served as a consultant to Wang Laboratories; Chase Manhattan Bank; Coopers and Lybrand; Tupperware International; Procter & Gamble; Harvard Community Health Plan; Mobil Oil Firestone/Bridgestone; Foley, Hoag & Eliot; and Pfizer Corporation. She frequently presents her work to national and international university and professional audiences. She received her Ph.D. from MIT's Sloan School of Management.

**Robert B. McKersie** has been at MIT since 1980. Before that he served as Dean of the New York State School of Industrial and Labor Relations at Cornell University, and prior to that he was on the faculty of the Graduate School of Business at the University of Chicago. His undergraduate training is in electrical engineering from the University of Pennsylvania, and his graduate degrees were received at the Harvard Business School.

His research interests have been in labor management relations with particular focus on bargaining activity. He co-authored *A Behavioral Theory of Labor Negotiations* in 1965. More recently, he focused attention on the subject of productivity (co-authoring the book *Pay, Productivity and Collective Bargaining*) and participated in a multiyear project at the Sloan School (resulting in the award-winning, co-authored book *The Transformation of American Industrial Relations*). He continues to do research on strategies being pursued in different industries to bring about more effective organizational arrangements. The auto and transportation sectors are of special interest. Recently, he organized a conference under the auspices of the Center for Transportation Studies to examine the transformation processes as they are unfolding in airlines, railroads, and the trucking industries.

He has served on several national Presidential Commissions, is a member of the National Academy of Arbitrators, and was President of the National Industrial Research Association. Within the Sloan School, he is Deputy Dean and Society of Sloan Fellows Professor as well as the Chair of the faculty committee for the Sloan Fellows Program.

**Bruce Patton,** Deputy Director of the Harvard Negotiation Project, is the Thaddeus R. Beal Lecturer on Law at Harvard Law School. A lawyer, he teaches negotiation to diplomats and corporate executives around the world and works as a negotiation consultant and mediator in international, corporate, labor management, and family settings. He is associated with the Conflict Management organizations, which he co-founded in 1984. He has both graduate and undergraduate degrees from Harvard University.

**Howard Raiffa,** Frank P. Ramsey Professor of Managerial Economics at Harvard University, currently holds a joint appointment between the Graduate School of Business Administration and the Kennedy School of Government. He previously held appointments at Harvard in the Department of Statistics and the Department of Economics. He obtained his Ph.D. in Mathematics from the University of Michigan.

He has published in the fields of game theory, statistical decision theory, decision analysis, risk analysis, and negotiation analysis. He was the first Director of the International Insititute for Applied Systems Analysis. He has published several prize-winning books, including *The Art and Science of Negotiation.*

**Mary P. Rowe** is Special Assistant to the President, Massachusetts Institute of Technology and Adjunct Professor at the Sloan School of Management. She received her Ph.D. in economics from Columbia University. She is one of two ombudsmen for MIT, whose responsibilities include hearing hundreds of concerns a year, consulting to managers, teaching, research, and writing. From time to time she acts as a consultant and lecturer for coporations, government agencies, and nonprofit institutions, advising on problems of work process such as nonunion complaint systems, intrainstitutional conflict management, harassment, and mentoring systems. She was a co-founder of the Corporate Ombudsman Association, now the Ombudsman Association. She has helped set up ombuds offices in dozens of corporations, government agencies, and academic institutions. She is the author of numerous published articles.

**Jeffrey Z. Rubin** is Professor of Psychology at Tufts University, Adjunct Professor of Diplomacy at the Fletcher School of Law and Diplomacy, and Associate Director of the Program on Negotiation at Harvard Law School. A Fellow of Divisions 8, 9, and 48, he is the author or co-author of 12 books, including *The Social Psychology of Bargaining and Negotiation; Dynamics of Third Party Intervention: Kissinger in the Middle East; Social Conflict: Escalation, Stalemate, and Settlement; Leadership and Negotiation in the Middle East; Negotiation Theory and Practice;* and *Mediation in International Conflict.* He has been the recipient of Guggenheim and Fulbright Fellowships.

**Frank E. A. Sander** is Bussey Professor and Associate Dean at Harvard Law School. He was born in Stuttgart, Germany, and received his A.B. and LL.B. from Harvard. Following graduation, he served as law clerk to Chief Judge Calvert Magruder of the U.S. Court of Appeals for the First Circuit (1952-1953) and Justice Felix Frankfurter of the U.S. Supreme Court (1953-1954). After brief stints with the U.S. Justice Department in Washington, D.C., and Hill and Barlow in Boston, he began teaching at Harvard Law

School in 1959, specializing initially in taxation and family law, and since 1975, in dispute resolution. He was a member of the ABA Standing Committee on Dispute Resolution from 1976 to 1989, serving as its Chair from 1986 to 1989. He has written and lectured extensively on various aspects of ADR.

**David Straus** is Chairman of the Board and founder of Interaction Associates, Inc., a management consulting and training firm specializing in the design and implementation of organizational change processes involving whole systems. Interaction's consulting services include cultural change, strategic planning, quality improvement, and public-private partnerships as well as the design and facilitation of task-oriented meetings, retreats, and conferences.

Working out of Interaction's Boston office, he is responsible for major change efforts in a wide variety of organizations, including health care and financial services. He is committed to helping organizations collaboratively align their direction, commitment, and capabilities and is working with social action partnerships in such cities as Newark, New Jersey, and Palm Beach County, Florida. He co-authored the widely read book *How to Make Meetings Work.*

**Lawrence Susskind** is Professor of Urban and Environmental Planning at MIT and Director of the MIT-Harvard Public Disputes Program at Harvard Law School. He is Senior Manager of Public Dispute Resolution Services with Endispute, Incorporated in Cambridge, Massachusetts, and publisher of *Consensus,* a quarterly newspaper distributed to all public officials in the United States and Canada that monitors efforts to resolve public disputes more effectively. He co-authored *Breaking the Impasse: Consensual Approaches to Resolving Public Disputes.*

**William Ury** co-founded Harvard's Program on Negotiation, where he directs the Negotiation Network. He has served as a mediator and adviser in negotiations ranging from acrimonious business partnerships to wildcat coal strikes to Middle East conflicts. Formerly on the faculty of Harvard Business School, he has taught negotiation to thousands of corporate executives, labor leaders, and government officials around the world. He has also served as a consultant to the White House on establishing nuclear risk reduction centers in Washington and Moscow. His most recent book is *Getting Past No: Negotiating With Difficult People.* He received his undergraduate degree from Yale and a Ph.D. in Anthropology from Harvard.

**Gerald R. Williams** is Professor of Law at Brigham Young University, where he teaches negotiation, dispute resolution, and remedies. A frequent lecturer for bar associations and law firms on negotiation and alternative dispute resolution, he is author of *Legal Negotiation and Settlement* and has taught negotiation as a Visting Professor at Harvard Law School. He is a member of the prestigious American Bar Association Standing Committee on Dispute Resolution, is on the editorial board of *Negotiation Journal: On the Process of Dispute Resolution,* is a member of the Council of Academic Advisors for the Center for Public Resources, is a member of the Board of Directors of the American Arbitration Association, is a member of CPR's Judicial Project Advisory Council, and is Chair of the ADR Subcommittee of the Civil Justice Reform Act Advisory Committee for the U.S. District Court for the District of Utah.